D1760344

Medieval Constructions in Gender and Identity:

Essays in Honor of Joan M. Ferrante

MEDIEVAL AND RENAISSANCE
TEXTS AND STUDIES

VOLUME 293

Medieval Constructions in Gender and Identity:

Essays in Honor of Joan M. Ferrante

Edited by

Teodolinda Barolini

Arizona Center for Medieval and Renaissance Studies
Tempe, Arizona
2005

About the Cover:
The Building of the City of Ladies, HARL.4431 f290.
By Permission of the British Library.

Having dug out and discarded the dirt of misogynous writings from the Field
of Letters, Lady Reason helps Christine to lay the foundations and build the
walls of the City of Ladies from the stones of womens' achievements.

Library of Congress Cataloging-in-Publication Data

Medieval constructions in gender and identity : essays in honor of Joan M.
Ferrante / edited by Teodolinda Barolini.
  p. cm. -- (Medieval and renaissance texts and studies volume ; 293)
Includes bibliographical references.
ISBN-13: 978-0-86698-337-2 (alk. paper)
ISBN-10: 0-86698-337-6 (alk. paper)
1. Literature, Medieval--History and criticism. 2. Civilization, Medieval.
I. Ferrante, Joan M., 1936- II. Barolini, Teodolinda, 1951- III. Medieval &
Renaissance Texts & Studies (Series) ; v. 293.
PN671.M376 2005
809'.02--dc22
                                                              2005027668

∞
This book is made to last.
It is set in Adobe Caslon Pro,
smyth-sewn and printed on acid-free paper
to library specifications.
Printed in the United States of America

TABLE OF CONTENTS

Tabula Gratulatoria

Michael Agnew
Suzanne Conklin Akbari
Hubert Babinski
John W. Baldwin & Jenny Jochens
Teodolinda Barolini
Jennifer Bell
Susan Leslie Boynton
Robert Brentano
Saul N. Brody
Elizabeth A. R. Brown
Caroline Walker Bynum
Joan Cadden
Theresa A. Carballal
Mary Carruthers & Dr. Erika Rosenfeld
Jo Ann Cavallo
Anne L. Clark
Giles Constable
Paul Creamer
Consuelo W. Dutschke
Kathy Eden
Susan L. Einbinder
David Eng
Scott Failla
Lesleigh & William Forsyth
Carmela Vircillo Franklin
Elaine K. Gazda
Linda Georgianna
Tobias Foster Gittes
Frederick Goldin
Manuele Gragnolati
Patricia E. Grieve
Mr. and Mrs. Edward R. Halpert
Barbara Russano Hanning
Robert Hanning
Carolyn G. Heilbrun
Jean E. Howard
Martha C. Howell
Laura L. Howes
Adnan A. Husain
Andreas Huyssen
Marion E. (Betty) Jemmott
Constance Jordan

Peter H. Juviler
David Scott Kastan
Joel Kaye
Laura Kendrick
Alice Kessler-Harris
Joseph Kissane
Christopher Kleinhenz
Patricia H. Labalme
Richard Lansing
David Levering Lewis
Susan Lloyd
Edward P. Mahoney
William McBrien
James McIntosh
Ken & Peggy McIntosh
Richard & Marjorie McIntosh
Letty Moss-Salentijn
John Hine Mundy
Kristina Olson
Margaret Aziza Pappano
David L. Pike
Sandra Pierson Prior
Esther Quinn
David Raybin
Roy Rosenstein
Jane E. Rosenthal
George Saliba
Karl-Ludwig Selig
Robert Somerville
Sarah Spence
Gayatri Chakravorty Spivak
David Staines
Robert Stein
Catharine R. Stimpson
H. Wayne Storey
M. Teresa Tavormina
Toy-Fung Tung
Nancy Vickers
Winthrop Wetherbee
Charles T. Wood
Mary Marsh Zulack

Bibliography of Joan M. Ferrante

Books

The Conflict of Love and Honor: *The Medieval Tristan Legend in France, Germany, and Italy*. De proprietatibus litterarum. The Hague: Mouton, 1973.

Guillaume d'Orange: *Four Epics*. Translation with commentary. Records of Civilization. New York: Columbia University Press, 1974. Reprinted in paper, 1991.

In Pursuit of Perfection: *Courtly Love in Medieval Literature*. Edited with George D. Economou. Port Washington: Kennikat Press, 1975.

Woman as Image in Medieval Literature from the Twelfth Century to Dante. New York: Columbia University Press, 1975. Reprinted in paper Durham, NC: Labyrinth Press, 1985, and Grand Rapids: Baker Books, 1995.

The Lais of Marie de France. Translation and commentary with Robert W. Hanning. New York: Dutton, 1978. Reprinted in paper Durham, NC: Labyrinth, 1982, and Grand Rapids: Baker Books, 1995.

The Political Vision of the Divine Comedy. Princeton: Princeton University Press, 1984.

W. T. H. Jackson. The Challenge of the Medieval Text: *Studies in Genre and Interpretation*. Edited with Robert W. Hanning. New York: Columbia University Press, 1985.

To the Glory of Her Sex: *Women's Roles in the Composition of Medieval Texts*. Bloomington: Indiana University Press, 1997.

Internet Databases

Epistolae: *Medieval Women's Latin Letters*. Database of letters and translations online through Columbia Center for New Media Teaching and Learning.

Articles

"The Frame Characters of the *Decameron*: A Progression of Virtues." *Romance Philology* 19 (1965): 212–26.

"The *Malebolge* as the Key to the Structure of Dante's *Inferno*." *Romance Philology* 20 (1967): 456–66.

"The Relation of Speech to Sin in the *Inferno*." *Dante Studies* 87 (1969): 33–46.
"The Conflict of Lyric Conventions and Romance Form." In *In Pursuit of Perfection*. Eds. George D. Economou and Joan M. Ferrante. Port Washington: Kennikat Press, 1975. 135–78.
"Narrative Patterns in the *Decameron*." *Romance Philology* 31 (1978): 585–604.
"Florence and Rome, the Two Cities of Man in the *Divine Comedy*." *Acta, Binghamton Conference on the Early Renaissance* 5 (1978): 1–19.
"Artist Figures in the Tristan Stories." *Tristania* 4 (1979): 25–35.
"Some Thoughts on the Application of Modern Critical Methods to Medieval Literature." *Yearbook of Comparative and General Literature* 28 (1979): 5–9.
"Ab joi mou lo vers e 'l comens." In *The Interpretation of the Medieval Lyric*. Ed. W. T. H. Jackson. New York: Macmillan, 1980. 113–41.
"The Education of Women in the Middle Ages, in Theory, Fact, and Fantasy." In *Beyond Their Sex, Learned Women of the European Past*. Ed. Patricia A. Labalme. New York: New York University Press, 1980. Reprinted in paper, 1984. 9–42.
"*Cortes' Amor* in Medieval Texts." *Speculum* 55 (1980): 686–95.
"Was Vernacular Poetic Practice a Response to Latin Language Theory?" *Romance Philology* 35 (1982): 586–600.
"Words and Images in the *Paradiso*: Reflections of the Divine." In *Dante, Petrarch, Boccaccio*: *Studies in the Italian Trecento in Honor of Charles S. Singleton*. Eds. Aldo Bernardo and Anthony Pellegrini. Binghamton: State University of New York Press, 1983. 115–32. Italian translation: "Parole e immagini nel *Paradiso*: riflessi del divino." In *Studi Americani su Dante*. Eds. Gian Carlo Alessio and Robert Hollander. Milan: Franco Angeli, 1989. 203–19.
"*Farai un vers de dreyt nien*: The Craft of the Early Trobadors." In *Vernacular Poetics in the Middle Ages*. Ed. Lois Ebin. Kalamazoo: Medieval Institute, 1984. 93–128.
"Male Fantasy and Female Reality in Courtly Literature." *Women's Studies* 11 (1984): 67–97.
"The French Courtly Poet: Marie de France." In *Medieval Women Writers*. Ed. Katharina M. Wilson. Athens: University of Georgia Press, 1984. 64–89.
"Self-Imprisonment of Man and Society in Courtly Codes." *Andrew W. Mellon Lectures*. New Orleans: The Graduate School of Tulane University, 1984.
"The Court in Medieval Literature: The Center of the Problem." In *The Medieval Court in Europe*. Ed. Edward E. Haymes. Houston German Studies 6. München: Wilhelm Fink, 1986. 1–25.
"Good Thieves and Bad Thieves: A Reading of *Inferno* XXIV." *Dante Studies* 104 (1986): 83–98.

"Public Postures and Private Manoeuvres: Roles Medieval Women Play." In *Women and Power in the Middle Ages*. Eds. Mary Erler and Maryanne Kowaleski. Athens: University of Georgia Press, 1988. 213–29.

"Usi e abusi della Bibbia nella letteratura medievale." In *Dante e la Bibbia: Atti del Convegno Internazionale*. Florence: Olschki, 1988. 213–25.

"A Frenchwoman in England Writes for a Norman Court: Marie de France." In *A New History of French Literature*. Ed. Denis Hollier. Cambridge: Harvard University Press, 1989. 50–56. (Also translated into French.)

"Notes Towards the Study of a Female Rhetoric in the Trobairitz." In *The Voice of the Trobairitz*. Ed. William D. Paden. Philadelphia: University of Pennsylvania Press, 1989. 63–72. Reprinted in *Classical and Medieval Literary Criticism*. Vol. 66 (2004).

"Images of the Cloister: Haven or Prison." In *A Miscellany of Medieval and Renaissance Studies in Honor of Aldo Bernardo*. Eds. Anthony L. Pellegrini and Bernard S. Levy. *Mediaevalia* 12 (1986; publ. 1989): 57–66.

"'Ez ist ein zunge, dunket mich,' Fiction, Deception and Self-Deception in Gottfried's *Tristan*." In *Gottfried von Strassburg and the Medieval Tristan Legend*. Eds. Adrian Stevens and Roy Wisbey. Cambridge: D.S. Brewer, 1990. 171–80.

"Dante's Beatrice: Priest of an Androgynous God." In *Center for Medieval and Early Renaissance Studies: Occasional Papers, 2*. Binghamton, NY: State University of New York Press, 1992.

"The Bible as Thesaurus in Medieval Literature." In *The Bible in the Middle Ages: Its Influence on Literature and Art*. Ed. Bernard S. Levy. Binghamton: State University of New York Press, 1992. 23–49.

"A Poetics of Chaos and Harmony." In *The Cambridge Companion to Dante*. Ed. Rachel Jacoff. Cambridge: Cambridge University Press, 1993. 153–71.

"Why did Dante Write the *Comedy*?" *Dante Studies* 111 (1993): 9–18.

"Alatiel, Politics, Finance, and Feminism in *Decameron* II, 7." *Studi sul Boccaccio* 21 (1993): 151–174.

"Whose Voice? The Influence of Women Patrons on Courtly Romances." In *Literary Aspects of Courtly Culture*. Eds. Donald Maddox and Sara Sturm-Maddox. Cambridge: Boydell and Brewer, 1994. 3–18.

"Beyond the Borders of Nation and Discipline." In *The Future of the Middle Ages: Medieval Literature in the 1990's*. Ed. William D. Paden. Gainesville: University Press of Florida, 1994. 145–63.

"Hell as the Mirror Image of Paradise." In *Dante's Inferno: The Indiana Critical Edition*. Ed. Mark Musa. Bloomington: Indiana University Press, 1995. 367–80.

"Women's Role in Latin Letters from the Fourth to the Early Twelfth Century." In *The Cultural Patronage of Medieval Women*. Ed. June Hall McCash. Athens: University of Georgia Press, 1996. 73–104.

"Dante and Politics." In *Dante: Contemporary Perspectives*. Ed. Amilcare A. Iannucci. Major Italian Authors. Toronto: University of Toronto Press, 1997. 181–94.

"'Scribe quae vides et audis': Hildegard, Her Language, and Her Secretaries." In *The Tongue of the Fathers: Gender and Ideology in Twelfth-Century Latin*. Eds. David Townsend and Andrew Taylor. Philadelphia: University of Pennsylvania Press, 1998. 102–35.

"Correspondent: 'Blessed is the Speech of Your Mouth'." In *Voice of the Living Light: Hildegard of Bingen and Her World*. Ed. Barbara Newman. Berkeley: University of California Press, 1998. 91–109.

"Canto XXIV: Thieves and Metamorphoses." *Lectura Dantis: Inferno*. Eds. Allen Mandelbaum, Anthony Oldcorn, Charles Ross. Berkeley: University of California Press, 1998. 316–27.

"Introduction." With Robert W. Hanning. In *Medieval Scholarship: Biographical Studies on the Formation of a Discipline*. Vol. 2. Literature and Philology. Ed. Helen Damico. New York: Garland, 1998. xiii–xxvi.

"History is Myth, Myth is History." In *Dante, mito e poesia. Atti del secondo Seminario dantesco internazionale*. Eds. Michelangelo Picone and Tatiana Crivelli. Florence: Franco Cesati, 1999. 317–33.

"Earthly Love in a Spiritual Setting: The Language of Friendship among Religious" and "Spiritual Love in an Earthly Context: Religious Allusions in Courtly Love Texts." In *Earthly Love, Spiritual Love, Love of the Saints*. Ed. Susan J. Ridyard. *Sewanee Medieval Studies* 8 (1999): 5–44.

"'Licet longinquis regionibus corpore separati': Letters as a Link in and to the Middle Ages." *Speculum* 76 (2001): 877–95.

"*Women in the Shadows of the Divine Comedy*." In *Reading Medieval Culture: Essays in Honor of Robert W. Hanning*. Eds. Robert M. Stein and Sandra Pierson Prior. Notre Dame: University of Notre Dame Press: 2005. 407–25.

Response to Carolyn G. Heilbrun, "From Rereading to Reading." Forum: Responses to Carolyn G. Heilbrun's Guest Column. *PMLA* 119 (2004): 320–21.

INTRODUCTION

The essays in this volume were commissioned for a conference held at Columbia University in November of 2001 in honor of Joan M. Ferrante's sixty-fifth birthday. All the speakers at the conference were one-time students of Ferrante's, now established scholars. The essays consequently reflect those areas that Ferrante herself has most cultivated in her distinguished career. They range through time, covering the period from the tenth through the fifteenth century, and across languages, discussing sources in Latin, Italian, French, Occitan, English, and Hebrew. They range also through a variety of cultural settings: from nunneries in Germany, Italy, France, and England to a Jewish community in France; from the Provence of the troubadours and the England of Chaucer to the Florentine scribal circles in which Dante's *Vita nuova* was copied.

As a group, the essays in *Medieval Constructions in Gender and Identity* mirror Ferrante's lifelong commitment to comparative medieval literature. Their breadth is both tribute to and *imitatio* of the extraordinary breadth demonstrated, singularly as well as collectively, by the books Ferrante published between 1973 and 1997: *The Conflict of Love and Honor: The Medieval Tristan Legend in France, Germany, and Italy* (1973), the first detailed comparison of five major medieval versions of the Tristan story, the French poems of Béroul and Thomas, the German poems of Eilhart and Gottfried, and the Italian prose *Tavola Ritonda*; *The Political Vision of the* Divine Comedy (1984), a study of the *Divine Comedy* as political propaganda in the context of contemporary political theory, the church-state conflict, economics, and social justice; *Woman as Image in Medieval Literature from the Twelfth Century to Dante* (1975), a major step in its day for medieval women's studies, focusing on the way women are presented in different literary genres, in contrast to the more recent *To the Glory of Her Sex: Women's Roles in the Composition of Medieval Texts* (1997), which concentrates on historical women who commissioned, inspired, or composed political, religious, and literary texts.

Ferrante's bibliography also includes two translations that are still in print and still being adopted as texts: *Guillaume d'Orange: Four Epics* (1974), and *The Lais of Marie de France* (1978), a work which she undertook with her longtime friend and colleague, Robert W. Hanning. (Hanning has contributed "In Praise of a Nonpareil Colleague" as an Afterword to this volume.) Nor should I overlook, in this tribute to my own doctoral sponsor, the two collections of essays inspired by W. T. H. Jackson, Ferrante's doctoral sponsor and the founder of the comparative medieval tradition at Columbia University, a tradition that Ferrante has since carried forward: *In Pursuit of Perfection* (1975), co-edited with George

D. Economou, which features essays on courtly love in various genres by Ferrante and Economou and several other Jackson students, and *The Challenge of the Medieval Text*, co-edited with Robert W. Hanning, which gathers Jackson's most important essays on medieval literature. Ferrante's own articles extend the range of subjects that interested her to Boccaccio as well as Dante, to various aspects of Provençal lyric poetry and of medieval narrative, to the education of medieval women and Hildegard of Bingen's relation to her texts.

Ferrante's current work is *Epistolae*. This enormous, groundbreaking, and generous project is a unique database of medieval women's correspondence, letters gathered by Ferrante over the last twenty years and now numbering more than two thousand. Culled from various sources — the *Patrologia Latina*, collections of letters, chronicles, and histories — these letters were written to and from women from the fourth to the thirteenth century. They are grouped by the woman, with a brief biography of each woman and historic information about each letter. Eventually there will be genealogies showing how many of the women are related and how major royal and noble houses are related through the women. The purpose of the database is to make generally available the more than two thousand letters that Ferrante has so far collected in both their Latin originals and in translations.

The *Epistolae* database makes a very important contribution to the history of women, and is indeed the culmination of a lifetime of important contributions to the history of women. In her work on women, Ferrante has always been drawn to showing not how mistreated they were but how culturally significant and active they were — how indeed they operated to the glory of their sex. The *Epistolae* database, which allows these women to speak in their own voices, will continue to make this fundamental and critical point. The letters demonstrate — and dramatize — how deeply involved medieval women were in politics, culture, and religion. Moreover, the letters reveal details about real life and the role women played in it that are not mentioned in most medieval or later histories, thus adding to our understanding of the past.

What the essays in the present volume share with Ferrante herself is a passionate interest in questions of women and identity formation. Ferrante's pioneering and profoundly political contribution to the history of women and their representation is a connecting thread through many of these essays. In "Hrotsvit von Gandersheim and the Political Uses of Astrology," Joan Cadden poses a problem — that "the search for a medieval Marie Curie, the gold standard of women scientists, has not been profitable, and historians of science and medicine have had to revise their questions and methods in order to understand and benefit from the veins of material uncovered by earlier scholars" — and suggests applying a Ferrantean approach as a solution:

The work of Joan Ferrante, particularly the ambitious synthesis presented in *To the Glory of Her Sex*, offers a model and even, in the case of particular women authors, a map. Ferrante's subtle treatment suggests that the significance, the contributions, indeed the glory of medieval women is often to be discerned in their participation in the cultural, religious, and political projects of their time; in their deployment of the intellectual and rhetorical resources available; in the very embeddedness of their experiences, actions, and utterances within networks of women and men. As her work shows, rather than obscuring the specificity of female vision and voice, this contextual approach highlights it.

Cadden interprets the tenth-century playwright Hrotsvit von Gandersheim's use of astrology in her verse legend of St. Dionysius as an act of political and cultural significance. Using as a springboard the model provided by Ferrante's *To the Glory of Her Sex*, Cadden makes a learned if "circumstantial case for reading Hrotsvit's advancement of astrology as part of an Ottonian agenda." The essay reflects an important new current in medieval feminist scholarship by placing a woman in the larger sphere of intellectual activity without insisting unduly on her gender. Showing us how "Hrotsvit put the science of the stars to work," Cadden forcefully concludes that "the issue is not whether Hrotsvit is a candidate for a Nobel prize in physics for her astrological expertise, though she ranks high on a tenth-century scale" but that she made skillful, active, and creative use of her astrological knowledge in ways that "advanced the larger social programs of her milieu."

Anne L. Clark's essay, "Under Whose Care? The Madonna of San Sisto and Women's Monastic Life in Twelfth- and Thirteenth-Century Rome," tells a sadder and less empowered story of male ecclesiastical intervention in the rhythms of a female religious community. Whereas Hrotsvit was a noble canoness at the imperial abbey of Gandersheim, Clark takes us to a monastery in Rome, known as Sancta Maria Tempuli or Sancta Maria in Tempulo, "best known not for any extraordinary woman who dwelt there" but for its ownership of a famous icon of the Virgin Mary, now commonly referred to as the Madonna of San Sisto. Clark's investigation focuses on the time when the nuns of Sancta Maria Tempuli and their icon were forced to join the Dominican community of nearby San Sisto. This transfer, which occurred in 1221, offers an opportunity for reflecting on "the self-identity of this women's community," a self-identity "articulated in terms of the nuns' relationship to their icon of the Virgin."

Using the eyewitness account of Cecilia, a nun who participated in the move to San Sisto from Sancta Maria Tempuli at seventeen and who years later refers to it in the stories she dictated about miracles worked by Dominic, Clark shows us that Cecilia's story of the transfer of the nuns is not only centered on "the drama of the fate of her community," linked indissolubly to the icon, but that it is also a story of loss, for at the time of the move both the sisters and the icon were removed from public view: "The enclosure of the nuns and the icon in a strictly cloistered environment removes both from public circulation. The nuns are no longer able to leave their monastery and their relatives will have much more restricted access to them. Their traditional way of life—one that in ecclesiastical hindsight will be called 'wandering all over the place' and the 'custom of inveterate liberty'—is being radically transformed to fit the new papal agenda of strictly cloistering all religious women." The cloistering of the nuns of San Sisto leads to the cloistering of the icon of the Virgin: "Thus neither the nuns nor the icon, as signs or embodiments of sacred presence, were to have an active role in the larger economy of Roman religious life after the transfer to San Sisto."

The theme of enclosure and resistance—of women exerting what power they could muster in their cloistered religious communities—returns in the contribution of Margaret Aziza Pappano. While granting that "The history of female monasticism in medieval Europe can be told as a relatively straightforward narrative of increasing clerical encroachment on female sources of power and expression," Pappano notes that "recent studies that examine particular institutional contexts, attentive to the daily negotiation of power on a micro-level, have made it apparent that practices like enclosure were highly contingent, related to such things as social status, nature of order, circumstances of foundation, and geographical location." In "Sister Acts: Conventual Performance and the *Visitatio Sepulchri* in England and France," Pappano attends precisely to "the daily negotiation of power on a micro-level," looking at liturgical drama as representing "a way in which the nuns could redraw the line between themselves and laywomen, promoting their special access to spiritual life through performance."

Considering liturgical drama from three nunneries, in particular the versions of the *Visitatio Sepulchri* performed on Easter morning at the nunneries of Barking and Wilton Abbeys in England and of the Abbey of Ste.-Benoîte-Origny in France, Pappano analyzes the use and non-use of touch as a means of mapping the relation of the nuns to power through their performances. Her essay examines the significance of the nuns who portray the three Marys at Barking touching and kissing the feet of the actor portraying Christ, a symbolic gauge of their access to the body of God: "Only in the *Visitatio Sepulchri* of Barking Abbey do the Marys fall to the ground and kiss the feet of Christ." Noting that "Barking's Easter drama is singular, perhaps as a testament to the particularly powerful and important position of this monastic institution, home to queens, princesses, and other nobility throughout its long history," Pappano then moves to Origny, where she focuses on the insertion into the liturgical drama of a vernacular female voice which "serves to dissociate spiritual knowledge from male, clerical, Latinate authority" and concludes that "This play is less interested in the signifier of the tomb's emptiness than in Mary's experience." By contrast, the female performers in the Wilton Abbey Easter drama were strictly regulated, the nuns' identities "produced as bodies which are not literally enclosed, because there is obviously a lay congregation present at the play, but symbolically enclosed."

If in these female religious communities performance is the site of a negotiation between repression and the expression of identity, in the larger community as well we can see forms of art functioning as a means of self-affirmation in the face of isolation and persecution. In "On the Borders of Exile: The Poetry of Solomon Simhah of Troyes," Susan L. Einbinder offers us an opportunity to glimpse a world rarely seen by those of us who work in more well-trodden fields, that of a "virtually unknown Jewish poet from northern France" who reflects "the state of intellectual life among northern French Jews just prior to their expulsion from France in 1306." Einbinder takes us to Troyes, not as the home of Chrétien and his canonical romances, but as the scene of Jewish martyrs: "In Troyes, famed through the twelfth century as a seat of Jewish learning, the competing interests of local, Dominican, and royal officials converged on the Jews memorably in the spring of 1288. That year, thirteen local Jews were burned at the stake following an accusation of ritual murder." In her analysis of Solomon's poetry, which includes his two laments for the Troyes martyrs, Einbinder explores the language of cultic sacrifice that "offered both mourners and the rabbi-poets a theological framework that encompassed senseless violence" and draws particular attention to "Solomon's use of cultic imagery as a metaphor for the act of composing poetry and prayer." Einbinder's essay expands the frame of reference for our theme of identity and further illuminates the paths of resistance and affirmation that humans take in the quest to maintain a sense of identity and of self. Like Cadden's treatment of Hrotsvit, moreover, Einbinder's presentation of Solomon Simhah of Troyes inserts a marginalized figure into the larger cultural context.

With Roy Rosenstein's "*Ubi Sunt?* Three Lost (and Found) Ladies in Troubadour Lyric," we remain in France and within the context of the historically lesser known, turning back however to women as exemplars of the disenfranchised within the dominant culture. As Rosenstein writes, his paper "recovers one unknown woman, one forgotten woman, and one legendary woman, all of them historical players behind the genesis of lyrics by as many and more troubadours: Guiraudo lo Ros, Jaufre Rudel, Uc de Mataplana, Raimon de Miraval, Uc de Saint-Circ." On the whole, as with the previous papers, Rosenstein is dealing with history—with retrieving the stories of actual women with whom male troubadours and/or their poetry engaged—rather than with the representation of women, to which we will turn in the essays of Akbari and Barolini.

Rosenstein embarks on the literal retrieval of identity in the case of Alis, "a woman whose identity is unknown because it is concealed beneath a codename or *senhal*, used by a troubadour to refer to his lady without betraying her identity."

In this instance, Rosenstein's sleuthing takes us to only a partial revelation, to "an Elis or Alis at the court of Dalfi d'Alvernha and others frequented by Guiraudo." With respect to Sarrazina, however, Rosenstein uncovers the wife of Hugh VII of Lusignan in Jaufre Rudel's "theme song of the Second Crusade," *Quan lo rius,* in which the troubadour affirms that there never was a nobler Christian woman than his beloved, neither Jewess nor Saracen woman ("Juzeva ni Sarrazina"). Here, in Rosenstein's convincing reconstruction, the common noun "Sarrazina" is also a proper name, indeed the name of the wife on whose grave, "in the presence of their five sons, [Hugh] had sworn to set out on the disastrous crusade from which he, like his friend and companion Jaufre Rudel, would not return." From the wife encoded by a poet into his poem as a tribute to her husband, Rosenstein moves to a woman poet in her own right, the trobairitz Gaudairenca—a poet, but unfortunately one whose poems do not survive. Consequently, the reconstruction of her colorful life—discarded by her husband the troubadour Raimon de Miraval, because "he did not want a wife who knew how to compose poetry," Gaudairenca promptly contracted a new marriage with her lover—is based on poetic exchanges between men and on the accompanying prose commentaries known as *razos.*

Whereas Rosenstein uses the Occitan *razos* and *vidas,* the prose "lives" of the troubadours, as aids in reconstructing historical identities, Laura Kendrick, in "Lives and Works: Chaucer and the Compilers of the Troubadour Songbooks," uses them to think about the creation of individual identity in a great literary text, Chaucer's *General Prologue* to the *Canterbury Tales.* Kendrick innovatively juxtaposes the troubadour *vidas* to Chaucer's pilgrim portraits, which she suggests "might more appropriately be called 'lives'." The proposed literary analogues for Chaucer's "lives," Benoît de Sainte-Maure's portraits of Trojan and Greek heroes and heroines in his twelfth-century *Roman de Troie,* do not make use of the past experiences of his characters. By comparison, Kendrick notes that, while the description in the *vidas* is certainly more formulaic than in Chaucer, "One of the most striking themes the troubadour *vidas* share with the pilgrim 'lives' is precisely what, according to Lumiansky, we do *not* find in Benoît de Saint-Maure's portraits: 'past experiences' or events of personal history." While Kendrick concludes that "Analogies between Chaucer's *General Prologue* 'lives' of the pilgrim storytellers and the collected *vidas* of the troubadours should not be pressed too hard," her essay illuminates both the creation of identity in the *vidas*—"Identity in the troubadour *vidas* is defined in terms of where one comes from and where one goes or has gone"—and by comparison in the *General Prologue,* whose "pilgrim storytellers remain more anonymous than do the troubadours."

From the identities of characters in a text, either historical like the troubadours in the *vidas* or fictive like the pilgrims in the *General Prologue,* we move to authorial, scribal, and textual identity in H. Wayne Storey's "Following

Instructions: Remaking Dante's *Vita Nova* in the Fourteenth Century." Indeed, Storey's essay demonstrates the importance of the material and codicological context in the creation of the Italian literary canon. Storey plunges us into the world of book production, which he engages through a discussion of the technical significance of *liber* versus *libello* and hence the technical significance of Dante's using the term *libello* for the *Vita nuova* (composed c. 1292–1294; for the different spellings see the note in the Barolini essay). Focusing on the "passages usually overlooked for their seemingly mundane technical instructions," he notes that in the *Vita nuova* "we find Dante the copyist guiding what he knew would be other copyists of his work on *how* to transcribe his *libello*." Storey speculates that "Dante's elaborate narrative frame might well have been designed not only to elucidate the poems' reconstructed compositional contexts and hidden meanings but also, as in the tradition of the *trobar clus*, to protect materially the little book's lyrics which could have otherwise been reordered outside the poet's narrative or even scattered from their collective form in disparate copies." In other words, Dante inserts instructions to future copyists of the *Vita nuova* in order to preserve the authorial integrity and identity of his book—his construction, his creation. And he was successful: for although Storey rightly alerts us to Boccaccio's prehumanist excisions of Dante's *divisioni*, ultimately the *Vita nuova*'s authorial constructedness withstood assaults on its textual identity.

Sarah Spence's "The Straits of Empire: Sicily in Vergil and Dante" moves from the construction of the Italian canon to the construction of Empire, or more precisely, to the construction of the "poetics of Empire." Spence reads the use of Sicily by Vergil in the *Aeneid* and by Dante in the *Purgatorio* as analogous to Shakespeare's use of Wales in Terence Hawkes's reading of *Henry V*: in each case the ancient land is used to validate the native and true culture upon which the new nation is founded. Spence shows that Dante follows Vergil in representing the home landscape in a way that grounds poetic support of Empire in the cultural geography of the nation, and then goes further, demonstrating that the politicized image of Sicily may be used as a means for fruitfully exploring anew both the *Aeneid* and the *Commedia*'s Vergilian intertextuality. Indeed, Spence effectively locates the origins of a rich tradition—the tradition of Sicily as Cicero's "jewel in the crown" of the Roman Empire—that has continued and developed into our own times: modern Italian literature boasts many instances of Sicily as the primal trope of the politicized landscape.

Noting that "the action of the *Aeneid* begins off Sicily ('vix e conspectu Siculae telluris') and the setting of the entire poem is limited to that part of the Mediterranean dominated by Sicily," Spence explores Sicily's liminal status as a place that "was but is no longer a part of the mainland": "Aeneas, in avoiding the straits, distinguishes himself from the earlier heroes and goes around Sicily, both marking and erasing the divide. Where other heroes and authors find and emphasize division, Vergil and Aeneas assert a more complex relationship as a new unity emerges from the divided land." With respect to Dante too, Spence locates in Sicily a trope of unity. Working with Ferrante's emphasis on the connection in Dante between politics and poetry, a hallmark of *The Political Vision of the* Divine Comedy, Spence shows that, for Dante, "Sicily, whose language, unlike its rivers, is not divided at Pelorus from the Italian peninsula, is the land of unity—of politics and poetry."

With Suzanne Conklin Akbari's essay, we circle back to women, now not to the vicissitudes of historical women but to the question of the representation of women. Akbari focuses on the representation of Muslim women in the figure of the "Saracen princess," a convention that she explores through the princess Floripas featured in the romance of *Fierabras*. Akbari frames her study with an appeal to the Ferrantean topos of "woman as image": "Since the publication in 1975 of Joan Ferrante's groundbreaking study, *Woman as Image*, much work has been done on women's roles in medieval literature: not just on their active participation as writers, patrons, and correspondents"—this is the work Ferrante contributes to in *To the Glory of Her Sex*—"but on their passive representation." In "Woman as Mediator in Medieval Depictions of Muslims: The Case of Floripas," Akbari concludes, "The case of Floripas illustrates the extent to which the 'image of woman' is not singular—not even within the tradition of a single romance."

Akbari focuses on the variable depiction of Floripas in three French versions of the romance *Fierabras*: the verse *Fierabras* (of which the earliest manuscript dates from the fourteenth century), the anonymous prose *Fierabras* (surviving in two early fifteenth-century manuscripts), and the prose version completed in 1478 by Jean Bagnyon. In her essay we witness the complex negotiations at the intersections between gender identity and religious/cultural identity. As Akbari notes, "the extended period during which Floripas is neither wholly Saracen nor wholly Christian repays examination, for it constitutes a liminal phase during which not only Floripas's identity, but also the feminine ideal itself, is in flux." Woman serves as link and conduit—as mediator—between otherwise alien cultures, for Saracen princesses can convert and marry Christian kings, but at the same time the conduit may be a source of contamination: "the pagan woman even after conversion may pollute the Christian world she enters." Akbari probes the unstable identity constellation embodied in the Saracen princess, illuminating the shifting authorial negotiations as we move from the early verse romance whose Floripas "must be understood within the terms of the ideology of the crusade," to Bagnyon, who explicates "the capricious and unrestrained behavior of Floripas in terms of woman's essential nature, rather than in terms of Saracen identity."

My essay, "Lifting the Veil? Notes toward a Gendered History of Early Italian Literature," continues the discussion of the representation of women by sketching a paradigm for evaluating the treatment of women in early Italian literature. I argue that the key to approaching the construction of gender in the authors of the early Italian tradition is their ambivalence, manifested in the competing ideological systems to which they subscribe: on the one hand, they subscribe to the ideology of courtly love, and, on the other to an often violently anti-courtly ideology that permeates their moralistic poetry. Poetry based in a courtly logic is always fundamentally narcissistic and centered on the male lover/poet; the female object of desire serves as a screen on which he projects questions and concerns about himself. Whether we are speaking of the courtly poetry of the Sicilian Giacomo da Lentini early in the thirteenth century or the later theologized courtliness of Dante and his fellow *stilnovisti* (poets of the "new style"), the fundamental logic of the courtly poem remains narcissistic. The didactic works of writers like Guittone d'Arezzo, Dante in his late moral canzoni, and Boccaccio, on the other hand, are marked by a utilitarian stamp: women are supposed to *use* this literature, to be instructed by it, to learn from it. In other words, this poetry, precisely by virtue of its moralistic and even paternalistic program, actually needs to communicate with women, to treat them as subjects who can learn, rather than as objects to be desired.

My argument, then, is that the tradition of male instruction of women in utilitarian and moralizing texts is in fact more *progressively* pro-feminist than the beautiful and much beloved courtly strand of Italian poetry because, by assuming that women can be taught, the writers of moralizing instruction assume that they have agency, the ability to make decisions to change their lives. In this essay, which advances a framework for a shift in our thinking about the early Italian tradition, I pursue this argument by starting with Dante, asking how we account for his development from a courtly poet into the poet of the *Commedia*, that is, into a poet who assigns agency to all human beings, including women. To answer that question, I focus on one of his late moralistic canzoni, *Doglia mi reca nello core ardire*, a poem that functions as a pivot between the earlier courtly poet and the poet of the *Commedia*. I then move back to one of Dante's lyric precursors, Guittone d'Arezzo (d. 1294), whose didactic poem on female chastity, *Altra fiata aggio già, donne, parlato*, influenced Dante's *Doglia mi reca*, and conclude with Boccaccio, whose *Decameron* exemplifies a male author's commitment to using discourse on behalf of women.

In fact, it is Boccaccio to whom we shall give the last word, for he beautifully ties together our volume's opening essays on monastic women, in their struggle with male regulation and suppression in the form of enclosure, with its concluding essays on the representation of women in literary texts. For Boccaccio attends to the enclosure of women. Indeed, he opens the *Decameron* by explaining that he offers his book as solace to women in love since their need is greater than that of men, and their need is greater because they are "racchiuse"—"enclosed": "ristrette da' voleri, da' piaceri, da' comandamenti de' padri, delle madri, de' fratelli e de' mariti, il piú del tempo nel piccolo circuito delle loro camere racchiuse dimorano" ("constrained by the wishes, the pleasure, and the commandments of their fathers, their mothers, their brothers, and their husbands, most of the time they remain enclosed in the small compass of their rooms" [*Proemio* 10]). Boccaccio is the early Italian author who most explicitly places the category "woman" (rather than just a particular woman) at the core of his opus and who, in a fashion that is contradictory, nuanced, and anything but ideologically doctrinaire, shines a light on the disenfranchisement of women, using them as emblematic for all those who are oppressed, cloistered away from society, and stripped of agency. Not just addressed to women, Boccaccio's work is also a vehicle for understanding their lives; not just an indictment of immobility and enclosure, the *Decameron* is a work that guides the reader in the construction of an alternate reality of mobility and fresh air. *Mutatis mutandis*, our tribute hopes to make the same point about the work of Joan Ferrante.

I would like to add a word of thanks to those who have helped in the making of this volume: the sagacious and helpful anonymous readers, from whose time and efforts we have all benefited; the supportive staff of Medieval & Renaissance Texts & Studies, in particular its Director, Robert Bjork, and its Managing Editor, Roy Rukkila; and my research assistants Kristina Olson and Juliet Nusbaum. I thank Juliet, who came late to this project, for her attention and care in bringing it to conclusion. Kristina's energy, determination, and friendship were essential and inspirational throughout the process, from the planning of the original conference through the editing of the manuscript. I couldn't have done it without her, and I am very grateful.

Teodolinda Barolini
Columbia University

HROTSVIT VON GANDERSHEIM AND THE POLITICAL USES OF ASTROLOGY

JOAN CADDEN

Recovering historical evidence of women's participation in science and medicine during the Middle Ages has been a laborious process, yielding fragmentary and often disappointing results. In its early phases, it was fueled by a necessary optimism—a refusal to take "none" for an answer—that succeeded in unearthing mother lodes we continue to mine today. The wishful belief that these veins would pan out to be pure gold led not only to the misinterpretation of the first assays but also to a failure to reflect on the crucial role of less noble metals in medieval civilization. As a more thorough examination of the evidence evolved, what had at first appeared to be a rich and untarnished record of female scientific accomplishment sometimes came to look debased. Margaret Alic, in her history of women in science, celebrated the early identification of foremothers: "Trotula and the 'Ladies of Salerno' . . . helped to bring about the medical renaissance that signaled the end of the Dark Ages in Europe" (1986, 50). By that time, however, new evidence was emerging that "Trotula" was not the author of the medical works usually attributed to her; her role in the production of that opus was circuitous. Moreover, the material that *can* be attributed to a woman named Trota, although of great interest, was no glorious forerunner of the medical renaissance.[1] Similarly, those who pointed to precious nuggets of astronomical and medical learning in the works of Christine de Pizan, a physician-astrologer's daughter, have recently been met with cautionary remarks like, "She doesn't even seem to be familiar with the notion of epicycles" and "It is clear . . . that [she] does not have a deep knowledge of the medical field."[2]

In short, the search for a medieval Marie Curie, the gold standard of women scientists, has not been profitable, and historians of science and medicine have

---

[1] Benton (1985) and Green (1999 and 2000) have applied paleographical and philological methods to a question previously debated largely in terms of what a woman "could not have" or "must have" written. Cf. Marie de France, "Les deus amanz" (1978), 128–30, ll. 95–140 and 129, n. 2. An edition of the work on practical medicine by Trota will be included in Green, *Women and Literate Medicine in Medieval Europe: Trota and the "Trotula"* (forthcoming).

[2] Ribémont 1995, 256: "Elle ne semble même pas connaître la notion d'épicycle qui pourtant figure dans le manuel de base de tout enseignement de l'astronomie depuis le XIIIe siècle"; Picherit 1995, 241: "Il est clair, à la suite de l'inventaire que nous venons de dresser, que Christine de Pizan n'a pas une connaissance approfondie du domaine médicale . . ." See also Ribémont 1994.

had to revise their questions and methods in order to understand and benefit from the veins of material uncovered by earlier scholars. The work of Joan Ferrante, particularly the ambitious synthesis presented in *To the Glory of Her Sex*, offers a model and even, in the case of particular medieval women authors, a map. Ferrante's subtle treatment suggests that the significance, the contributions, indeed the glory of medieval women is often to be discerned in their participation in the cultural, religious, and political projects of their time; in their deployment of the intellectual and rhetorical resources available; in the very embeddedness of their experiences, actions, and utterances within networks of women and men. As her work shows, rather than obscuring the specificity of female vision and voice, this contextual approach highlights it.

Hrotsvit, Saxony, and an Astrologer-Saint

This paper about the uses of science draws on the substance and method of Ferrante's work in an attempt to place a few lines in the writings of Hrotsvit von Gandersheim (c. 935–c. 1000) into one dimension of its context: the legitimation of the Ottonian dynasty that controlled the Holy Roman Empire from 962 to 1024. Hrotsvit was a noble canoness at the imperial abbey of Gandersheim, which Liudolf, duke of Saxony (d. 866), and his wife Oda (d. 912) had founded within their core domains near the northeastern frontier of Christian Europe.[3] Its abbesses, like those of the nearby house at Quedlinburg, were powerful regional lords and participants in the regime of this family that ascended from dukes to kings to emperors. These women's houses safeguarded the spiritual well-being of the family and its dependents, but they also offered special opportunities for the consolidation of land and power. The sisters, daughters, and nieces of the ruling family who were withheld from the marriage market often presided over these institutions, where their resources and talents reflected and enhanced the status of Liudolf and his descendants (Ferrante 1997, 76–78; Edwards 1996; Leyser 1979, 64–71; Althoff 1991).

By the time Liudolf's great-grandson Otto I, dressed in Frankish garb, became King of Francia and Saxony at Aachen in 936, the dynasty had already involved itself in marital, political, and military affairs to the west and south, where the old, rich, and populous centers of European power were located. Nevertheless, its resources and strength were still rooted in the eastern marches of the Empire, which remained a precarious frontier. For example, in 983, when Otto I had been emperor for more than twenty years and Hrotsvit was about fif-

---

[3] On the political history of the dynasty, especially in relation to their royal and imperial status, see Müller-Mertens 1999 and Lees 2004.

ty, groups of Slavs raided Saxon religious houses, including the convent at Hillersleben about seventy miles northeast of Gandersheim (Leyser 1979, 64). Gandersheim as an institution and Hrotsvit as an individual did much to contribute to the formation of Ottonian authority in the mid- to late tenth century beyond supplying financial and military support. Hrotsvit's plays, for example, though set in patristic times and formed on classical models, persistently conveyed messages about good and bad rulers that reflected the political conditions and forces of her environment (Schütze-Pflugk 1972; Wailes 2001). Her verse accounts of the founding of Gandersheim and the deeds of Otto I, among the few narrative histories produced in the region, not only celebrated the family and its retainers but also shaped their images (Ferrante 1997, 78–81). Justly celebrated for her rhetorical skills, Hrotsvit was one of the very few writers of her time to integrate mathematical sciences into her historical and religious writings. In the early Middle Ages the quadrivium—arithmetic, geometry, astronomy, and music—had its home mainly in encyclopedic works, such as that of Macrobius, and in the specialized tracts of *computus* that addressed such problems as calendrical calculation (McCluskey 1998; Lindgren 1976, 13–39). Hrotsvit may have been familiar with some of these texts. She could also have drawn upon literary references, as well as on the expertise of contemporary scholars with whom she had contact through connections with the imperial court.

Vigilant readers of Hrotsvit's works, Ferrante among them, have remarked on the moment in the play *Sapientia* at which the character Wisdom demonstrates her command of arithmetic principles, wielding her expertise as a weapon against a pagan oppressor (2001e, sc. III, § 13–21; Ferrante 1997, 183; Wilson 1987). And they have likewise recognized the significance of the lessons the saintly Pafnutius teaches about musical and celestial harmonies in the play *Thais*, where proportion and equilibrium ultimately prevail over the fleshly passions of a corrupt city (1970a, sc. I, § 7–17; Ferrante 1997, 183; Chamberlain 1980). In each case, the learned discipline provides the basis for important structural elements within the works, at the same time that the learned displays enhance the prestige of the characters, the author, and the social elite of which she was a part. The goal of this paper is to add the science of astrology to the list of disciplines that Hrotsvit employed, and to develop some specifically political aspects of the authority that her writing supports. Her deployment of astrological knowledge evoked the classical glories of the older power centers of France and Italy at the same time that it addressed the newer stresses of the Northeastern regions from which the Ottonians emerged.

Although the study of celestial bodies had clearly distinguished divisions and uses, early medieval authors often employed the terms "astronomy" and "astrology" interchangeably. Isidore of Seville (d. 636), whose authoritative and encyclopedic *Etymologies* circulated widely, includes "astrology" in his discussion of "astronomy" (1911, bk. 3, chap. 27). There he condemns some astrological practices but finds others acceptable. He does not use the word "astrology" in his chapter on *magi*, which is devoted to forbidden activities such as augury, divination, magic, and sorcery (bk. 8, chap. 9). As evidence from her works will suggest, Hrotsvit was aware of both the ambiguities and the distinctions among these terms. In the following discussions and translations of particular texts, the English mirrors the terms that occur in the Latin.

Astrology makes an appearance at the opening of Hrotsvit's verse legend of St. Dionysius. Her main source is the *vita* by Hilduin, Abbot of St. Denis, written in the mid-ninth century to glorify his monastery's patron saint.[4] Hilduin begins with the story of a distinguished scholar, "dedicated to philosophy and to the vain superstitions in the cult of the pagans." St. Paul's preaching leads him to abandon these "demonic trifles and heathen fictions," and to accept Christ.[5] Paul later meets Dionysius, famous for his extensive knowledge of the divinities, and asks him about an altar labeled "Unknown God" that he sees among the pagan shrines in Athens.[6] Dionysius explains that he had gone to Egypt with a fellow philosopher who was a votary of astrology. There, at what Paul later tells him was the moment of Christ's death, day was turned into monstrous night. "Astonished by the [celestial] sign of these shadows—one never before seen or heard of—[Dionysius, who was] educated in the disciplines of all subjects, said: 'This night, which, with our eyes, we wonder at having descended suddenly, has given a sign of the coming true light of the whole world, and a God that will shine forth to humankind.'"[7] Following a dialogue with the apostle, he becomes Paul's disciple. Only after he witnesses a miracle, however, are Dionysius and his household baptized.

Hrotsvit starts her own version of the story with the moment when the sun goes dark. Dionysius himself is the astrologer (the companion has disappeared), and he is in Egypt drinking deeply from the streams of that art. Whereas Hilduin's Dionysius regards the event as unprecedented, Hrotsvit's protagonist, though taken by surprise, at first seeks an explanation in the ordinary operations of nature.

---

[4] Homeyer, in Hrotsvit 1970, 188–91. Hilduin's *vita* was written shortly after 834.

[5] Hilduin 1864, chap. 4, col. 26: ". . . deditusque esset philosophiae, et vanis superstitionibus ritu paganorum.

. . . daemonicas ludificationes et gentilitias [sic] adinventiones . . ."

[6] The altar to the unknown god and the conversion of Dionysius on the basis of Paul's preaching about it figure in Acts 17.

[7] Hilduin 1864, chap. 5, col. 27: ". . . earumdem tenebrarum signo antea inviso et inaudito attonitus, ut omnium litterarum disciplinis edoctus, dixit: haec nox, quam nostris oculis novam descendisse miramur, totius mundi veram lucem adventuram signavit, atque Deum humano generi effulsurum, serena dignatione dictavit."

Thus he applies his specific scientific expertise: astrology. This is, she explains, "the art that teaches the motion of the stars and also the course of the sun." The *magus*, as she calls him, "was astounded and began to seek in the books he had gathered, whether there could be an eclipse of the sun at that time." Having assured himself that there could not, he recorded the day and year. "And he conjectured, with [these] propitious signs as evidence, that a beneficent god as yet unknown was soon to be shown to the world."[8] Dionysius returns home to Athens, where he adds the "unknown god" to his pantheon and explains the story to Paul. He is won over to the faith, witnesses a miracle, gets baptized, travels west, receives his commission from the Pope, suffers among the Gauls, gets executed, and carries his head to the site of Hilduin's abbey.

Hrotsvit's telling of Dionysius's conversion takes fewer than thirty lines but it contains clues about the status and uses of the mathematical sciences, especially the one called alternately "astronomia" and "astrologia." First, Hrotsvit is unflinching in her identification of the future saint as an astrologer. In addition to describing him as *astrologus* and *magus*, she defines the science, alludes to its texts, mentions elements of its subject matter, describes some of its methods, and, finally, emphasizes the protagonist's expertise in the art. Furthermore, although, like Hilduin's pagan idolater, Dionysius abandons the Greek pantheon for the one true God, Hrotsvit does not dismiss his art with phrases like "vain superstitions" or "demonic trifles." Indeed, we find nothing even slightly derogatory in the diction of this passage. Rather it is by the careful application of his skills that he is brought to the brink of conversion.

In the early Middle Ages, astrology had not only all the usual drawbacks of pagan learning, such as a concern with worldly matters, but also a general connection with other forms of divination, against which the early church fought persistently, and a specific incompatibility with free will. Under these circumstances, we might ask, "What possessed her?" In fact, Hrotsvit's very awareness of these problems gave her the resources to meet the commonplace objections to the activities of "mathematicians," as astrologers were often called. Her definition of astrology derived directly or indirectly from Isidore of Seville. That science, the respected bishop held, can be either licit ("natural") or illicit ("superstitious"). The former corresponds to Hrotsvit's definition and has to do with "the

---

[8] Hrotsvit 2001d, ll. 6–16: "Quo mox astrologus viso Dyonisius almus, / Qui tunc Memphitidis artem discebat in oris, / Quę docet astrorum motus solis quoque cursum, / Obstupuit libris coepitque requirere lectis, / Si tunc eclypsis posset consistere solis. / Ast ubi non solitas sensit magus esse tenebras, / Descripsisse diem dignum ducebat et annum / Non dubitans designari quid forte stupendi, / Quod post mysterium declarasset tenebrarum; / Coniectatque deum signis testantibus almis / Actenus ignotum mundo mox esse probandum." Homeyer reads "lectis" as meaning "collectis" (1970,193, note to l. 9).

courses of the sun and the moon, or the fixed positions of the seasons' stars"; the latter involved using celestial signs as augurs of the spiritual or bodily states of individuals.[9] She has placed Dionysius's methods squarely on the acceptable side of the science, even if she has not entirely distanced him from the divinatory practices of its superstitious branch.

If Isidore's distinction gave her permission to incorporate astrology, it did not provide an imperative to do so. What reasons can we discern for the prominence Hrotsvit gives to its practice by a Christian martyr? I would suggest two answers, each of which illustrates something about the way this science functioned in Hrotsvit's specific historical context. The first and more general concerns the quadrivium and the liberal arts; the second returns to the relationship between astrology and divination.

The Functions of the Quadrivium

Taken together, the liberal arts formed a significant element of the Ottonian cultural agenda (Newell 1987, 130–32). After a period of serious disruptions in what had been the Carolingian empire, felt especially in Saxony at the eastern boundaries of northern Christendom, the formation of a regional dynasty was hard enough; the reconstitution of the Roman Empire required a vast array of resources including military, marital, and ecclesiastical strategies. As members of noble families, landlords over vast territories, and suppliers of armed men, the women who led Gandersheim and other imperial religious houses played a direct role in Ottonian politics, but they also provided many cultural products, such as Hrotsvit's *Deeds of Otto [the Great]*, that served to legitimize imperial claims. Among the raw materials at their disposal were the remnants of Charlemagne's similar project, including the substance and symbolism of classical learning as embodied in the liberal arts. Alcuin of York (d. 804), as head of the palace school, had written school texts on each of the arts; and the emperor's biographer Einhard tells us that Charlemagne had his sons and daughters educated in them, mentioning that the king himself especially supported scholarship on astronomy and "investigated most eagerly the course of the stars."[10]

---

[9] Isidore of Seville 1911, vol. 1, bk. 3, chap. 27, § 2: "Naturalis, dum exequitur solis et lunae cursus, vel stellarum certas temporum stationes. Superstitiosa vero est illa quam mathematici sequuntur, qui in stellis auguriantur, quique etiam duodecim caeli signa per singula animae vel corporis membra disponunt, siderumque cursu nativitates hominum et mores praedicare conantur."

[10] Einhard 1911, § 25, 30: "siderum cursum curiosissime rimabatur." On Charles's children, § 19, 23.

What had been for the long-Christian Franks a reminder of their links with classical Rome was for the never-Romanized Saxons a much more alien enterprise, making the role of Hrotsvit and other scholars all the more difficult. Like most of her contemporaries, Hrotsvit drew first and foremost upon the resources associated with grammar and rhetoric. Her greatest accomplishment in this vein was undoubtedly the fusion of the plays of Terence with the tales and lessons of early Christian history. Members of the educated elite were far less likely to be familiar with the particulars of the mathematical arts, or quadrivium, than with literary subjects (Newell, 1987, 130). Gerbert of Aurillac (c.945–1003), the greatest mathematician of the tenth century, had to search throughout Europe for books on astronomy and mathematics. But, like the most learned of her contemporaries, Hrotsvit grasped elements of these less common arts as well. Her command of celestial science was limited compared to her greater proficiency in music and arithmetic. Yet she was familiar with important concepts and vocabulary, so that her insistence on astrology in *St. Dionysius* is sufficient to stand in as the third of the four mathematical arts codified by encyclopedists like Macrobius and Isidore. Like Gerbert, she made no comparable use of geometry.[11]

The mathematical sciences had their own particular functions within early medieval culture. First, just as the trivium of grammar, rhetoric, and logic was valued as a set of tools that could be brought to bear in the interpretation of scripture, so the quadrivium — arithmetic, geometry, astronomy, and music — played crucial practical and theoretical roles in medieval religious life. The subject of *computus*, which, by Hrotsvit's time, incorporated a variety of elements from tracts on calculation to agricultural advice, centered on the knowledge of solar and lunar astronomy, indispensable for the measurement of liturgical hours, days, and years (McCluskey 1998, chs. 5 and 6). This was the sort of knowledge Dionysius used to determine eclipse times. Secondly, just as the literary sciences unified and validated the textual foundations of elite culture and, as such, accorded quasi-magical powers to those who controlled both the arts and the texts, so the mathematical sciences unified and validated the order and proportion of body, soul, society, and cosmos and, similarly, accorded a sort of transcendent authority to those who defined and interpreted measure, ratio, and harmony. Hrotsvit invoked this order in the lessons her character Pafnutius taught about the microcosm and the macrocosm in *Thais*.

---

[11] Bubnov (in Gerbert 1899, 46, n. 1) does not accept the *Isagoge geometriae* attributed to Gerbert as genuine. See also Lattin in Gerbert 1961, 6.

The Powers of Astrology

The specific relation of these functions to the particular historical circumstances in which Hrotsvit was writing will become clearer in connection with the second reason for her incorporation of astrology into a saint's life: the association of astrology with divination and its attendant cultural status. Auguries, auspices, and other means by which the course of human events could be predicted were precisely the practices Isidore and others had associated with forbidden superstitions of astrology, and it was precisely the accusation of divination that Hrotsvit dodged by identifying Dionysius's astrology with the natural (and thus acceptable) knowledge of heavenly motions. But in her telling of the story, the saint employed *both* branches of the science; indeed he *had to* do so in order to arrive at his awe and reverence for this "unknown god." First, that is, he consulted the astronomical tables that contained the positions of the sun and the moon, and he did the calculations necessary to ascertain that the darkness was not the result of an eclipse. These were practices of "natural" astrology. They led him to conclude, however, that this was not a natural occurrence. Hrotsvit continues to describe his next moves in language consistent with the procedures of respectable natural philosophy. He hypothesizes (*coniectat*) on the basis of the evidence (*signis testantibus*) that the existence of a new god would be verified (*esse probandum*). He even notes down the exact day and hour. Nevertheless, what he is doing is interpreting these "signs" as an omen and attempting to evaluate their human consequences. Thus he has crossed over into what Isidore had characterized as the forbidden side of astrology. He is, in short, a *magus*, which Isidore had defined as a sorcerer.[12] Yet in Hrotsvit's narrative, if there is anything wrong with this aspect of his learning it is not that it is superstitious but that, unlike his expertise on eclipses, it is incomplete: Paul has to supply the missing element.

To make sense of this curious picture, we must consider the circumstances in which the Saxon rulers and their talented retainers carried out their cultural politics. Hrotsvit wrote the vita before 972, after which, with the marriage of Otto II to the Greek princess Theophanu and the death of Otto I, the iconography of empire took on a Byzantine hue.[13] For Otto I and for Hrotsvit, the political and cultural line of Roman imperial authority passed through the Carolingians. But if Otto the Great was able in many respects to represent himself as the political heir to Charlemagne, there were practical limits to the comparison. Like Charles, the Ottonians contended with intractable heathens to the east (the

---

[12] Isidore 1911, vol. 1, bk. 8, chap. 9, § 9: "Magi sunt, qui vulgo malefici ob facinorum magnitudinem nuncupantur."

[13] Lafontaine-Dosogne 1995. McKitterick (1995) emphasizes the continuity of intellectual traditions, however.

Slavs), but not much more than a century earlier the Saxons themselves had *been* the intractable heathens to the east. The Saxon campaigns had been among the most brutal and protracted wars prosecuted by Charlemagne (Lampen 1999). Although the Christian emperor may be said to have won by 804, he did not accomplish the project of a secure conversion, and his successors did little to incorporate Saxony into the Frankish sphere (Althoff 1999, 267). The original and most secure power bases of the Ottonians lay not in the older and more cosmopolitan diocese of western and northern Saxony, but at its eastern edge. Until 967, when Otto I secured approval of several new sees, there was only one bishop east of Gandersheim, where most of his royal lands were concentrated.[14] Record-keeping and the production of lasting artifacts were dominated by the clergy and the Christianized aristocracy, nevertheless signs of surviving pagan traditions have come down to us. Among the earliest texts in the German language, for example, are a pair of verse conjurations. Known as the "Merseburg Charms," they were written down during the tenth century, perhaps a hundred miles south of Gandersheim.[15]

In the course of the gradual conversion of Europe, everything from the location of an altar to the role of relics was the product of contestation, negotiation, and synthesis. Even an idealist in tenth-century Saxony would have been a fool to ignore the powerful magical forces that inhabited earth and sky—and the Ottonians were neither idealists nor fools. Gods and spirits that had exercised power over their land and people, along with the practices and practitioners required to tame and exploit them, were far too effective instruments of authority to be passed over by rulers making their way from dukes to kings and from kings to emperors. On the other hand, they could not take advantage of these supernatural and social forces by embracing a patently heterodox theology or relying on under-educated local clergy. Much of their political, diplomatic, and administrative success depended on the institutions of a transnational church and the talents of clergy recruited from across Europe, including such figures as Gerbert, who became Pope Sylvester II. As Valerie Flint has pointed out, the most opportune area of convergence between pagan occult practices and Western Christianity was that dealing with the heavens (1991, 128–46). Thus, in a limited and always

---

[14] For landholdings, see Müller-Mertens 1999, 234–35. The appointment of the first bishops of Magdeburg, Merseburg, Meissen, and Zeitz in 968, after resistance from older dioceses, considerably enhanced Ottonian power and prestige. The sees were the first to be formed in the region since those of Hildesheim, north of Gandersheim, and Halberstadt, just to its east, were established in the wake of Charlemagne's victory.

[15] The *Merseburger Zaubersprüche* may have originated in the eighth century. They were recorded in the tenth century on the flyleaf of a ninth-century missal at the monastery of Fulda.

somewhat precarious form, astrology held and gained ground, leading to what she calls a "rush toward respectability" in the tenth century (142). Flint suggests three circumstances favorable to the "rescue" of astrology: it was not as objectionable as other forms of divination and magic; authoritative (including scriptural) support was available; and it could be associated with the mental discipline of asceticism (129).

Although Hrotsvit's portrait of Dionysius does not itself constitute a political appropriation of judicial astrology, it does represent the process by which such an appropriation was rendered possible and desirable. First, she emphasizes the scriptural invitation to read human history in the heavens: the end of Christ's life, like its beginning, is marked by a celestial omen which the adept, the *magus*, can at least partially interpret. Second, only those with books can determine such things as the timing of eclipses; thus, from a practical point of view, the adept in early medieval Europe are the clergy. This ascription of authority was a particular advantage in Ottonian Saxony, where abbots, bishops, and counselors were routinely selected by the king from among the clergy groomed in the royal chapel. Otto the Great's brother was archbishop of Cologne; his illegitimate son was archbishop of Mainz.

Finally, the place of astrology in the bosom of the liberal arts, qualified though it was, brings us back to the status and uses of the quadrivium. Unlike the various forms of earth magic, astrology belonged to a body of learning that had, for other reasons, already become a part of early medieval cultural politics. Along with music and arithmetic, the science of the heavens conveyed and explicated the integrated harmonies of the cosmos, human relations (now seen through the lens of Christian community), and the human body. It suited the Neoplatonic cast common to much early medieval interpretation of scripture and Creation. What is more, because the quadrivial subjects were less widely taught in schools and because they were highly technical, what they may have lacked in terms of demonic hocus-pocus was more than made up for in abstract virtuosity. We see the effects of quadrivial brilliance in the amazement of Pafnutius's disciples in *Thais*, as he explains the overlapping harmonies laid out in Boethius's *De musica*, and see them even more dramatically in the literally stunning proficiency with which Hrotsvit's Sapientia uses Boethian arithmetic to overwhelm her pagan adversaries. In a similar way, Gerbert of Aurillac astounded his contemporaries by the speed with which he calculated unimaginably large numbers, quickly moving marked tokens on a metal board specially inscribed with Arabic ciphers (Gerbert 1961, 46, n.1). During Hrotsvit's lifetime, Gerbert had sought out Muslim mathematical wisdom and returned from Spain with a working knowledge of the astrolabe, just as Hrotsvit's Dionysius had sought astrological secrets in Egypt. It was undoubtedly his association with the Saracen mathematical arts that led a twelfth-century chronicler to question Gerbert's orthodoxy.[16] These sciences thus enjoyed a powerful combination of authority and mystery that enhanced their usefulness in the hands of Hrotsvit and her contemporaries.

This circumstantial case for reading Hrotsvit's advancement of astrology as part of an Ottonian agenda is strengthened by the relationship of astrology to kings. The association in turn bolstered the newly emergent family's claim to royal status at a time when the politics of succession were still unsettled (Lees 2004). Of course, the sun and moon affected everyone through the cycle of the seasons and the ebb and flow of bodily fluids. Belief and practice, however, especially tied celestial signs, whether discerned in the regular motions of the heavenly bodies or in prodigious appearances like comets, to great events, such as pestilence and war, and to great personages. Indeed, in early Germanic law the primary secular reason for outlawing astrology had to do with the politically dangerous practice of predicting the deaths of kings (Flint 1991, 95 and n. 17). In the world of the Ottos, we find evidence hinting at the exploitation of such celestial powers and meanings. Writing about the Nativity in a poem on the Virgin Mary, Hrotsvit specifically calls the magi mentioned in the gospel of Matthew not only "astrologers," but also "kings."[17] The royal status of these figures did not become widely accepted until the twelfth century, so here, as in the legend of Dionysius, Hrotsvit has made a deliberate choice. And (as in *Dionysius*) her phrasing invokes the technical nature of the science: the magus-kings come *solis de cardine*, from the cardinal point of the sun, that is, the East, in search of the newborn King.[18]

Hrotsvit made no astrological references in her poem on the life of Otto the Great but she did so in the history of her abbey. Liudolf and Oda, Otto's great-

---

[16] William of Malmesbury edited in Gerbert 1899, 387.

[17] Hrotsvit 2001c, ll. 635–41: ". . . Reges astrologi solis de cardine lecti / Advenere, magi stellarum lege periti / Quęrentes urbem famosam denique Salem / Necnon Herodem constanti pectore regem / Sollicitant regis de nativitate recentis / Se vidisse novam fantes nuperrime stellam, / Quę regem natum demonstraret Iudęorum." Homeyer 1970, note on l. 635, interprets "solis de cardine" as "out of the East," and suggests comparison with Statius, *Theb.* 1, 158. As at the opening of *Dionysius*, she reads *lecti* as "together." There may also be an echo of the Christmas hymn "A solis ortu cardine": *Liturgia horarum* (1985) 337. Lewis and Short, *A Latin Dictionary*, s.v. *cardo*, includes several technical meanings, including pole, meridian line, center, cardinal point, with reference at this last to Statius.

[18] Her use of *demonstraret* may also allude to astrological methods, though (like *probandum* in *Dionysius*, 2001d, l. 16) it did not yet have the strongly philosophical connotations it later acquired.

grandparents, have royal and papal permission to establish the house. They need to determine—or perhaps to divine—the proper site. Celestial lights appear in the forest, first seen by swineherds, who are astounded by them. Duke Liudolf himself interprets the heavenly sign: the monastery is to be founded on that spot (2001f, ll. 185–226). Another miraculous bit of divination—based on the signaling of a bird—leads Hathumoda, daughter of the cofounders and abbess designate, to the quarry that will be used (ll. 238–269). With its connections both to the light in the sky that announced the birth of Jesus and to the forest magic of Saxon swineherds, this account of the ruling family and its religious foundation, whose abbess was also the lord of such rustics, reinforced the multilayered power of the dynasty.

Astrological omens and wisdom are hardly a pervasive theme in Saxon historiography, but Hrotsvit was not alone in invoking them. Liutprand (920–c. 972), an influential cleric in the imperial entourage, also took advantage of their resonance, connecting celestial omens to the fates of several kings.[19] He recorded Otto I's expedition to enforce his authority against the pope. In a brief chapter cluttered with the words *imperator, caesar, augustus* and *rex*, Liutprand tells how Otto paused before Rome while the sun was in the sign of Cancer—both inauspicious and hot. He entered the city successfully, welcomed by most of its leaders, under the more auspicious and temperate sign of the "virginal star," Virgo—colored, of course, with Christian connotations.[20] One of the emperor's first acts was to inquire into the misdeeds of Pope John XII (955–964). The chronicler suggests a contrast at this point, between the dignified and politically blessed uses of astrology and the debased, pagan, magical practices of the discredited enemy, who, according to his accusers, "begged for the help of Jupiter, Venus, and other demons, when he played dice."[21] More royal than popular, more Christian than pagan, the control of astrological signs as framed by Hrotsvit and Liutprand was also more classical than vulgar, containing echoes of Statius and Terence respectively. At the convergence of all these radii was imperial authority, sustained by institutions of the imperial church, like Gandersheim, and by the talent and learning of ecclesiastical supporters, like Hrotsvit and Liutprand.

---

[19] In addition to Otto I, the celestial bodies affected the Byzantine emperor Leo VI (an ill omen involving the sun, the moon, and all five planets) and Ludwig IV of East Francia (including a meteorological menace): Liutprand 1971a, bk. 1, chap. 9, 260 and bk. 12, chap. 4, 302.

[20] Liutprand 1971b, chap. 8, 504: "Haec dum aguntur, Phoebi radiis grave cancri sidus inaestuans imperatorem Romanis arcibus propellebat. Sed cum virginale sidus gratam rediens temperiem ferret, collectis copiis, clam Romanis invitantibus, Romam advenit." After *inaestuans*, the editors refer to Boethius, *De philosophiae consolatione*, 1.6.

[21] Liutprand 1971b, chap. 10, 508: "In ludo aleae Iovis, Veneris ceterorumque demonum adiutorium poposcisse dixerunt." The accusation is repeated in chap. 12, 512.

The textual dimension of such cultural politics was reinforced by the well-known splendor of Ottonian iconography. The treasury at Quedlinburg, like Gandersheim once a female abbey and lordship held closely within the ruling family, still contains an ivory reliquary representing Christ as the king and the sun, and depicting the twelve apostles, each accompanied by a sign of the Zodiac. And Henry II (1003–1024), the last of the Saxon emperors, had a magnificent cloak embroidered with those constellations (O'Conner 1980). The most elaborate illustrations of a secular text circulating and copied in the tenth century were the depictions of the signs of the zodiac in the astrological treatise known as the *Aratea*.[22] This network of associations was neither the invention nor the sole property of this particular dynasty. The Ottonians got the *Aratea* from the Carolingians and we may surmise that Charlemagne's special interest in astronomy among the seven arts was not entirely academic. Yet, along with the elevation of the quadrivium, the expansion of *computus*, the reproduction of zodiacal manuscripts, and the application of astrological imagery, the careful positioning of astrology in the works of Ottonian authors served a particular historical moment.

Hrotsvit put the science of the stars to work. First, she placed astrology at the service of the general, classicizing cultural movement that tied the imperial regime to their Carolingian predecessors and ultimately to ancient Rome; second, in the hands of Hrotsvit and others, the mathematical sciences, including astrology, exercised particular functions in this Ottonian renaissance; and, finally, Hrotsvit's astrological references had specific utility in the more local context of East Saxony. Seen in this light, the issue is not whether Hrotsvit is a candidate for a Nobel prize in physics for her astrological expertise, though she ranks high on a tenth-century scale. Rather, it is the skill and persistence with which she forged the serviceable metals available to her into useful rhetorical tools, and the extent to which her works in turn reflected and advanced the larger social programs of her milieu. As with Terence, so with astrology, she conjured up pagan demons and pressed them into service in the integrated interests of classical learning, Christian understanding, and Saxon legitimacy—goals she shared with the abbesses of Gandersheim and Quedlinburg, the historian Liutprand, and the teacher and pope Gerbert. A similar observation might be made about the astrological elements in Christine de Pizan's biography of Charles V. True, she does not mention epicycles, but it is not her purpose to *do* astrology. Rather, like Hrotsvit, she is responding to her specific cultural and political envi-

---

[22] It is impossible to know where all the extant manuscripts were in Hrotsvit's time or whether there were others that have not come down to us. At least one was produced in Aachen in the ninth century (Mostert and Mostert 1990; Mütherich 1990). For later in the ninth century, see McGurk 1981. A tenth-century example: Vienna, Österreichische Nationalbibliothek, MS. Palatinus 107.

ronment, engaging in a contemporary debate about power and expertise.[23] Both of these women made skillful, active, and creative use of astrological knowledge, and, in this way, they were participants in a gradually developing culture of sciences. Each, in her particular context, acted with purpose and spoke with a clear voice — to the glory of her sex.[24]

---

[23] On Christine and astrology, see Cadden 1997. For her position with respect to medical knowledge, particularly about women, see Green 1998.

[24] I am grateful to Joan M. Ferrante, Margaret L. Zimansky, and Monica H. Green for their comments on drafts of this paper.

Works Cited

Alic, Margaret. 1986. *Hypatia's Heritage: A History of Women in Science from Antiquity through the Nineteenth Century.* Boston: Beacon Press.

Althoff, Gerd. 1991. "Gandersheim und Quedlinburg: Ottonische Frauenklöster als Herrschafts- und Überlieferungszentren." *Frühmittelalterliche Studien* 25: 123–44.

———. 1999. "Saxony and the Elbe Slavs in the Tenth Century." In *The New Cambridge Medieval History*, vol. 3, *C. 900–c. 1024*, ed. Timothy Reuter, 267–92. Cambridge: Cambridge University Press.

Benton, John F. 1985. "Trotula, Women's Problems, and the Professionalization of Medicine in the Middle Ages." *Bulletin of the History of Medicine* 59: 30–53.

Cadden, Joan. 1997. "Charles V, Nicole Oresme, and Christine de Pizan: Unities and Uses of Knowledge in Fourteenth-Century France." In *Texts and Contexts in Ancient and Medieval Science: Studies on the Occasion of John E. Murdoch's Seventieth Birthday*, ed. Edith Sylla and Michael McVaugh, 208–44. Studies in Intellectual History. Leiden: Brill.

Chamberlain, David. 1980. "Musical Learning and Dramatic Action in Hrotsvit's *Pafnutius*." *Studies in Philology* 77: 319–43.

Davids, Adalbert, ed. 1995. *The Empress Theophano: Byzantium and the West at the Turn of the First Millennium.* Cambridge: Cambridge University Press.

Edwards, Carolyn. 1996. "Domestic Sanctity in Two Early Medieval Women's Lives." In *Medieval Family Roles: A Book of Essays*, ed. Cathy Jorgensen Intyre, 3–19. Garland Medieval Casebooks. New York: Garland.

Einhard. 1911. *Vita Karoli Magni.* Ed. G. H. Pertz and G. Waitz. 6th edition. Scriptores Rerum Germanicarum in Usu Scholarum; Monumenta Germaniae Historica. Hannover: Hahn.

Ferrante, Joan M. 1997. *To the Glory of Her Sex: Women's Roles in the Composition of Medieval Texts.* Women of Letters. Bloomington: Indiana University Press.

Flint, Valerie I. J. 1991. *The Rise of Magic in Early Medieval Europe.* Princeton: Princeton University Press.

Gerbert of Aurillac [Sylvester II]. 1899. *Gerberti postea Silvestri II papae opera mathematica (972–1003).* Ed. Nicolaus Bubnov. Berlin: [R. Friedländer]. Repr. Hildesheim: Georg Olms, 1963.

———. 1961. *The Letters of Gerbert with His Papal Privileges as Sylvester II.* Trans. and annot. Harriet Pratt Lattin. Records of Civilization, Sources and Studies 60. New York: Columbia University Press.

Green, Monica H. 1998. "'Traitté tout de mençonges': The *Secrés des dames*, 'Trotula,' and Attitudes Towards Women's Medicine in Fourteenth- and Early Fifteenth-Century France." In *Christine de Pizan and the Categories of Difference*, ed. Marilynn Desmond, 146–78. Medieval Cultures 14. Minneapolis: University of Minnesota Press. Reprinted in *Women's Healthcare in the Medieval West: Texts and Contexts*, item 6. Variorum Collected Studies. Aldershot, Hampshire: Ashgate, 2000.

———. 1999. "In Search of an 'Authentic' Women's Medicine: The Strange Fates of Trota of Salerno and Hildegard of Bingen." *Dynamis* 19: 25–54.

———. 2000. *The Trotula: A Medieval Compendium of Women's Medicine*. Middle Ages Series. Philadelphia: University of Pennsylvania Press.

Hilduin, Abbot of St. Denis. 1864. *Areopagitica sive sancti Dionysii vita. Patrologia Latina* 106. 13–50. Paris: J.-P. Migne.

Hrotsvit von Gandersheim. 1970. *Hrotsvithae Opera*. Ed. with intro. and comm. by H. Homeyer. Paderborn: Ferdinand Schöningh.

———. 2001. *Opera omnia*. Ed. with intro. by Walter Berschin. Bibliotheca Scriptorum Graecorum et Romanorum Teubneriana. Munich and Leipzig: K. G. Saur.

———. 1970a. *Conversio Thaidis meretricis* [= *Pafnutius*]. In *Opera omnia*, ed. Berschin, 218–44.

———. 1970b. *Gesta Ottonis*. In *Opera omnia*, ed. Berschin, 276–305.

———. 1970c. *Historia nativitatis laudabilisque conversationis intactae dei genitricis quam scriptam repperi sub nomine sancti Iacobi fratris domini* [=*Maria*]. In *Opera omnia*, ed. Berschin, 4–35.

———. 1970d. *Passio sancti Dionisii egregii martiris*. In *Opera omnia*, ed. Berschin, 104–13.

———. 1970e. *Passio sanctarum virginum fidei spei et karitatis* [= *Sapientia*]. In *Opera omnia*, ed. Berschin, 245–67.

———. 1970f. *Primordia coenobii Gandeshemensis*. In *Opera omnia*, ed. Berschin, 306–29.

Isidore of Seville. 1911. *Etymologiarum sive originum libri XX*. Ed. W. M. Lindsay. 2 vols. Oxford Classical Texts. Oxford: Oxford University Press.

Lafontaine-Dosogne, Jacqueline. 1995. "The Art of Byzantium and Its Relation to Germany in the Time of the Empress Theophano." In *The Empress Theophano: Byzantium and the West at the Turn of the First Millennium*, ed. Adelbert Davids, 211–30. Cambridge: Cambridge University Press.

Lampen, Angelika. 1999. "Sachsenkriege, sächischer Widerstand und Kooperation." In *799, Kunst und Kultur der Karolingerzeit: Karl der Große und Papst Leo III. in Paderborn*, ed. Christoph Stiegemann and Matthias Wemhoff, 1:264–331. 3 vols. Mainz: Philipp von Zabern.

Lees, Jay T. 2004. "Hrotsvit of Gandersheim and the Problem of Royal Succession in the East Frankish Kingdom." In *Hrotsvit of Gandersheim: Contexts, Identities, Affinities, and Performances*, ed. Phyllis R. Brown et al., 13–28. Toronto: University of Toronto Press.

Leyser, K. J. 1979. *Rule and Conflict in an Early Medieval Society: Ottonian Saxony*. London: Edward Arnold.

Lindgren, Uta. 1976. *Gerbert von Aurillac und das Quadrivium: Untersuchungen zur Bildung im Zeitalter der Ottonen*. Sudoffs Archiv, suppl. 18. Wiesbaden: Franz Steiner.

Liturgia horarum iuxta ritum romanum. 1985. Vol. 1, *Tempus adventus, tempus nativitatis*. The Vatican: Libreria Editrice Vaticana.

Liutprand of Cremona. 1971a. *Liber antapodoseos*. In *Quellen zur Geschichte der sächsischen Kaiserzeit: Widukinds Sachsengeschichte, Adalberts Fortsetzung der Chronik Reginos, Liutprands Werke*, ed. Albert Bauer and Reinhold Rau, 244–494. Ausgewählte Quellen zur deutschen Geschichte des Mittelalters, 8. Darmstadt: Wissenschaftliche Buchgesellschaft.

———. 1971b. *Liber de Ottone rege*. In *Quellen zur Geschichte der sächsischen Kaiserzeit: Widukinds Sachsengeschichte, Adalberts Fortsetzung der Chronik Reginos, Luitprands Werke*, ed. Albert Bauer and Reinhold Rau, 496–522. Ausgewählte Quellen zur deutschen Geschichte des Mittelalters, 8. Darmstadt: Wissenschaftliche Buchgesellschaft.

Marie de France. 1978. "Les deus amanz." In *The Lais of Marie de France*, trans. Robert Hanning and Joan Ferrante. Durham, N. C.: Labyrinth.

McCluskey, Stephen C. 1998. *Astronomies and Cultures in Early Medieval Europe*. Cambridge: Cambridge University Press.

McGurk, Patrick. 1981. "Carolingian Astrological Manuscripts." In *Charles the Bald: Court and Kingdom: Papers Based on a Colloquium Held in London in April 1979*, ed. Margaret Gibson and Janet Nelson with David Ganz, 317–32. BAR International Series 101. Oxford: B.A.R.

McKitterick, Rosamond. 1995. "Ottonian Intellectual Culture in the Tenth Century and the Role of Theophano." In *The Empress Theophano*, ed. Davids, 169–93.

Mostert, Richard, and Marco Mostert. 1990. "Using Astronomy as an Aid to Dating Manuscripts: The Example of the Leiden *Aratea planetarium*." *Quaerendo* 20: 248–61.

Moulinier, Laurence. 2001. "Hildegarde ou Pseudo-Hildegarde? Réflexions sur l'authenticité du traité 'Cause et cure'." In *"Im Angesicht Gottes suche der Mensch sich selbst": Hildegard von Bingen (1098–1179)*, ed. Reiner Berndt, 115–46. Erudiri Sapientia: Studien zum Mittelalter und zu seiner Rezeptionsgeschichte 2. Berlin: Akademie Verlag.

Müller-Mertens, Eckhard. 1999. "The Ottonians as Kings and Emperors." In *The New Cambridge Medieval History*, vol. 3, *c. 900–c. 1024*, ed. Reuter, 233–66.

Mütherich, Florentine. 1990. "Book Illumination at the Court of Louis the Pious." In *Charlemagne's Heir: New Perspectives on the Reign of Louis the Pious, 814–840*, ed. Peter Godman and Roger Collins, 593–604 and plates. Oxford: Clarendon Press.

Newell, John. 1987. "Education and Classical Culture in the Tenth Century: Age of Iron or Revival of Learning?" In *Hrotsvit of Gandersheim: Rara Avis of Saxonia?*, ed. Katharina M. Wilson, 127–41. Medieval and Renaissance Monograph Series 7. Ann Arbor: Medieval and Renaissance Collegium (MARC).

O'Conner, Elizabeth Carroll Waldron. 1980. "The Star Mantle of Henry II." Ph.D. diss., Columbia University.

Picherit, Jean-Louis G. 1995. "Les références pathologiques et thérapeutiques dans l'oeuvre de Christine de Pizan." In *Une femme de lettres au moyen âge: Études autour de Christine de Pizan*, ed. Liliane Dulac and Bernard Ribémont, 233–44. Medievalia, 16. Orleans: Paradigme.

Ribémont, Bernard. 1994. "Christine de Pizan et l'encyclopédisme scientifique." In *The City of Scholars: New Approaches to Christine de Pizan*, ed. Margarete Zimmermann and Dina De Rentiis, 174–85. European Cultures: Studies in Literature and the Arts 2. Berlin: Walter de Gruyter.

———. 1995. "Christine de Pizan: Entre espace scientifique et espace imaginé (*Le livre du Chemin de long estude*)." In *Une femme de lettres au moyen âge: Études autour de Christine de Pizan*, ed. Dulac and idem, 245–61.

Schütze-Pflugk, Marianne. 1972. *Herrscher- und Märtyrerauffassung bei Hrotsvit von Gandersheim*. Frankfurter historische Abhandlungen 1. Wiesbaden: Steiner.

Wailes, Stephen L. 2001. "Beyond Virginity: Flesh and Spirit in the Plays of Hrotsvit of Gandersheim." *Speculum* 76: 1–27.

Wilson, Katharina M. 1987. "Mathematical Learning and Structural Composition in Hrotsvit's Works." In *Hrotsvit of Gandersheim: Rara Avis of Saxonia?*, ed. Wilson, 99–111.

UNDER WHOSE CARE? THE MADONNA OF SAN SISTO AND WOMEN'S MONASTIC LIFE IN TWELFTH- AND THIRTEENTH-CENTURY ROME

ANNE L. CLARK

We have come to know much about religious women of the later Middle Ages.[1] Their sometimes anxious and sometimes exultant reflections on their religious experiences expressed in their confessional literature or their hagiographic dossiers compiled by admirers point to a wide array of religious aspirations and commitments, frustrations and joys. Even though the literary expressions of these experiences were constructed in complex processes of scribal interaction, confession, interrogation, idealization, imaginative re-creation, and political infighting (Mooney 1999), they are nonetheless valuable documents for enriching our understanding of the possibilities and parameters of women's religious lives. But striking and numerous as the documents attesting to women's devotional lives are, they are tied to a small fraction of the women who committed themselves—or were committed by others—to the professed pursuit of religious life in the later Middle Ages. There were many, many more women who lived in communities where there were no outstanding exemplars of piety to attract the attention of a hagiographer, where no sister declared that she had been visited by the hand of God and thereupon labored to create a text expressing her sense of this visitation. My focus in this essay is one such community, a monastery in Rome known as Sancta Maria Tempuli or Sancta Maria in Tempulo. During the ninth through twelfth centuries, it was a women's community best known not for any extraordinary woman who dwelt there, at least not any woman who dwelt there in the flesh. Then—as now—its reputation was based on its ownership of a famous icon of the Virgin Mary, an image now commonly referred to as the Madonna of San Sisto.

Art historians have long been interested in this icon, whether it be as a subject for study of Byzantine and Byzantine-style icons in Rome, or the more recent

[1] I am grateful to have the opportunity to offer this essay in celebration of Joan Ferrante's achievement and her generous support of others which have so richly contributed to the study of medieval religious women. I began this research while at the Institute for Advanced Study in Princeton and continued it with the support of the College of Arts and Sciences, the Graduate College, and the Women's Studies Program of the University of Vermont. I wish to thank these institutions for their support of this project. I would also like to thank Ramón Hernández, O.P., Archivist at l'Archivio Generale dell'Ordine dei Praedicatori, and Luke Dempsey, O.P., Prior of San Clemente, for their generous help in using the materials of their libraries.

work of scholars like Hans Belting, Gerhard Wolf, and William Tronzo who are interested in the role of icons in the cultural and political life of Rome. Yet despite this concern with the power and politics of icons, the role of this image in the convent's history has not been fully addressed. It is the nuns of Sancta Maria in Tempulo that I would like to bring into the stories told about the Madonna of San Sisto.

This small image (71.5 x 42.5 cm), variously dated from the sixth to the ninth century, has gold casing on the hands and a gold-leaf cross on Mary's shoulder, which, as Belting suggests, may have been part of the original image. The posture of the Virgin—her two hands extended in prayer while she looks to the one looking at her—conveys her role as advocate, and it is this function that is evoked in the title Madonna Avvocata.[2]

This is a very mobile icon. Its verifiable peregrinations can be summarized as follows: though we do not know how and when the image came to be at the convent of Sancta Maria Tempuli, it was probably not there before 806, the date at which Pope Leo III made a donation to the chapel of Saint Agatha the martyr at the monastery of Tempulo (Ferrari 1957, 225). (The dedication of the chapel was changed from Agatha to the Virgin with the arrival of the icon.) It was certainly there by 905, the year in which Pope Sergius III made a donation to the Virgin Mary at the monastery, repeatedly referring to the nuns as servants of the blessed Virgin (Carbonetti Vendittelli 1987, 7). In 1221 the icon was moved to nearby San Sisto when the nuns of Sancta Maria Tempuli joined the Dominican community of San Sisto; in 1575 it moved again with the nuns to San Domenico e Sisto in the city center (on the south edge of the Quirinal Hill [Magnanapoli], now the University of St. Thomas [Angelicum University]), and in 1931 it reached its present location in Monte Mario, at the convent of La Madonna del Rosario, still possessed by the Dominican nuns who are the successors of the early community (Belting 1994, 324–25; Boyle 1977, 4). I will focus on the time in Sancta Maria Tempuli, and on the movement of the icon from Tempuli to San Sisto. It is the movement of the image to San Sisto that is the crucial turning point in the story about women's religious life.

According to Bernard Hamilton, the fact that the community survived the late ninth-century religious decline was "almost certainly due to the veneration in which the miraculous icon was held in Rome, and the need to provide for its due cult." The patronage of Sergius III ensured its continued existence. Though it was still not wealthy enough to support a large community, yet women from

---

[2] Belting (1994, 315) suggests a sixth-century origin for the icon; Hamilton (1970, 197) cites Carlo Bertelli, who restored the icon and dated it to the late eighth or early ninth century. The image before restoration is reproduced in Belting 1994, fig. 190, and after restoration in pl. 5 following p. 264.

among noble families of Rome did go there (Hamilton 1970, 199–201). Thus from an early date, the fortunes of this women's community were linked to its possession of the icon.

The creation of the icon, its transport to the convent, and the patronage of Pope Sergius are all enshrined in a legend that circulated in several versions in Rome at least from the early twelfth century. The legend begins before the beginning, before the creation of the world, casting everything that follows in the omniscient foreknowing of God. After a summary of salvation history, highlighting the conception, birth, death, resurrection, and ascension of Jesus, the legend turns to Mary, whose physical beauty the apostles so appreciated that they "decided among themselves" that her most lovely appearance should be painted. The Evangelist Luke drew her likeness but the image was later found to be glowing with such a marvelous beauty that it was "not the work of carnal hands" but the result of a supernatural intervention. The icon, although often referred to both in the Middle Ages and today as a Lukan painting, is considered not a human rendering by an eyewitness painting the living authentic model, but a miraculous product of Luke's unintended collaboration with a supernatural artist. So the legend does not aim at affirming historicity or authenticity but rather the miraculous essence of the icon (cf. Belting 1994, 58).

Next the legend briefly disposes of the problem of the presence of the icon in Rome by saying that by God's will it was brought "here" (*in hac civitate*; *in hanc romanam civitatem*) by a holy man. More attention is given to its cultic establishment in Rome. Three pious brothers, exiles from Constantinople living in Rome at a shrine dedicated to Saint Agatha, were divinely commissioned to acquire the icon and set it up in the church of Saint Agatha, which was then rededicated to Mary. Because of these miracles, the three brothers remained there until their deaths. The reference to the exiles from Constantinople is very interesting. It may enshrine some historical memory of the presence of Eastern religious who fled to Rome during the struggles over icons, often bringing icons with them (Koudelka 1961, 27). It also hints at acknowledging the Eastern style of the icon itself, even as the legend denies its origins in mere human styles of painting.

It is only in the third and final part of the legend that there is reference to religious women at the church of Sancta Maria. Here the nuns' presence at Sancta Maria and their ownership of the icon is asserted without being explained. The legend instead focuses on a threat to the nuns' ownership. During the pontificate of Pope Sergius (904–911), certain clergy convince the pontiff that such a valuable and powerful icon should be relocated to the Lateran palace, a more appropriate site for it. With his blessing, they go and take the icon, to the great grief of the nuns. But en route to the Lateran, their progress is eerily thwarted, as the icon becomes unmovable. The pope learns that they have been halted, hurries to the spot, prays, and then is able to move it. He carries it to the Lateran palace and sets it up next to the icon of the Lord. The next night, however, the icon miraculously returns to Sancta Maria in Tempulo. The Pope goes to the convent and interrogates the abbess who reports seeing it come into the church through a window. Consulting with his clergy, the Pope acknowledges that the miraculous return of the icon to the nuns' care demonstrates that it should remain there. He celebrates Mass there and makes generous donations to the convent to honor the icon.

The legend as I just summarized it survives in several distinct versions. There are two different versions that circulated in Rome in the twelfth and thirteenth centuries; there are other versions—abbreviated, sometimes versified, sometimes translated into vernaculars—that circulated outside of Rome in collections of Miracles of the Virgin. For the history of the nuns at Sancta Maria in Tempulo, the two Roman versions are most relevant. Each of these versions is found complete in only one medieval manuscript,[3] in both cases a liturgical manuscript. One manuscript, BAV, Fondo S. Maria Maggiore, MS. 122, is a homiliary from Santa Maria Maggiore, dating from about 1100 (Salmon 1971, 4: 46); the legend is found among the readings for the dedication of the basilica. This is the version that has attracted the attention of Belting and Wolf in their discussions of Roman icons. Belting suggests that the legend was included in the manuscript as a reflection of the fear that the icon at Santa Maria Maggiore might be lost to "the greed of the curia, which sought to hoard all the sacred relics of the city in the Lateran" (1994, 316). Wolf has suggested that its inclusion in a homiliary of Santa Maria Maggiore, a traditionally papal-friendly basilica which already possessed its own cult image, was perhaps aimed at encouraging papal support of the ancient Marian images and shrines, especially, of course, Santa Maria Maggiore itself (Wolf 1990, 168). This latter explanation seems a bit odd—a story about a rather ambiguous papal action hardly seems calculated to win papal favor, and a story about one miraculous icon does not seem to be a very efficient way to seek support for another icon.

The other Roman version of the legend is found in a lectionary written around 1300, Collegio San Clemente, MS. 1, which was owned by the nuns who owned the icon (Boyle 1958, 370, 382; Boyle 1978, 188). Here the legend is found as a

---

[3] The San Sisto version is found in at least two post-medieval manuscripts: It was copied after the colophon in BAV, MS. Vat. Lat. 6075 (Paulus Sfrondratus, Passionale, 1601), and it is included in Nicolo Cassiani, *Di tante imagini della Madre S. quali si conservano e riversiscono in Roma* (17th century), in BAV, MS. Fondo Reginense, MS. Lat. 2100. Although Vat. Lat. 6075 is a copy of an eleventh-century manuscript (Cape Town, National Library of South Africa, MS. Grey 48.b.4–5), the legend of the icon is not found in that earlier manuscript. A transcription of the S. Maria Maggiore version is in Wolf 1990, 318–20; a transcription of the San Sisto version is in Mamachi et al. 1756, Appendix I, cols. 9–13; this text may be based on Rome, Collegio San Clemente, MS. 1 or perhaps on an earlier printing (Boyle 1958, 382–83).

reading for the Saturday office of the Blessed Virgin Mary. A comparison of the two texts reveals significant differences. First, in the text from the nuns' lectionary, there is much more attention to the miraculous nature of the icon. Both texts affirm that Mary's appearance had only been sketched by the hands of the evangelist Luke and both affirm that the finished product was shining with such a marvelous beauty that it could not be the work of carnal hands, but only the nuns' version makes it explicit that it was *painted* by the ineffable power of God, whereas the Santa Maria Maggiore version leaves the actual artistic process undescribed and says that it was done at God's command. The Santa Maria Maggiore text says that the name of the shrine of Saint Agatha was changed because of the icon's presence; the nuns' version says it was changed because of the frequent miracles worked there through the icon. Where the Santa Maria Maggiore version simply says that the icon could not be moved, the nuns' version has terrifying thunder and lightning at the site of its proposed removal. The Santa Maria Maggiore version says that the abbess "saw it [the icon] enter through the window of the church" (BAV, Fondo S. Maria Maggiore, MS. 122, fol. 142v); in the nun's version the abbess is said to declare to the pope, "Suddenly I saw it coming in through the window like some winged animal and behold, it promptly stationed itself in the place where, with God ordaining, it had been" (Rome, Collegio San Clemente, MS. 1, fol. 191r). Here, the icon's strenuous activity—*semetipsam strenue collocantem*—suggests not just the intervention of God but the supernatural agency of the icon itself. While it may be all well and good for the chapter clergy at Santa Maria Maggiore to include this story in their homiliary, there was no need to dwell on the miraculous power of someone else's icon.

In addition to the greater attention given to the miraculous nature of the icon, the version of the legend from the nuns' lectionary pays much more attention to the nuns themselves. For example, in the Santa Maria Maggiore text, the miraculous immobility of the icon when the Lateran clergy took it from the convent is said to be due to the Lord's desire to magnify the glory of his mother. In the nuns' lectionary, the cause of the icon's immobility is described thus: "The omnipotent Lord, who did not wish *this place* to be defrauded of its protective relic in this way, deigned to perform such a miracle *for its honor* that, as long as the wheel of this rotating world turns, *this most sacred place*, where it was established by heaven that this power had come, would be held greatly in honor" (Rome, Collegio San Clemente, MS. 1, fol. 190v; emphasis added). Verbose perhaps, but repeatedly drawing attention to *this place*, its honor, its divine favor. Where the version in the Santa Maria Maggiore homiliary never characterizes the nuns, the version associated with the nuns refers to them as living most chastely and to the abbess as being of great seriousness and sanctity. Likewise the nuns' version gives much more attention to the nuns' anguish at the loss of the icon and gives the abbess a more active, speaking role as leader of her community. The abbess, it declares, having let out a great wail, threw herself at the pope's feet and said,

"In the middle of the night, while I was greatly distressed with grief because the image of my extraordinary Lady had been carried off and I was praying with my arms outstretched to the omnipotent Lord for my sins, suddenly I saw it coming in through the window . . ." (Rome, Collegio San Clemente, MS. 1, fol. 191r).

Not only does the nuns' version of the legend pay more attention to the icon and to the nuns, it also emphasizes the evil done by the pope and the Lateran clergy. This is seen in the already mentioned passage in which the icon's immobility is attributed to the Lord's refusal to let the convent be cheated of its powerful source of supernatural patronage. In both versions of the legend, Pope Sergius acknowledges that he was guilty, but in the nuns' version, the Lateran clergy were said to be "impiously incited by the goad of envy; . . . in no way were they providing for divine honor but they were evilly consulting their own avarice"; they are said to be "stealing the icon"; and the icon is said to have returned to the place from which "it had been violently rather than piously carried away" (Rome, San Clemente, MS. 1, fols. 190r–191v).

Considering all these differences, the nuns' version of the legend cannot be seen as simply more elaborate in some neutral way; it is a more dramatic story of a confrontation between clergy inclined toward evil and the good nuns who owned a powerful, miraculous icon by divine right. The existence of this version of the legend sheds some interesting light on the ways in which this women's community remembered itself: as a community of holy nuns committed to the veneration of their patron whose presence was embodied in the icon; as a community of holy women whose way of life and property were threatened by the greed of the Lateran clergy and even the pope; as a community of holy women who were protected by their patron, the Madonna Avvocata.

This self-identity of the community is particularly interesting in light of a later set of circumstances in which the nuns of Sancta Maria Tempuli experienced the intervention of a pope and other male ecclesiastical leaders in the affairs of their life and property. In 1221, the nuns of Sancta Maria in Tempulo moved to the newly created monastery of San Sisto. The founding of San Sisto and the transfer of the nuns of Sancta Maria Tempuli there in 1221 is the setting for further reflection on the self-identity of this women's community, and this reflection is again articulated in terms of the nuns' relationship to their icon of the Virgin.

The transfer from Sancta Maria Tempuli to San Sisto, which to date has been most extensively studied by Vladimir Koudelka (1961), was anticipated by the efforts of Pope Innocent III to reconstruct the basilica of San Sisto as a monastery for all the nuns in Rome.[4] The *Gesta Innocentii III* records his substantial subsidy

---

[4] There is earlier evidence of Innocent III's interest in "reforming" Roman nuns, e.g., his letter of 7 December 1204 to the abbesses of all Roman convents (Bolton 1990, 107).

in 1208 for the construction *ad opus monialium* (Koudelka 1961, 45; Bolton 1990, 109). At his death, the work was near enough to completion that it could be finished in the fourteen-month period from Christmas 1219 to Lent 1221, now under the patronage of Honorius III. Honorius made the Gilbertines relinquish their claim on the basilica and engaged Saint Dominic, whom he knew as the guardian of Prouille, a "reformed" or strictly cloistered women's monastery, to orchestrate the transfer of the nuns of Rome to the new monastery (Koudelka 1961, 44–46, 51). In fact, not all the nuns of Rome were gathered into the new establishment. The core of the new community was the nuns of Sancta Maria Tempuli.

There is a text that gives us some insight into at least one nun's perspective on this move. Cecilia, one of the nuns of Sancta Maria Tempuli who was seventeen at the time of the move, recounted her memory of this move many years later. She remained at San Sisto for only two years until she was assigned to go to the new Dominican foundation of Saint Agnes in Bologna, where she became prioress in 1237. In the later years of her life, sometime between 1272 and 1288, she dictated to a Sister Angelica stories about miracles worked by Dominic (Walz 1967, 12). Cecilia has been chided by Marie-Humbert Vicaire, the influential historian of the Dominican Order, for some of her accounts which "border on indecency or childishness" and for her "taste for the marvelous [which] has distorted proven facts" (Vicaire 1964, 345; cf. Koudelka 1961, 40). Yet her accounts are invaluable for her perspective on the monumental changes which reshaped her life and that of her sisters.

There are two places in this text where Cecilia refers to the founding of San Sisto. In Chapter Two, Cecilia tells of Dominic's resurrection of Napoleon, the dead nephew of Stephen of Fossanova, Cardinal of the Twelve Apostles (cf. Jordan of Saxony 1982, 25). In setting the context for the miracle, Cecilia declares:

> Pope Honorius of good memory commissioned blessed Dominic to gather in one place all the nuns who were staying in monasteries in the various districts of Rome, and to make them live together in the monastery constructed at San Sisto. Blessed Dominic asked Honorius to deign to concede to him suitable allies in helping him achieve such a great affair. So Honorius gave him Lord Ugolino, bishop of Ostia, who would later be pope, lord Stephen of Fossanova, Cardinal of the holy Apostles, and lord Nicholas, bishop of Tusculum, so that they could help Dominic in everything that he required. However, when all the nuns objected and did not want of their own will to obey the lord Pope and blessed Dominic in this, the abbess of Sancta Maria Tempuli, together with all her nuns except one, offered herself to blessed Dominic with all the possessions and revenues which pertained to the monastery (Walz 1967, 12).

Cecilia goes on to describe the announcement of Napoleon's death, the Mass that Dominic celebrated, and his subsequent calling back to life of the dead youth. But this chapter is particularly important for it is Cecilia's first indication of the reaction of Roman nuns — those of her own community and those of others — to the plan for gathering all the nuns of the city into a common foundation. Cecilia tells this story as a member of the community that was in fact most amenable to the initiatives of Honorius and Dominic, as someone who seems herself to have been particularly eager to embrace this transformation of her community, as becomes clear in Chapter Fourteen of this text. At least this is how she seems to have represented herself many years later, in the words of Sister Angelica's rendering of her stories. The narration in Chapter Fourteen has so many striking elements that it is worth quoting at length:

> Following the order of the lord Pope Honorius, blessed Dominic was gathering the nuns who lived in various monasteries in the city so that he could bring them together in the church of San Sisto where the brothers had till then been staying. Among the others, the abbess of Sancta Maria in Tempulo, where there was that image of the blessed Virgin that is now in the church of San Sisto, made her profession in the hands of blessed Dominic, together with sister Cecilia and her other nuns, except for one, promising that she together with the others would enter if the image of the blessed Virgin would remain with them in the church of San Sisto. But if that image were to return to its own church, just as it had once done, she and all the others would be wholly absolved from that profession. Then blessed Dominic freely accepted this condition.
>
> After the profession, blessed Dominic told them that he did not want them any longer to go outside the cloister to visit their relatives or any one else. And so, when their relatives heard what had happened, they came to the monastery and began to argue heatedly with the abbess and the nuns, objecting that they were going to ruin such a noble monastery and moreover put themselves in the hands of that unknown and coarse man.[5] Thus it happened that some of the nuns regretted the profession which they had made.

---

[5] Whether or not Sancta Maria in Tempulo was a noble monastery, it is the case that San Sisto was hardly a place to be recommended. The fifth-century basilica dedicated to Pope Sixtus II was progressively sinking into what had become a swampy terrain. The reconstruction had begun for the Dominican friars, who received it in 1219. Cecilia's comment about the Romans' suspicion of Dominic refers to the mistrust that the friars had encountered in Rome. A fatal accident during the renovation of San Sisto was particularly dreadful to the friars who feared that the Romans would see this as a sign of divine disapproval of their mission (Vicaire 1964, 288–91).

Knowing this through the spirit (*per spiritum*), blessed Dominic came to them one morning and, having said Mass and given the sermon, said to them: "My daughters, now you regret and wish to withdraw your foot from the path of the Lord. Therefore, I wish that all you who by your own will wish to enter to again make profession in my hands." Then the abbess with others, indeed, many of those who had regretted but were called back by Dominic's merits, again made profession in his hands.

When all had professed under the same condition as they had at first, blessed Dominic took all the keys of the monastery and assumed full control of the monastery from then on. Blessed Dominic established lay brothers who would guard the monastery day and night and administer food and necessities to the enclosed sisters, and he did not permit the sisters to speak alone with their relatives or other people.

. . . So, on the first Sunday of Lent, they went to live there . . . .

On the following night after the sisters had entered, blessed Dominic was fearful of the Romans who did not want the image of the blessed Virgin to be removed from its place since they were better able to see it there. So he, together with two cardinals, namely lord Nicholas and lord Stephen, whose nephew he had raised, and many other people, all coming in bare feet, with many lamps preceding and following, carried that image on his own shoulders to the church of San Sisto. And with the sisters, barefoot and gathered in prayer and waiting for it, it was set up with great reverence in the church of the sisters. It remains there to this day with the same sisters, for the praise of the Lord Jesus, to whom is honor and glory for ever and ever. Amen (Walz 1967, 42–43).

Although the context of this story is the miracles of Dominic, Cecilia's greatest interest here is in the drama of the fate of her community. And for Cecilia, there was a very real connection between the community of women and their icon of the Virgin. There are two related issues here: first, presence—the presence of the icon is linked with the presence of the community; where the icon goes, the women will go. The self-identity of the community is constructed in relationship to this embodiment of their patron. The account also affirms the autonomous agency of the icon, suggesting its own ability to choose where it wants to be, and evoking the legend of the thwarted "theft." Dominic is portrayed as agreeing to the terms, due—we can assume—to either his faith in divine approval of the move or his cynicism about the icon's power to move on its own.

But this story is also about loss, the removal of the icon and the removal of the women's community. The enclosure of the nuns and the icon in a strictly cloistered environment removes both from public circulation. The nuns are no longer able to leave their monastery and their relatives will have much more restricted access to them. Their traditional way of life—one that in ecclesiastical hindsight will be called "wandering all over the place" and the "custom of inveterate liberty"—is being radically transformed to fit the new papal agenda of strictly cloistering all religious women.[6]

This "re-formation" of the lives of these nuns in a new physical environment is evidenced throughout the text in details about claustration. Chapter Two, portraying a time before their move to San Sisto, describes the nuns leaving the convent to attend Mass celebrated by Dominic and going with him to the house where he raises the dead Napoleon. But in Chapter Fourteen, after their move to San Sisto, the nuns wait expectantly at the convent for the procession to bring their icon to them. Even a procession with their own icon no longer includes them, because they must now remain within the cloister. And now their interactions with Dominic are limited to the window at which they gather to hear him preach in the church. The fourteenth-century chronicle of the monastery written by Prior Benedetto da Montefiascone attests to the inconvenience if not outright danger of the nuns being completely enclosed in a locked cloister with the keys held by the pope who did not exactly live next door (Rome, AGOP, MS. XII. 9003b, fols. 7v–8v).

But not only are the nuns being cloistered; so is the icon of the Virgin. The icon was placed in the nuns' chapel (*in ecclesia sororum*), not in a public part of the basilica, a fact that is noteworthy given Jeffrey Hamburger's reminder that enclosed nuns sometimes had no access to the objects that stood in the public parts of convent churches (Hamburger 1992, 120).[7] Cecilia's reference to the displeasure of the Romans at the removal of the icon from Sancta Maria Tempuli is testimony to the fact that the devotion to the Madonna Avvocata was not restricted to the nuns who possessed the icon. Dominic had to orchestrate a nocturnal transfer of the image since the Romans would resent its withdrawal from a place where they had ready access to it.

---

[6] *Per diversa vagantes* is a phrase used by Benedetto da Montefiascone, O.P., prior of San Sisto, who wrote a description of the founding of the community, to describe the agenda of Innocent III: ". . . ut mulieres Urbis et moniales aliorum monasteriorum Urbis per diversa vagantes possent ibi sub arcta clausura et diligenti custodia Domino famulari": Rome, Archivio Generale dell'Ordine dei Praedicatori, MS. XII. 9003b, fol. 3v (1667). *Consuetudine inveterate libertatis* is a phrase used by Thierry of Apolda in his *vita* of Dominic, completed c. 1298, to describe the resistance of the Roman nuns: "consuetudine inveterate libertatis absorte eius persuasionibus quadam stolida audacia et feminea pertinacia omnes pariter recusabant": BAV, MS. Vat. Lat. 1218, fol. 28r.

[7] According to the seventeenth-century convent chronicle, when the nuns moved to San Sisto e Domenico, the icon was mounted with a device so that it could be turned to be viewed by either the nuns or the public (Spiazzi 1993, 544).

Further evidence for the icon's role—and loss thereof—in the wider devotional life of Rome can be see in two circumstances outside the range of the
convent's own documentation. William Tronzo has argued that there is evidence
that in the eleventh and twelfth centuries the icon of the Madonna Avvocata was
part of the major procession celebrated on the Vigil of the Assumption (Tronzo
1989, 175–80). In the procession, the "unpainted" icon of the Savior was pro-
cessed from the Lateran, to greet the Lukan icon of the mother of the Savior.
The Virgin's intercession, represented by her outstretched arms, was affirmed as
efficacious and salvific in the celebration of the Feast of the Assumption (Tronzo
1989, 182). It was this very well-known and powerful association of the Madonna Avvocata with the Assumption that led it to be quoted in two major monu-
ments of Roman art, the apse mosaics in Sancta Maria in Trastevere and in Santa
Maria Maggiore (Tronzo 1989, 184). But the trail of evidence for this icon disappears after the twelfth century, and at some point, perhaps with other icons
intervening, the so-called Salus Populi Romani, the icon of Madonna and Child
at Santa Maria Maggiore, enters the Assumption ceremony. Art historians who
have noticed this eclipse in the role of the San Sisto icon have attributed it to
various causes: the competition of the madonnas in Rome, the preference for images of Mary with her son, the multiplication of copies of various ancient cult
images, its location in a monastic church rather than a major basilica, its vulner-
ability to theft as hinted at in the legend (Belting 1994, 322–29; Wolf 1990, 167;
Tronzo 1989, 179). None of these explanations takes seriously the history of the
nuns who owned the icon. But the "enclosure" of the icon in a strictly cloistered
monastery offers a more concrete circumstance to account for the disappearance
of the icon from the public ritual life of Rome. Cecilia's reference to the anger of
the Roman people at their loss of contact with the Madonna supports this interpretation. Neither the nuns nor the icon, as signs or embodiments of sacred presence, were to have an active role in the larger economy of Roman religious life
after the transfer to San Sisto.

There are many more aspects of the history of this women's community to be
told. A cartulary exists and has been edited, and there are some fourteenth-century account books from San Sisto. There are references to the icon in medieval
Dominican texts about Rome. There are also theories to be spun out about the
composition of the legend of the icon. But for now, I close with a reflection on
the dynamics of a women's community shaped by their ownership of a valuable
religious object, one that they seemed to identify with as it became the "coin" in
their interactions with the Roman society, both lay and ecclesiastical. This is just
one of many stories that could be told about the shifting possibilities for women's
religious life in this period. And although we may recognize in it the familiar dynamics of the increasing ecclesiastical influence being brought to bear on
women's communities to accept strict claustration, we should be mindful of two

other things. First, despite the "party line" about claustration that can be seen in the papal and Dominican documents, this was not an inevitable development; in fact, this was a great period of religious experimentation, witnessing the emergence of the Franciscan and Dominican orders and the beguines or *pinzochere*, as well as the flourishing of "open monasteries" (Gill 1992, 17–24). Second, the legend of the icon and Cecilia's *Miracula* give us some insight into the collective representation of this community—a group of women who saw their fate inextricably linked with a painting which itself had repeatedly testified to its own desire to be with them. Without the kind of textual evidence from which we often more readily recognize representations of women's religious aspirations—confessional or hagiographical literature—these documents, the legend about the beloved icon of the Virgin and Cecilia's narratives about the move to San Sisto, offer us a glimpse of how a community of religious women saw themselves in relation to the world of powerful ecclesiastics who would intervene in and even radically transform the rhythms of their life.

Works Cited

Manuscripts

Cape Town, National Library of South Africa, MS. Grey 48.b.4–5.
Rome, Archivio Generale dell'Ordine dei Praedicatori, MS. XII. 9003b.
Rome, Collegio San Clemente, MS. 1.
Vatican City, Biblioteca Apostolica Vaticana, Fondo Reginense, MS. Lat. 2100.
Vatican City, Biblioteca Apostolica Vaticana, Fondo S. Maria Maggiore, MS. 122.
Vatican City, Biblioteca Apostolica Vaticana, MS. Vat. Lat. 1218.
Vatican City, Biblioteca Apostolica Vaticana, MS. Vat. Lat. 6075.

Printed works

Belting, Hans. 1994. *Likeness and Presence: A History of the Image Before the Era of Art.* Trans. Edmund Jephcott. Chicago: University of Chicago Press.
Bolton, Brenda M. 1990. "Daughters of Rome: All One in Christ Jesus." In *Women in the Church*, ed. W. J. Sheils and Diana Wood, 101–15. Studies in Church History, 27. Pp. 101–15. Oxford: Basil Blackwell.
Boyle, Leonard E. 1958. "Dominican Lectionaries and Leo of Ostia's *Translatio S. Clementis.*" *Archivum Fratrum Praedicatorum* 28: 362–94.
———. 1977. "San Sisto and San Clemente." In idem, *San Clemente Miscellany I: The Community of SS. Sisto e Clemente in Rome, 1677–1977*, 1–26. Rome: Collegio San Clemente.
———. 1978. "The Date of the San Sisto Lectionary." In idem, Eileen Kane, and Federico Guidobaldi, *San Clemente Miscellany II: Art and Archeology*, 179–94. Rome: Collegio San Clemente.
Carbonetti Vendittelli, Cristina, ed. 1987. *Le più antiche carte del convento di San Sisto in Roma (905–1300).* Rome: Società Romana di Storia Patria.
Ferrari, Guy. 1957. *Early Roman Monasteries: Notes for the History of the Monasteries and Convents at Rome from the V through the X Century.* Città del Vaticano: Pontificio Istituto di Archeologia Cristiana.
Gill, Katherine. 1992. "Open Monasteries for Women in Late Medieval and Early Modern Italy: Two Roman Examples." In *The Crannied Wall: Women, Religion, and the Arts in Early Modern Europe*, ed. Craig A. Monson, 15–47. Ann Arbor: University of Michigan Press.
Hamburger, Jeffrey. 1992. "Art, Enclosure and the *Cura Monialium*: Prolegomena in the Guise of a Postscript." *Gesta* 31: 108–34.
Hamilton, Bernard. 1970. "The House of Theophylact and the Promotion of the Religious Life Among Women in Tenth-Century Rome." *Studia Monastica* 22: 195–217. Repr. in Bernard Hamilton 1979. *Monastic Reform, Catharism and the Crusades (900–1300)*, London: Variorum Reprints.

Jordan of Saxony. 1982. *On the Beginnings of the Order of Preachers*. Trans. Simon Tugwell. Dublin: Dominican Publications.

Koudelka, Vladimír J. 1961. "Le 'Monasterium Tempuli' et la fondation dominicaine de San Sisto." *Archivum Fratrum Praedicatorum* 31: 5–81.

Mamachi, Tommaso Maria, Francisco Maria Pollidori, Vincenzo Maria Badetto, Hermannus Dominicus Christianopulus, and Vincenzo Maria Ferretti. 1756. *Annalium Ordinis Praedicatorum*, vol. 1. Rome.

Mooney, Catherine M., ed. 1999. *Gendered Voices: Medieval Saints and Their Interpreters*. Philadelphia: University of Pennsylvania Press.

Salmon, Pierre. 1971. *Les manuscrits liturgiques latins de la Bibliothèque Vaticane*. Vol. 4. Città del Vaticano: Bibliotheca Apostolica Vaticana.

Spiazzi, Raimondo, ed. 1993. *Cronache e fioretti del monastero di San Sisto all'Appia*. Bologna: Edizioni Studio Domenicano.

Tronzo, William, 1989. "Apse Decoration, the Liturgy and the Perception of Art in Medieval Rome: S. Maria in Trastevere and S. Maria Maggiore." In *Italian Church Decoration of the Middle Ages and Early Renaissance: Functions, Forms and Regional Traditions*, ed. idem, 167–93. Villa Spelman Colloquia 1. Baltimore: Johns Hopkins Press.

Vicaire, M. H. 1964. *Saint Dominic and His Times*, trans. Kathleen Pond. London: Darton, Longman, and Todd.

Walz, Angelus. 1967. "Die 'Miracula Beati Dominici' der Schwester Cäcilia." *Archivum Fratrum Praedicatorum* 37: 5–45.

Wolf, Gerhard. 1990. *Salus Populi Romani: Die Geschichte römischer Kultbilder im Mittelalter*. Weinheim: VCH, Acta Humaniora.

Sister Acts: Conventual Performance and the *Visitatio Sepulchri* in England and France

Margaret Aziza Pappano

The history of female monasticism in medieval Europe can be told as a relatively straightforward narrative of increasing clerical encroachment on female sources of power and expression. The preponderance of ecclesiastical legislation concerned with enforcing enclosure and limiting nuns' access to sacramental religion readily supports such a teleological account. But recent studies that examine particular institutional contexts, attentive to the daily negotiation of power on a micro-level, have made it apparent that practices like enclosure were highly contingent, often determined as much by social status, the nature of the order, the circumstances of foundation, or geographical location.[1] Enclosure moreover was not always suppressive, for it might be aligned with privileged introspective devotional practices. The astounding popularity and financial success of Syon Abbey in England, founded in 1415 with a practice of strict enclosure, demonstrates the predominant ideal of seclusion for women's spiritual expression in the later Middle Ages. But for other foundations with less secure endowments, enclosure was not a practical possibility, nor did it always reflect the way that a particular institution organized its spiritual practices.[2] Powerful female monasteries had participated in secular social and political life over the course of centuries,[3] and some depended upon various forms of public repute for their ability to attract gifts and endowments. The increasing emphasis on the performance of devotion in private for lay women and on strict enclosure as the authoritative index of the nun's spiritual status have led many to stress the continuities in female spiritual experience across the lay-monastic divide in the late Middle Ages.[4] Liturgical drama represents a counter-tradition to this trend, especially since both lay men and women attended these special services which, in a decidedly public way, manifested the spiritual authority of the nuns. Liturgical drama might even represent a way in which the nuns could redraw the line between themselves and lay women, promoting their special access to spiritual life through performance.

Liturgical drama has been an overlooked source for the study of female monastic culture in the Middle Ages, yet this important genre allows us to glimpse something of the dynamics of communal life that constituted such a crucial component of monastic identity. In recent years there have been important studies

---

[1] See Oliva 1998, Warren 2001, Lee 2001, and Salih 2001.
[2] See Makowski 1997 for a discussion of the uneven practices of enclosure in England.
[3] Wogan-Browne 2001.
[4] Hutchinson 1989, 215–27; Gilchrist 1994.

that document the individual nun's narrative of spiritual experience, whether in the form of mystical vision or *vita*, but a concentration on these forms has emphasized the singular, mystically-talented nun's experience over communally-oriented spiritualities and their particular institutional contexts. By considering the liturgical drama from three nunneries, Barking and Wilton Abbeys in England, and the Abbey of Ste.-Benoîte-Origny in France, this essay will explore how specific devotional issues around public performance and affective piety were manifested differently in each institutional setting, adumbrating variations in ways that convents conceived of their communal culture.

This essay focuses on the tradition of the *Visitatio Sepulchri*, the short dramatization that was performed on Easter morning in conjunction with the matins liturgy and served to represent and announce Christ's resurrection to the expectant congregation. Easter plays were a tremendously popular genre in the Middle Ages; Walter Lipphardt's eight-volume edition of Easter drama contains approximately 830 extant plays,[5] performed in cathedrals, monasteries, and parish churches throughout western Europe from the tenth through sixteenth centuries. Twenty-three female monasteries can be identified as sites of Easter drama amongst the hundreds of edited plays, constituting a small but significant *oeuvre*.[6] The prominence of female figures in the events of resurrection provides a resonant opportunity to dramatize feminine spirituality and may have appealed to nuns for this reason.[7] Furthermore, the emphasis in these plays on the Marys as a *group* of women who process together to the grave and undergo a collective religious experience corresponds to the communal nature of devotion in the convent, allowing the nuns to shape their own vision of what O. B. Hardison termed, from the perspective of Christianity, the central event in world history.[8] The *Visitatio*s from nunneries tend to expand the role of the Marys, not just in terms of actual lines but also in terms of their role as witnesses and, in some cases, as the translators of spiritual experience to the audience. The texts of this study emphasize the emotional state of Mary Magdalen and the other Marys by adding special laments and rejoicings to the traditional liturgical dialogue. The

---

[5] Lipphardt 1975–1981. Despite its impressive breadth, this work is scarcely complete, since many liturgical manuscripts across Europe remain unedited. Lipphardt does not, for instance, include the plays from Wilton Abbey, perhaps because of their questionable preservation status (discussed below).

[6] It is important to note that there are other kinds of convent drama, most famously the plays identified with Hrotsvit of Gandersheim and the liturgical play, the *Ordo Virtutum*, of Hildegard of Bingen. In addition, the nuns of Huy appeared to produce nativity plays. As Elissa B. Weaver has recently documented, there is a rich tradition of convent performance in Italy, in comedy as well as sacred representation. See Weaver 2002.

[7] See Yardley 1986, 22.

[8] Hardison 1965.

women's sorrow and joy become the essence of the drama, and therefore the pro-
fundity of the event of resurrection is conveyed to the congregation through the
framework of female affective piety.

The earliest examples of Easter drama focus on the Marys' apprehension
of the empty grave and joyful announcement of the resurrection. In the eleventh century, the disciples John and Peter, who race to the grave and confirm
the truth of the Marys' report, begin to appear in the *Visitationes*. The addition
of the *noli me tangere* dialogue between the risen Christ and grieving Magdalen,
derived from the Gospel of John 20:15–17, can also be traced to around this time.
In the traditional approach to the *Visitationes*, pioneered by Karl Young, the ad-
ditions of these scenes correspond to three distinct "stages" of development in
the drama.[9] But six extant *Visitationes* also contain the scene of Christ's meeting
with the group of Marys on the road to Galilee, the account of resurrection from
Matthew 28:9: "Et ecce Iesus occurrit illis dicens havete. Illae autem accesserunt
et tenuerunt pedes et adoraverunt eum" [and behold Jesus met them saying hail.
They approached and touched his feet and worshipped him].[10] (The earliest of
these plays, Fleury, has been dated in the late twelfth century.) Since this scene
provides an opportunity for the three women to express their intimacy with the
risen Christ, it is significant that of the six plays that include this scene, three are
associated with nunneries: Wilton, Barking, and Origny. Matthew 28:9 appears
to be an important site of biblical authority for these nuns, promoting female
conventual experience as a source of spiritual value. Yet, although this scene is
found in six *Visitationes*, it is also notable that five of these alter the events of the
Gospels, explicitly leaving out the emphasis on tactile devotion—the action indicated by the phrase "tenuerunt pedes." Only in the *Visitatio Sepulchri* of Barking Abbey do the Marys fall to the ground and kiss the feet of Christ—only at
Barking, then, do the women touch the body of God.

The inclusion of Matthew 28:9 in the female *Visitatio* tradition, even if in
altered form, is all the more surprising given its infrequency in other genres of
the later Middle Ages. Although this Gospel event is represented in various
contexts —visual, exegetical, instructional— of the early Middle Ages, there is
a marked shift in the later Middle Ages which favors the *noli me tangere* as a locus of discussion of female spiritual access. In contrast, in the earlier period the
account of Matthew is deployed in contexts explicitly associated with female monasticism in order to authorize the nun's special relation to God.[11] For instance,

---

[9] Young 1933.

[10] I cite from the Vulgate *Biblia Sacra*.

[11] Gregory the Great's influential commentary maintains that the *noli me tangere*
does not mean that Christ forbid women *per se* to touch him, citing Matthew 28:9 as evidence. See his Homily XXV.5, in *Homiliae in Evangelia, PL* 76. 1193A.

in his letter to his sister, known as *De Institutione Inclusarum*, Aelred explains that Jesus did not forbid Mary Magdalen to touch him but simply deferred the moment of bliss until she returned with the other women, citing Matthew 28:9 as his authority:

> Redit, sed cum aliis mulieribus. Quibus ipse Iesus occurrens blanda saluta-tione, deiectas erigit, tristes consoletur. Adverte. Tunc est datum, quod fuit ante dilatum. Accesserunt enim, et tenuerunt pedes eius.[12]

> (She returned, but with the other women. Jesus goes to meet them with a soothing greeting; he cheers the dejected women; he comforts the sad ones. Observe, what then occurs, what was delayed before. "They approached him and touched his feet.")

Similarly, in his second letter to Heloise, Peter Abelard used the example of Christ's appearance to the group of Marys to exalt the special salvational value of female monasticism:

> Quae de Domini Jesu Christi sepultura sollicitae eam unguentis pretiosis et praevenerunt et subsecutae sunt et circa eius sepulcrum studiose vigilan-tes et sponsi mortem lacrimabiliter plangentes, sicut scriptum est: Mulieres sedentes ad monumentum lamentabantur flentes Dominum.[13] Primo ibi-dem de resurrecione eius angelica apparitione et allocutione sunt consola-tae, et statim ipsius resurrectionis gaudia, eo bis eis apparente, percipere meruerunt et manipus contrectare.[14]

> (Women cared for the tomb of our Lord Jesus Christ, they went ahead and followed after with precious ointments, keeping close watch around this tomb, tearfully lamenting the death of their bridegroom, just as it is writ-ten: "The weeping women sitting at the tomb lamented for the Lord." And there they were first reassured about his resurrection by the appearance of an angel and the words he spoke to them; and by his two appearances to them, they were found worthy of the joy of his resurrection and to touch him with their hands.)

In both of these examples, touch indicates a special relationship—bliss and joy—that the holy women enjoyed with Christ; moreover, this special rela-tionship serves both Aelred and Abelard to authorize the spiritual privileges of

---

[12] Aelred Rievaliensis 1971, 673. (Also in *PL* 32.1471).
[13] This is an Easter antiphon (cf. *PL* 78.769A): it quotes Luke 23:27.
[14] Abelard 1996, 212. English translation modified from the translation by Betty Radice. See Abelard 1974, 125.

cloistered women. However, this emphasis on female touch is so troubling to the later Middle Ages that it becomes excised from the dramatic depictions and is rarely found in sculptural programs and manuscript illuminations.[15] For it is precisely women's touch that is at issue in canonical legislation that seeks to bar women from altar service and handling liturgical objects,[16] radically diminishing nuns' access to ritual practice and exacerbating their dependence upon priests.[17] The scene of Christ's prohibition of women's touch—his severe and forbidding words, *noli me tangere*—massively increases in popularity precisely as Matthew 28:9 virtually disappears from the representational landscape.

As I have noted, five of the six *Visitationes* that contain the scene of Christ's meeting with the Marys choose not to represent the act of touching; most of the plays leave out the scene altogether, ending with Mary's announcement to the disciples, who then provide the authoritative voice confirming the truth of the resurrection. The heightened role of the disciples in many of the *Visitationes* may also be influenced by the thirteenth-century re-emergence of Ambrose's interpretation of *noli me tangere* that privileges the status of male interpreters of divine knowledge.[18] Given the charged context around female touching and access to the divine, it is quite provocative that the Easter drama of three convents should contain, in some form, the scene of Christ's meeting with the Marys. Yet, despite this unusual inclusion of Matthew 28:9 in the female *Visitatio* tradition, it is important to emphasize that only at Barking is the Gospel text literally enacted to dramatize female tactile devotion to the divine body.

Barking's Easter drama is singular, perhaps as a testament to the particularly powerful and important position of this monastic institution, home to queens, princesses, and other nobility throughout its long history.[19] Although Barking draws from a *Visitatio* tradition identified with the cathedral of Rouen, it alters the text in slight but significant ways to emphasize the role of the nuns.[20] For the purposes of comparison with Wilton and Origny, it is important to note that Barking includes Matthew 28:9 immediately after the *noli me tangere* scene.[21] The rubrics indicate that after uttering those enigmatic words of prohibition, the "persona" [Christ] disappears [*persona disapparuerit*]. Mary then communicates

---

[15] See "Appearances of the Risen Christ," in Duchet-Suchaux 1994, 41 for reference to the rarity of Matthew 28:9 in the later Middle Ages.

[16] See particularly the appendices of Lauwers 1992.

[17] McNamara 1996, 344.

[18] Ambrose 1902, 517–20. (Also *PL* 15.1841–1845).

[19] Loftus 1932.

[20] Young 1933, 1: 370–372.

[21] All citations to the Barking plays will be drawn from the edition by Tolhurst 1927–1928.

her joy to the other Marys, who join with her in verses of rejoicing. Another set of the rubrics indicate that the "persona" reenters, coming to the right side of the altar, where he addresses the women with the greeting from Matthew, "avete noli timere." At this point the three women prostrate themselves on the ground and hold Christ's feet [*teneant pedes*] and kiss them [*deosculentur*]. The Barking *Visitatio* alters the more ambiguous "adoraverunt" to "deosculentur," accentuating physical intimacy with the resurrected body, but it is otherwise derived from the Gospel account. The rarity of this dramatic performance, found only at Barking, exemplifies the success of the ecclesiastical establishment in limiting women's access to divine power and specifically the sacramental body of Christ.

Barking's decision to dramatize the touch of the women speaks to both the abbesses' role in designing and promoting the ceremony and also the institutional traditions that contested the male, clerical monopoly of Christ's body. Although the extant text from Barking does not provide us with clues about who played Christ in the *Visitatio*, in the accompanying *Harrowing of Hell* play the nuns take on the roles of the disciples and the patriarchs. In an institution where the abbess and nuns held the power and made the important decisions, clerical authority, even sacramental authority, could be marginalized and transformed into the perfunctory performance of duties. The Barking nuns could and did manage their own spiritual and temporal affairs, which included pastoral work, except in those areas that were under the explicit scrutiny of the bishop. Although such scrutiny may have intensified in the later Middle Ages, the strength and continuity of Barking's traditions are reflected in its liturgical and spiritual practices, which do not seem to have conformed to enclosure regulations but maintained a publicly-oriented religious life, at least at the time of the *Ordinale*'s creation in 1404. It is instructive to note that although Matilda of Newton, a nun of Barking, was selected to be the first abbess of the newly founded Syon, her leadership was shortlived. After only about a year, she was replaced and subsequently returned to Barking, probably, it has been suggested, because of her refusal to be under the direction of the male confessor general.[22] Barking nuns were accustomed to female self-governance, and their use of Matthew 28:9 appears designed to dramatize their agency and privileged relation to the very center of spiritual power — the body of Christ.

Although Matthew 28:9 represents the possibility for displaying female monastic authority, its performance was not uniform in convent liturgical practice. The extant *Visitationes* from German convents leave it out altogether, as do those of Ste. Croix in Poitiers and Notre-Dame of Troyes. Notably, both Origny and Wilton play the scene differently from Barking and from each other. All three of these nunneries were wealthy, prestigious, and ancient Benedictine

---

[22] Deanesly 1915; see also the recent discussion in Krug 2002, 163–66.

foundations where prohibitions against women's touch were at odds with the dynamics of power governing other arenas of institutional life, but all three represent Matthew 28:9 in different ways. Why do the nuns touch at Barking while they stay their hands at Wilton and Origny? Why does one Benedictine nunnery fly in the face of convention as the others appear to uphold it? My proposals will necessarily be speculative, but my argument seeks to suggest that within the broad category of women's aristocratic monasteries one can witness important variations, attesting to the highly contested and necessarily strategic nature of female spiritual authority. Even wealthy and socially prominent nuns could not always transform dominant ecclesiastical codes, for clerical sacramental authority could contravene other sites of power — precisely those to which cloistered women could lay some claim. Moreover, as I shall discuss below, Matthew 28:9 was used to explore other means of spiritual expression aside from touch that promoted modalities of female piety.

1. "Douce Dame": The Female Voice at Origny

The *Visitatio Sepulchri* from Origny Sainte-Benoîte, a Benedictine abbey in northeastern France, departs significantly from the usually terse ceremonies by incorporating extensive vernacular into the traditional Latin dialogue.[23] The alternate use of Latin and vernacular is highly significant in the context of the play, reflecting different alignments of gender with spiritual authority. The drama begins and ends in Latin and utilizes the traditional *quem quaeritis* dialogue, but the Marys express their deepest longing and sorrow for their beloved Lord in the vernacular. In this *Visitatio*, the vernacular female voice serves to dissociate spiritual knowledge from male, clerical, Latinate authority. Moreover, as the nuns move between the vernacular language of affective devotion and the Latin liturgical language, they are situated as translators, bringing knowledge of and devotion to Christ to the lay public. Origny was an important aristocratic nunnery which wielded power in its area and over the canons from the local college of Saint-Vaast who served them. Telchilde de Montessus explains, "A Origny, l'abbesse a tout pouvoir sur le clergé local: elle nomme, présente les curés à l'évêque, installe elle-même ses douze chanoines, reçoit leur hommage et leur serment, les

---

[23] All citations to the play from Origny will be from the edition by de Coussemaker 1964, 256–79. While vernacular is found in other Easter dramas, it is generally of a much more limited nature. In Origny's version, the stage directions are also in French, which is unusual. However, since the entire manuscript, the *Livre de la trésorye*, was copied into French in the late thirteenth century, this feature may represent a formal continuity within the manuscript.

corrige et les révoque au besoin, assistant une fois l'an à leur chapitre général et à l'élection de leur prévot."[24] The sense of female spiritual authority is manifested in the *Visitatio*, even to the extent that one of the nuns played the role of God.[25]

Origny is particularly notable for its lengthy *unguentarius* scene: two of the Marys negotiate with a merchant to purchase ointments to anoint the body of Christ, an exchange which takes place entirely in French. The merchant is so moved by the Marys' love for their Lord that he sells his best ointment to them for the low price of two *bezants*. The Marys' lament pervades every line of this exchange, a consistency that runs counter to the usual dynamic language of commercial transaction and ultimately leads the merchant to join them in expressing his devotion to Christ. Indeed, as the transaction proceeds the merchant's compassion increases so that he even expresses desire to go with the women to the grave; although he does not in fact follow them, he becomes like a member of the audience, eager to witness the sign of resurrection through the holy women. The vernacular merchant scene is framed by Latin, demonstrating the Marys' move out of the liturgical register as they cross from the space of the theological lament to the commercial transaction and back again. And it is explicitly in this crossing that the Marys demonstrate the unique power of holy women, their ability to mediate between God and the laity, moving the laity to exalt the spiritual above the material practices of life.

After the scene with the merchant, the play switches back to Latin and continues with the traditional *Visitatio* dialogue, "Quis revolvet" and "Quem queritis," and so on. Although the angels relay the news of the resurrection to the women and remind them of Christ's own words which foretold it, the Marys' response is one not of joy but of intense, paralyzing sorrow—they are "infelices" because they haven't found the body of their beloved Lord. At this point the two Marys depart and Mary Magdalen continues her lament alone in Latin. The angel's response, "Mulier, quid ploras?" is a traditional one, derived directly from the Gospel of John (20:13). When Mary explains that she grieves because her Lord's body has been taken away, the angel urges her not to cry because her Lord has been resurrected: "Noli flere, Maria. Alleluia! Resurrexit Dominus. Alleluia!" But even the added Alleluias, the traditional liturgical signs of seasonal mood shifts, fail to assuage Mary's sorrow. She cries with increased passion that her heart is burning—"ardens est cor meum"—and she repeats that she desires to see her Lord, but she doesn't know where they've put him. The

---

[24] de Montessus 1972, 250. Montessus's information is drawn from the unedited *Livre de la trésorye de l'abbaye d'Origny-Saincte-Benoicte* (Saint-Quentin Bibl. Mun., ms. 86), which contains information concerning the preparation of liturgical rites and other customary practices.

[25]The *Livre de la trésorye* refers to "celle qui fait dieu." Quoted by Muir 1985.

dense melismata of this musical passage stress the throbbing of the female voice, a voice riven with sorrow and pain. Then, in what must rank as one of the most beautiful and moving moments in all of liturgical drama, the angel switches into the vernacular to offer comfort to the lamenting Magdalen: "Douce dame," he sings gently: "Douce dame, qui si ploures." From this moment their exchange continues in French, the angel offering comforting words to the weeping woman and Mary responding in kind, revealing her sorrow: "Je cuit de deul me tuerai" [I think that I will die of sorrow]. Over the next few stanzas, the angel's words serve to reflect and validate Mary's depths of grief and despair—"I believe very well that your heart burns for the Lord," "I know that you grieve very greatly for him," he says. Then he tells her, "Don't cry any more, because your King Jesus will come soon to you to assuage your great pain." "Bonnes nouvelles vous aport . . . Ne plourés plus, ma douce amie," he concludes. The extended exchange in the vernacular between the angel and Mary Magdalen is singular among *Visitationes* and forms the heart of the Origny ceremony. In the midst of the formulaic Latin drama, Mary's grief is so great that it spills over the liturgical frame, moving the angel, the heavenly being, played by a priest, to acknowledge her sorrow, simultaneously acknowledging the limitations of the liturgical ritual by speaking in the language of female devotion. This dialogue stages the very centrality of female devotion in opening up a space, in one of the most familiar and formulaic rites of the liturgical year, for the voice of the woman's lament. In utilizing the vernacular, the play emphasizes that this is a gendered voice, a voice of spiritual truth and power embodied in a nun.

The shift into the vernacular serves to emphasize the primacy of Mary's feeling, the truth of the emotion, over the mode of expression. This shift in registers is staged as unexpected, a sudden accommodation to the intensity of Mary's emotions. As the language of liturgy, Latin has the effect of uniformity and repetition, marking an authoritative tradition passed down that is repeated in regular cyles throughout the year and from one year to the next. The vernacular voice halts this cyclical pattern, inserting an immediacy into the diachronous liturgical structure. The voice of Mary Magdalen's lament, in the language of the nuns, emphasizes the continuity between the holy women and the sisters of Origny: the intensity of their grief connects them, as the nuns experience this emotion and make it present in the space of their monastery. Liturgical time cedes to the here and now of theatrical embodiment.

The appearance of Christ marks the play's return to the Latin register. While on one level this reflects the solemnity of the occasion of Christ's manifestation as divinity, on another, it also represents Mary Magdalen's spiritual healing. Having seen the resurrected Christ, her grief is assuaged and she expresses her solace by returning to the Latin liturgy, singing a verse of joy together with the other Marys. The Magdalen's emotional state thus becomes the sign by which the truth of the resurrection is confirmed and the rebirth of humankind

conveyed to the populace. This play is less interested in the signifier of the tomb's emptiness than in Mary's experience. Her deep sorrow is endowed with spiritual value as her identification with Christ's suffering is represented as generative, rewarded by his appearance to her. According to the angel, Christ will appear to her *because* she grieves so deeply—women's piety is shown to have particular force and value, which in larger terms, serves to authorize and exalt the spirituality of the nunnery itself.

Christ's entry into the choir brings the ceremony back to the point where it left off with Mary's lament and commences the usual pattern of recognition, joy, and the *noli me tangere*. Although much of Origny is traditional from here on in, what is unusual is that after his words of prohibition to Mary Magdalen, Christ addresses himself to the two Marys separately and in terms that depart from the Gospel: "Avete vos, michi dilecte, et me de morte surrexisse fideliter certum habete" [Hail to you, my beloved ones, and have faithful certainty that I have risen from death]. "Michi dilecte" is a term expressing familiarity and affection, showing that the other Marys are also beloved of Christ. The two Marys fall to the ground at his feet when he greets them, but there is no suggestion that they touch or kiss him. The Gospel of Matthew reads "illae autem accesserunt et tenuerunt pedes eius et adoraverunt" (28:9), but the rubrics of Origny merely direct that "Ces deus Maries gisent as piés nostre Signeur" [the two Marys lie at the feet of our Lord]. More explicit action would surely be indicated, as it is elsewhere in the ceremony.

While Origny includes the scene of Christ's meeting with the other Marys and reveals some fidelity to the Gospel rather than the *Visitatio* tradition in doing so, it stops short of physical contact between the Marys and the risen Christ. Yet it is indeed troubling in the compressed space of a liturgical play that one woman should be prohibited from touching while the others are not. Although Mary Magdalen is certainly the star of this show, the play seems concerned that she not be spiritually privileged over or separated from the other two Marys—hence the use of the special term "michi dilecte" that serves to bring the other Marys into the fold of Christ's beloved ones. The inclusion of this scene demonstrates the nuns' desire to show spiritual expression as a shared and communal experience. Thus, at Origny, the lack of touch between Christ and the Marys may not be so much a result of influence by contemporary misogynist theological currents as an attempt to harmonize spiritual privilege amongst the women and express devotion in communal terms.

The Origny *Visitatio* does contain the scene of Peter and John's race to the sepulchre, but it does not allow the male disciples to displace the authority of the Marys' announcement of the resurrection. A curious detail is included in this *Visitatio* which is not found elsewhere in the tradition. After the Marys' joyful announcement, there is a rubric which indicates the following action: "Li doi apostre vienent devant les Maries, et prendent le manche le Magdelainne un peu de lon" [the two apostles come before the Marys, and they hold onto the sleeve of the Magdalen for a little while]. "Tell us, Maria, what did you see on the way," they ask as they tug on her sleeve. Although this spoken line is common to the liturgical tradition from the *Victimae paschali* sequence, the action of holding the sleeve, a traditional way of getting the attention of a nun, lends it a specific significance. Rather than subsuming the Marys' announcement into their own, as is found elsewhere, here the apostles seek information from Mary Magdalen in the position of supplicants. Perhaps Origny includes this stage direction in order to underscore the primacy of the women's role in resurrection. Although Peter and John run to the sepulchre, their actions bespeak belatedness rather than confirmation. It is made clear that they hear the news through Mary, who is privileged as the first and most authoritative messenger of Christ's divinity.

It is instructive to compare the *Visitatio* from Origny with that from the *Fleury Playbook,* a manuscript which has been associated with the monastery of St.-Benoît-sur-Loire.[26] There are a number of similarities between Fleury and Origny, in both verbal lines and music, suggesting that they had a common source or that Origny descended from Fleury.[27] In Fleury's version, drawn very closely from John 20, Mary's visit to the sepulchre is bisected by the scene with Peter and John. Indeed, after Mary's first lament at the grave, "Heu dolor," directed to the angel, the rubrics indicate that she should proceed swiftly to those playing Peter and John [deinde pergat velociter ad illos qui in similitudine Petri et Johannis sunt]. She directs the next section of her lament—"Tulerunt Dominum meum, et nescio ubi posuerunt eum"—to the apostles. Organized in this way, Mary's verse is transformed from lament to bewilderment, which serves to position the disciples as authorities from whom she seeks an explanation concerning Christ's disappearance. In response, Peter and John immediately run quickly to the grave, where they also view the empty sepulchre and, significantly, provide exegesis to the audience. "Has the Lord been taken away secretly," John asks. "No, as he predicted while living, the Lord has risen, I believe," Peter answers. "But why do the napkin and shroud lie in the sepulchre?" John again inquiries. "For this reason," Peter tells him, "that to the one rising from the dead they were not necessary; yes, certainly they remain here as proofs of the resurrection." Although traditionally the resurrection is presented dramatically in the play—the audience experiences the horror of the empty tomb with Mary and then experiences the joy of the resurrection when Christ appears—the experiential status of this sequence is complicated by Peter's and John's intervention as clerical exegetes.

---

[26] This association is only conjectural. For a discussion about the possible provenance, see Campbell 1985. The text is edited by Bevington 1975, 39–44; citations will be to this edition.

[27] Wright 1936, 148–52; Rankin 1989.

In order for the *noli me tangere* scene to take place, Mary Magdalen must process a second time to the grave, an awkward sequence dramatically and hence largely excluded from the *Visitatio* tradition, though supported by the narrative arrangement of the Gospel account. Organizing the drama in this way allows the male disciples increased precedence in the events of resurrection, and it also significantly recasts the Magdalen's role. Her laments now appear superfluous, a sign of women's lack of comprehension of the divine. She might be the first to see the risen Christ, but she is not the first to *know* that Christ has risen: that role has been given to Peter and John, who can interpret the meaning of the empty grave when she cannot. The *Visitatio* from the *Fleury Playbook* is a long and ambitious play; like that of Origny, it encompasses all of the major sequences of the tradition, including a version of Matthew 28:9. Yet, despite the inclusion of this scene, the play explicitly subordinates the holy women's role in resurrection. Not only is the scene of touching excised, but Mary's lament is disrupted and stripped of its emotional power.

The comparison between Fleury and Origny demonstrates the way that specific institutional contexts shaped the dramatization of resurrection. In particular, the gendering of monastic experience is inflected in the *Visitatio* tradition, as male and female institutions interpreted the events differently, even as they drew from common sources. While the earliest *Visitationes* date from a period of monastic life characterized by relative mutuality, or even indifference to gender in the pursuit of a shared vocation,[28] those from the high and late Middle Ages show the marks of changed monastic culture. As nuns struggled for access to power in the monastery, their plays reveal efforts to promote and legitimize specifically female-oriented modes of piety in the face of the ecclesiastical focus on sacramentalism. It is thus particularly intriguing to note the existence of a shared *Visitatio* tradition among female monasteries: five nunneries, Barking, Wilton, Origny, Ste. Croix in Poitiers and Notre-Dame in Troyes, have characteristics in common, particularly in their laments, that are found nowhere else.[29]

---

[28] McNamara 1996 used the term "syneisactism" to characterize the early monastic ideal: "men and women living together chastely without regard for gender differences."

[29] Wright 1936, 40 notes that the *Visitatio Sepulchri* from the convents of Ste. Croix in Poitiers, Notre-Dame in Troyes, and Origny all contain similar laments not found elsewhere.

2. Words and Action: Regulating Performance at Wilton Abbey

Wilton Abbey's *Visitatio* shares melodies and lines from the ceremony at Origny to the extent that Susan Rankin has postulated that "both must have some common ancestry."[30] Yet there is much that is unique about Wilton's play, and it is quite different in spirit from Origny. Like Barking, Wilton was an elite, well-endowed Benedictine house of Anglo-Saxon foundation (possibly ninth-century), whose abbess held the title of "baroness." Wilton's *Visitatio*, like that of Origny and Barking, includes special laments assigned to the Marys, but unlike Origny (and like Barking), is composed entirely in Latin. In contradistinction to other *Visitationes*, the role of Christ as character is ambiguous in the text. "A priest clothed in amice and alb" [sacerdos amictu indutus et alba], plays the angel at the sepulchre, but seems to double in the role of Jesus. After directing the Marys to go to Galilee, the priest appears to take on the role of Jesus, speaking his lines in the first person, although still designated as "Angelus" in the text. There are no rubrics to indicate a change in character, and indeed in most other *Visitationes* another figure is designated to play the role of God (there are occasions in the briefest *Visitationes* when the line "resurrexi" is assigned to the chorus). The unexpected appearance of the risen Christ at the grave, sometimes disguised as a gardener (cf. John 20:15), would seem to demand a separate role; some rubrics indicate that he comes unexpectedly, "per aliam viam" for instance at Mont St. Michel.[31] Many plays use the term "interim," a directional notation indicating that Christ enters the scene while another action is taking place, thus distracting the audience's attention from his approach. The traditional climactic point of the *Visitatio* drama, the first vision of the resurrected Christ, may have had as much theatrical impact as the sudden appearance of the ghost of Hamlet's father did three hundred years later, but it is curiously altered and much diminished in the Wilton play.

The Marys sing several verses of laments together as they approach the sepulchre, some of which are identical with those of Origny and found at other convents as well. After the exchange with the angel seated at the grave, the women

---

[30] Rankin 1991 has edited the Wilton *Visitatio*: 3. All citations will be to this edition. The original manuscript, a processional, has been lost; the only extant text is represented by copy made by a monk of Solesmes, Dom Jausions, in the nineteenth century, currently MS. 596 in the Abbaye St.-Pierre at Solesmes. There are a number of corrupt lines in the copy, some of which Rankin has corrected in her edition but some of which defy explanation. I would like to thank Father Daniel Saulnier for his kind help when I consulted the manuscript.

[31] Young 1933, 1:373.

maintain the form of a chorus, narrating the events of the resurrection morning in their song rather than acting them through their bodies. While this is a formal technique found in the German tradition, its appearance in England is unusual. Standing before the sepulchre, the Marys sing:

> Adest ihesus carne innovatus,
> visu pulchro nimisque amabilis
> Salutans feminas purificans animus
> Pedes eius strinxerunt venerantes eis pia oscula prebuerent.

> (Jesus is present, renewed in flesh,
> a beautiful sight of loveliness beyond measure
> The cleansing spirit greets the women
> The worshipping women grasped his feet and bestowed pious kisses on them.)

There is no indication that the actions described in these lines are acted. Immediately following this verse, the rubrics indicate that a subdeacon appears and extends a cloth ("textum") to the Marys, which they "adore and kiss" and which is afterwards ("postea") passed to the congregation to be kissed.[32] Although the women have just sung of meeting Jesus and kissing his feet, clearly alluding to the action of Matthew 28:9, rather than representing the action of touching the resurrected body, the play inserts a substitute object in the form of a cloth. At the same time, the Wilton Marys' version departs significantly from the Gospel verse of Matthew, using the more specific terms of "stringere" and "praebere pia oscula" rather than "tenere" and "adorare." This choice of verbs specifically emphasizes the tactile nature of the meeting, filling out a descriptive scenario of the event narratively rather than dramatically. "Stringere" is a particularly strong verb, suggesting not just to touch or hold his feet, but to hold them tight as if with a grasping action; the vague term of "adorare" has changed to specify the act of kissing, the pressing of lips to the divine body. Although the play does not represent the action of touching through the bodies of the nuns, the alterations made to the Gospel account portray an image of intense female tactile devotion. However, the play suggests that such devotion is appropriate only in narrative meditations or through the medium of objects. Even in this representational space, female bodies do not touch God.

Wilton uses the Matthean verse to emphasize female tactile devotion; although it circumscribes this within a context of meditational piety, such devotion was nonetheless an important aspect of female monastic practice. Jeffrey

---

[32] "Subdiaconus accipiat textum; ostendat eis quem ipse adorent prius, et osculetur postea omnis et populus." Ogden 2002, 226 n. 5, interprets this line differently, translating "textum" not as cloth but as book.

Hamburger argues that "rather than a concession to a debased form of religiosity, late medieval devotional imagery should be seen as a response to a new set of religious aspirations in which the image plays a central role."[33] Through intense relations with images, cloistered women found new modes of access to spiritual power, particularly in the form of visionary experience. The Wilton verse encourages the congragation to imagine this scene of the Marys' fervent devotion—and perhaps it also recalls, for the nuns, their private performance of such tactile devotion with Christ images in their cells. While Hamburger is correct to stress the powerful nature of this image-oriented spirituality, it must be noted that such visionary experience was largely individual, even in the context of convents where widespread visionary activity is documented among the nuns. Such personal relations with images removed the site of spiritual value from communally-constituted worship, placing it in individual, interior dialogues with God.

The Wilton *Visitatio* demonstrates this orientation towards individual piety in other ways. While Wilton does not include a *noli me tangere* scene, it contains some elements of the *hortulanus*. This part of the play occurs after the verses of the Marys cited above in which they describe the meeting with Christ, thus altering the sequence of events described in the Gospels. The Marys continue to narrate the events of the resurrection morning, although now in the singular rather than the plural, indicating that these verses refer to the experience of Mary Magdalen alone. In fact, in Wilton's account, the Magdalen appears to come to the grave and converse with the angels without the other Marys: "mane valde diliculo venit nimis ardens,/ corpus querens in sepulchro, quod continet omnia./ En prospexit; vidit angelos; non esse ibi Jhesum; nimis tristatur animo" [in the morning at dawn, she came, exceedingly ardent, seeking the body which contains all things in the grave; she looked in and saw the angels (who said) that Jesus was not there, and she was greatly saddened in her spirit]. At this point, the rubrics indicate that Mary Magdalen prostrates herself before the sepulchre, as the other two Marys continue to sing in the form of a chorus: "flere cepit. Dicunt angeli, cur ita tuas genas perfudit lacrimis? / Tunc conversa, vidit Dominum, hortulanum putat ignara fatur taliter" [she began to weep. The angels said, "Why do you wet your cheeks with tears?" Then turning around, she saw the Lord, but she, unaware and thinking he was a gardener, spoke in this way].[34] Genuflecting before the sepulchre, Mary Magdalen sings in the first person: "Meum namque hic Dominum quesieram. Si tu eum scis, dicito michi, ut inde eum auferam" [I have

---

[33] Hamburger 1998, 148.

[34] There may be a minor corruption in the text here. I have treated "perfudit" as though it were "perfudis" to make sense of this line.

sought my Lord here. If you know him, tell me, so that I may take him away (cf.
John 20:15)]; after this line, the rubrics indicate that she changes from genuflec-
tion to a fully prostrate position before the sepulchre.

It is now that the character playing the angel reveals himself to be Christ,
although there is no indication that he has assumed the tokens of a gardener,
which the verses refer to as the basis of Mary's misrecognition. (The verses also
refer to "angeli" in the plural, although the rubrics of the play do not designate
more than one.)[35]

> Si tu scire vis quisnam ego sum
> Jhesus vocitor Dei sum unicus filius.
> Tuum agnosce Deum redemptorem.
> Tu es Maria quam ego amo
> meos omnium tibi primo cupio
> isus monstrare, nomen ut tuum inde sit laudabile,
> cum gloria per secula.

> (If you want to know who I am, I am called Jesus; I am the only son of God.
> Acknowledge God, your redeemer. You are Maria whom I love over all my
> other ones. I want to show that I was seen first by you so that thence your
> name shall be praised with glory through centuries.)

Although Christ's words proclaim his special love for Mary Magdalen, the
focus is on Christ's divine authority to attribute this status to her rather than
her deep grief that generates this recognition; indeed, although some laments are
used, the expression of Mary's sorrow is much minimized in comparison with
Origny. Perhaps most surprisingly, the scene of recognition between Jesus and
Mary that leads to the *noli me tangere*, the acts of reaching and drawing away, is
oddly absent here as Christ reveals his identity while the Magdalen lies prostrate
before the grave. Is the *noli me tangere* left out because of the conflict it raises with
the Marys' verse about holding and kissing Christ's feet? Possibly, but unlike Origny, Wilton's play does not seem particularly concerned about expressing communal spiritual experience through the group of Marys. Mary Magdalen is singled
out and honored as the one beloved of Christ above all others. And indeed, perhaps the absence of the *noli me tangere* speaks to this special status. Mary's reaching to touch can be seen as a transgression, as a seeking to probe the spiritual,
which is forbidden to women. The absence of the *noli me tangere* thus emphasizes
the depiction of the Magdalen as an obedient woman, honored by Christ for her
submissive and passive devotion. Indeed, the growth in the fifteenth century of

---

[35] The Gospels of Matthew and Mark both designate a single angel, while Luke and
John describe two angels at the grave.

the legend that Christ honored Mary by touching her forehead when he forbade her from touching him testifies to the reshaping of the Magdalen as an exemplar for submissive female piety.[36]

After this speech in which the "Angelus" speaks as Christ, he appears to shift back to the character of the angel, or perhaps he resumes his priestly office. The corrupted stage directions indicate that he is to pick up the *sudarium* together with Mary. The sudary cloth, the "napkin" of John 20:7, is an object with mortal associations, the head wrapping of the grave clothes that represent the human nature of Christ, as the Fleury play explained. When Christ rises from the dead, he leaves these clothes behind. It is notable that in most liturgical plays the angels and Christ do not touch the grave clothes, although there are some exceptions.[37] The angel at the tomb often points out the cloth to the Marys, or in some cases Peter and John, who then seize upon the cloth as a special object (cf. Luke 24:12; John 20: 5–7): both as evidence of Christ's absence—the body is gone, only the covering remains—and as a holy object—something that touched the body of Christ during his process of resurrection. Because of the mortal associations of the grave clothes, it is unusual that the heavenly angel/Christ character should handle them, but since the priest has no more lines in this role but speaks again as "Sacerdos," it is likely that he returns to his status as priest when he touches the cloth. Priests indeed often displayed relics for veneration, so the character's actions here are consonant with the sacerdotal office. This multiple characterization of the priest's role as angel/Christ/priest points to an unusual elasticity in male identities.

In Anthony Kubiak's analysis, the empty tomb is a "doubled sign" of both desire, for the absent divinity, and terror, of death, emptiness, the lack of divinity. As he writes, "the divine signifier of the empty tomb, mimicking signification itself, is forever hollow and absent to itself."[38] The very emptiness enables relations to be organized around the absent body, designating different levels of understanding and authority as they map out different channels and positions of access to God, even as they are subtended by a radical contingency, by the impossibility of breaching the gulf between human and divine. The sudary cloth plays an important role in organizing these relations. As the Easter drama evolved, the empty grave was not enough, or its terror was too great. The *sudarium* and *lintheum* were necessary as objects that could be touched and displayed and passed around to signify evidence, a physical remain, but also to satisfy longing by proximity, to get close to the precious body. Absence required presence,

---

[36] Jansen 2000, 329.

[37] These occur in the German versions; other similarities suggest that Wilton may have had access to an example from this tradition.

[38] Kubiak 1991, 51.

a tactile object, to register the body's disappearance. In some Easter ceremonies the cloths are stained to represent the bleeding of Christ's wounds so that a trace of the body could be made visible.[39] In the same way, the development of the drama to include the impersonation of the risen Christ addressed the audience's fear and desire.

The grave cloths displacing the absent body also came to have regulatory power; they could be touched by the people precisely because the body itself could not. In the Wilton play, the sudary cloth has largely a liturgical status, a status that depends upon its participation in a prescribed arena of meanings sanctioned by the clergy. As the subdeacon enters onto the stage and hands a cloth to the Marys, who kiss it and adore it before it is passed to the audience and congregation, the cloth is designated as an object invested with clerical authority, much like the *pax*, the carved object passed around the congregation after consecration which functioned as a substitution for the Eucharist. The meaning of the *textum* is not generated from the theatrical hermeneutics of the play but imposed from outside, intersecting with the play at just the point when female access to the sacred is at issue, when the Marys are describing their moment of touch, their moment of intimacy with the divine body. The entrance by the subdeacon reminds the audience that the play is but an imitation and that ecclesiastically-defined rules must be preserved even in dramatic space. Even though the Marys are defined by the play as *Christicolae*, and Mary Magdalen is given a special status, the cloth associates the nuns playing the holy women with the *populus*, magnifying a division between theatrical roles and liturgical identities. For the women, there is an unbreachable distinction between representational and spiritual and the channels running between these sites are mediated by the priest.

The merging of Christ's role with that of the angel, played by a priest, emphasizes that Christ has passed beyond the human state; he is aligned with the "superi cives" [citizens above; cf. Ephesians 2:19] and represented not simply by a human body on stage but by a priest playing an angel "playing" Christ. This configuration endows the priest with authority to represent the unearthly beings and associates sacerdotal status with the heavenly as it simultaneously aligns the male with the sacred. Unlike the nun, the priest is able to move through the registers of divine and human, dramatic and liturgical, in the space of the play; the concept of the sacred nature of sacerdotal identity, its fixity across registers, is not contested but firmly upheld in this dramatic arena. When the actor takes up the

---

[39] Many of the entries compiled in Pamela Sheingorn's "Catalogue of Easter Sepulchres" from England, the appendix to her study, refer to "a sepulcre cloth steyned" or "payntyd." See Sheingorn 1987, 77–368. For instance, in the entry from the church of St. Mary of Charity in Faversham, Kent, there is a reference to "a steyned clothe of red with clowdys [tears] for the sepulcre" (179).

sudary cloth at the end of the play, I have proposed that he does so in a priestly role. Although frequently Mary Magdalen bears the cloth because she displays it to the disciples (and audience), the priest's hands on the cloth designate it simultaneously as theatrical and liturgical object; he cannot touch it except as priest, but his touch splits it off from its theatrical function as Christ's graveclothes to render it part of the liturgical apparatus whose sacred status is controlled by the priesthood. The text does not indicate whether the priest or the nun playing Mary performs the action of displaying the cloth ("extendat sudarium contra populum"), but when the cloth is placed on the altar at the conclusion of the play ("supponatque sudarium altari"), it is likely the priest does this, since the play specifies that he is stationed there for the closing *Te Deum* ("sacerdos dicat ante altare: 'Te Deum laudamus'") and ecclesiastical legislation forbade the nuns from touching the altar. This cloth then functions to displace the value of the "textum" circulating amongst the *populus*, emphasizing that it is a double, a secondary representation of the sacred cloth that touched the body of Christ.

By minimizing the use of bodily expression in the dramatic schema, the Wilton play specifically de-emphasizes the devotional potentialities of somatic piety. Action is represented in word rather than in body; the range of acts allotted to the performing female body is minimized to prostrating, genuflecting, processing, and touching and kissing the cloth, and these are highly regimented, largely detached from verbal expression. Similarly, Mary's grief is narrated by the group of women rather than assigned to the nun playing the part. While one could say that Wilton's *Visitatio* simply represents a dramatic form less detached from the liturgy,[40] one must also remember that Origny and Wilton very likely drew from a common source and, given the popularity of the ceremony, that other models were also available.[41] The Wilton *Visitatio* is unusual in many respects, though perhaps none as striking as the limited signifying capacity with which the female body is endowed. Female spectacularity is scrupulously avoided; the nuns do not perform any bodily actions significantly different from those in the range of normal liturgical movements. The nuns' identities are in this way produced as bodies which are not literally enclosed, because there is obviously a lay congregation present at the play, but symbolically enclosed; they are bodies that act out a solemn façade seemingly designed to abrogate any suggestion of interior being, of difference, of person underneath the habit. While performance allows for divergence from the text that may well escape written record, Wilton's *Visitatio* differs from those of Origny and Barking by maintaining more clearly established boundaries between the Marys and the nuns. By policing these boundaries between character

---

[40] Although Young did not deal with the Wilton plays, his analytical framework assesses the "dramatic promise" in liturgical elements that include "impersonation."

[41] Rankin 1981, 1–2.

and the performing bodies of the nuns who play them, the Wilton *Visitatio* severs
the experiences of the holy women from the contemporary life of the nuns. The
presentness of drama is foreclosed; the here-and-now potential of theatrical identification is limited by the extensive use of narration and breaking of the frame by
clerical mediation.

Given the complexities of the transmission of the Wilton text and the subsequent difficulty in dating it, the play presents particularly vexing problems
to modern interpreters. While the redactive nature of the tradition of liturgical drama allows us to note the importance of subtle transformations from one
text to another, it is difficult to account for these. Wilton was a well-endowed
and prestigious institution, like Barking and Origny, but it may have been more
closely tied to and monitored by local clerical authorities than the others. It is
particularly important to note that, although a single "sacerdos" appears to play
the role of angel and Christ, this was not because of a shortage of clerical staff
in the convent. At the end of the play, five monks [*quinque monachi*] enter into
the play, assigned the lines "Dic nobis Maria" and "Credendum est." This male
monastic presence in the Wilton *Visitatio* is unusual, perhaps testifying to the
influence of a local institution in its production. It is possible too, in the absence
of rubrics suggesting otherwise, as at Barking and Origny, that a monk or priest
was involved in its composition. Wilton contains elements of both a male and
female *Visitatio* tradition, intimating that the nuns of Wilton may not have had
as free a hand in defining and representing their institutional spirituality as at
Barking and Origny. However, such points are highly conjectural, so they must
remain at the level of speculation.

3. Performance in the Convent

In the late Middle Ages, women's dramatic performance was rare, though not
unknown: men commonly played female roles, which, as Catherine Sanok has
argued, "rooted public [devotional] practices, even those associated with female
saints, in male bodies."[42] Convents constituted an exception, for the nuns not
only played women's roles but might even, as at Barking and Origny, take on
male roles. Sanok focuses on secular production practices which prohibited female performance, especially performances of female saints whose *vitae* represented challenges to the authoritative structures of governing civic and institutional ideologies; by dissociating female saints from contemporary women
through cross-dressing practices, the performance of these plays commonly also
served to reinforce the ascription of female devotion to private, highly controlled

---

[42] Sanok 2002, 286.

spaces. Given this history, when nuns play the Marys their potential identification with the holy women is highly charged, as is their assumption of spiritual power in a public arena. Convent performance provides one of the few opportunities for medieval women to enunciate their links with female saints and publicly to inhabit the authoritative and sometimes transgressive female roles.[43]

Although the Wilton *Visitatio* does not cross-dress its female characters, its circumscription of potential identifications between the nuns and the Marys is in keeping with contemporaneous secular theatrical practices which sought to limit the dynamic interplay between saintly figure and female body as a nexus of devotion. While aristocratic and vocational status often permitted nuns greater access to spiritual expression than laywomen, even nuns of high birth were subject to enclosure practices by which their public expressions of piety were regulated and minimized. Increased information about dramatic activities in female monasteries is now emerging,[44] but even so, we might ask why more nunneries did not have Easter drama, given the popularity of the custom and the opportunities it afforded for female devotional expression. One reason is certainly that nuns were dependent upon priests to perform these plays, since the handling of the sacrament in the accompanying *depositio* and *elevatio* ceremonies was an important aspect of them. Therefore, such plays depended upon the priest's willingness to play their parts in nuns' drama. At poorer nunneries, where complaints of inadequate sacramental services from priests are common, Easter drama would have been impossible for reasons connected with inadequate resources and control over their clerical staff.

In other contexts, it may be that the proscriptions of feminine lay performance in public invaded the monastic space and influenced the ability of nuns to conceptualize and realize such a practice. Certainly at Syon, the Breviary encourages the nuns to conceive of their liturgical performance as private, "for God alone." In the late Middle Ages, episcopal authorities mandated changes to architecture so that laity who shared parish churches with nuns could not spy the women at their services.[45] Although a *Visitatio* may have been performed for the monastic community alone, it is notable that, despite the marked divergences of the plays from Barking, Wilton, and Origny, all are designed around

---

[43] There is greater evidence in France than in England for both the performance of saint plays and women's acting in them. See Muir 1985. The Origny *Visitatio* moves close to secular saint plays, as it includes extensive apocryphal material and vernacular language.

[44] "Drama, Ritual, and Ceremony in the Female Monastery," panel at Kalamazoo, May 2003.

[45] Oliva 1998, 148–49; Paxton 1992, 145–46; see also Hamburger's discussion of the architectural arrangements made on the continent (1998, 35–110).

a lay presence and all are concerned, in different ways, with their relations to laity. Even in the context of Wilton, where this lay presence may lead to limitations on female performance, the nuns perform their very status as cloistered women publicly. Their spiritual status is thus explicitly linked, not to the walls that shield them, as the episcopal authorities would have it, but to their special knowledge of and access to a divine tradition. Spiritual value is placed not in enclosure, not in invisibility, but in a visibility, in women seeing God, and being seen seeing God. *Dic nobis, Maria, quid vidisti?*

The plays also serve to focus attention on the convent as the site of spiritual renewal in a way that highlights the collective nature of the community. As the nuns performed the plays for the laity, they constituted themselves as a community involved in the act of generating faith in the attending spectators. The decision to have Easter drama is important, as Katherine of Sutton knew as she arranged for or possibly created the Barking plays, for it bolsters the role of the institution in the life of the laity and locates the convent as the site where the annual resurrection is announced. By highlighting the role of the three Marys meeting the resurrected Christ, the parallel is made clear: holy women then, as now, played a special role in transmitting faith. The female monastery thus has an important role to play during the season of Easter, the center of the liturgical year in medieval Christianity. While the focus of spiritual life at Syon is, as Rebecca Krug has recently described, "individual identification with Bridget,"[46] even in a communal context, the liturgical plays demonstrate a countertradition of collective spirituality. The inclusion of Matthew 28:9 in the nuns' *Visitationes* as well as the public performances themselves may have served to oppose the trend towards fragmentation in the community and the turn towards interior piety.[47] Sister acts were important for the nuns to perform their identifications with one another as well as to establishing their difference from the laity: thus the costuming of these plays often involved the veiling of the Marys, accentuating the veil not as cover but as sign of shared identity.

---

[46] Krug 2002, 182.
[47] See Gilchrist 1994 for a discussion of the fragmenting of the female monastic community into separate "households," which occupied distinct living quarters in the convent.

Works Cited

Abelard, Peter. 1996. *Lettere di Abelardo e Eloisa*. Ed. and trans. Cecilia Scerbanenco. Milan: Biblioteca Universale Rizzoli.

———. 1974. *The Letters of Abelard and Heloise*. Trans. Betty Radice. New York: Penguin.

Aelred Rievaliensis. 1971. *Opera omnia*. Ed. A. Hoste and C.H. Taylor. Vol. 1. Turnhout: Brepols.

Ambrose. 1902. *Expositio Evangelii secundum Lucam*. In *Opera*, ed. C. Schenkl, 4: 517–520. CSEL 32. Vienna: Tempsky.

Bevington, David. 1975. *Medieval Drama*. Boston: Houghton Mifflin.

Bible. 1969. *Biblia Sacra*. Stuttgart: Bibelgesellschaft. Repr. 1983.

Campbell, Thomas P., and Clifford Davidson, eds. 1985. *The Fleury Playbook: Essays and Studies*. Kalamazoo: Michigan Institute Publications.

de Coussemaker, E. 1964. "Les Trois Maries." In *Drames Liturgiques du Moyen Age*, 256–82. New York: Bronde Bros.; repr. of Rennes: Vatar, 1860.

Deanesly, Margaret. 1915. *The Incendium Amoris of Richard Rolle of Hampole*. Manchester: Longman.

Duchet-Suchaux, G., and M. Pastoureau, eds. 1994. *The Bible and the Saints*. Paris: Flammarion.

Gilchrist, Roberta. 1994. *Gender and Material Culture: The Archaeology of Religious Women*. London: Routledge.

Hamburger, Jeffrey F. 1998. *The Visual and the Visionary: Art and Female Spirituality in Late Medieval Germany*. New York: Zone.

Hardison, O. B. 1965. *Christian Rite and Christian Drama in the Middle Ages: Essays in the Origin and Early History of Modern Drama*. Baltimore: Johns Hopkins University Press.

Hutchinson, Ann M. 1989. "Devotional Reading in the Monastery and in the Late Medieval Household." In *De Cella in Seculum: Religious and Secular Life and Devotion in Late Medieval England*, ed. Michael G. Sargent, 215–27. Cambridge: D. S. Brewer.

Jansen, Katherine Ludwig. 2000. *The Making of the Magdalen: Preaching and Popular Devotion in the Later Middle Ages*. Princeton: Princeton University Press.

Krug, Rebecca. 2002. *Reading Families: Women's Literate Practice in Late Medieval England*. Ithaca: Cornell University Press.

Kubiak, Anthony. 1991. *Stages of Terror: Terrorism, Ideology, and Coercion as Theatre History*. Bloomington and Indianapolis: University of Indiana Press.

Lauwers, Michel. 1992. "'Noli Me Tangere': Marie Madeleine, Marie d'Oignies et les pénitents du XIIIe siècle." *Melanges de l'École Française de Rome–Moyen Age* 104: 209–68.

Lee, Paul. 2001. *Nunneries, Learning and Spirituality in Late Medieval English Society: The Dominican Priory of Dartford.* York: York Medieval Press.

Lipphardt, Walter. 1975–1981. *Lateinische Osterfeiern und Osterspiele.* 8 vols. New York and Berlin: Walter de Gruyter.

Loftus, E. A. and H. F. Chettle. 1932. *A History of Barking Abbey.* Barking: Wilson and Whitworth.

Makowski, Elizabeth. 1997. *Canon Law and Cloistered Women: Periculoso and Its Commentators, 1298–1545.* Washington, DC: Catholic University of America Press.

McNamara, Jo Ann. 1996. *Sisters in Arms: Catholic Nuns through Two Millennia.* Cambridge, MA: Harvard University Press.

de Montessus, Telchilde. 1972. "Note sur le rituel de 1315 de l'abbaye d'Origny-Sainte-Benoît." *Revue Bénédictine* 82: 241–62.

Muir, Lynette. 1985. "Women on the Medieval Stage: The Evidence from France." *Medieval English Theatre* 2: 107–19.

Ogden, Dunbar H. 2002. *The Staging of Drama in the Medieval Church.* Newark: University of Delaware Press.

Oliva, Marilyn. 1998. *The Convent and Community in Late Medieval England: Female Monasticism in the Diocese of Norwich.* Rochester: Boydell.

Paxton, Catherine. 1992. "The Nunneries of London and Its Environs in the Late Middle Ages." D. Phil. Diss., University of Oxford.

Rankin, Susan K. 1981. "A New English Source of the *Visitatio Sepulchri.*" *Plainsong and Medieval Music* 4: 1–11.

———. 1989. *The Music of the Medieval Liturgical Drama.* 2 vols. New York: Garland.

Salih, Sarah. 2001. *Versions of Virginity in Late Medieval England.* Cambridge: D.S. Brewer.

Sanok, Catherine. 2002. "Performing Feminine Sanctity in Late Medieval England: Parish Guilds, Saints' Plays, and the Second Nun's Tale." *Journal of Medieval and Early Modern Studies* 32: 269–303.

Sheingorn, Pamela. 1987. *The Easter Sepulchre in England.* Kalamazoo: Medieval Institute Publications.

Tolhurst, J. B. L. 1927–1928. *The Ordinale and Customary of the Benedictine Nuns of Barking Abbey.* 2 vols. Henry Bradshaw Society 65, 66.

Warren, Nancy Bradley. 2001. *Spiritual Economies: Female Monasticism in Later Medieval England.* Philadelphia: University of Pennsylvania Press.

Weaver, Elissa B. 2002. *Convent Theatre in Early Modern Italy: Spiritual Fun and Learning for Women.* Cambridge: Cambridge University Press.

Wogan-Browne, Jocelyn. 2001. *Saints' Lives and Women's Literary Culture c. 1150–1300.* Oxford: Oxford University Press.

Wright, Edith A. 1936. "The Dissemination of the Liturgical Drama in France." Ph.D. diss., Bryn Mawr College.

Yardley, Anne Bagnall. 1986. "'Ful weel she soong the service dyvyne': The Cloistered Musician in the Middle Ages." In *Women Making Music: The Western Art Tradition, 1150–1950*, ed. Jane Bowers and Judith Tick, 15–38. Chicago: University of Illinois Press.

Young, Karl. 1933. *The Drama of the Medieval Church*. Vol. 1. Oxford: Clarendon Press.

ON THE BORDERS OF EXILE:
THE POETRY OF SOLOMON SIMḤAH OF TROYES

Susan L. Einbinder

For Manhattan, 2001.

Solomon Simḥah bar Eleazar of Troyes is an unusual and virtually unknown Jewish poet from northern France. In a number of ways, both his idiosyncrasy and his obscurity reflect the state of intellectual life among northern French Jews just prior to their expulsion from France in 1306. A great era of talmudic scholarship was waning along with the prestige of the scholar-rabbis known as Tosafists, brilliant dialecticians whose bold innovations are still admired today. The burning of the Talmud in Paris in 1242, the banning of Jewish books, crippling social and economic restrictions, and a combination of official violence and popular antipathy had battered Jewish communities over the thirteenth century. The impact of these developments upon the Jewish elite was particularly severe.

Recent scholarship has suggested that the contrasting stereotypes of the proud and rational Tosafists and their Pietist rivals in the Rhineland were never terribly accurate (Kanarfogel 2000). Like the Pietists, many Tosafists also honored esoteric traditions, some of them associated with Pietist practice, and some apparently stemming from pre-Crusade traditions. As Ephraim Kanarfogel has shown, the growing popularity of mysticism among northern French Jews corresponds (unsurprisingly) to the period of Tosafist decline; Solomon Simḥah may be an extreme representative of this trend. At the same time, his poetry illustrates attitudes and concerns shared by Christian writers around him, unwittingly testifying to the degree to which Jewish and Christian lives were still enmeshed even on the eve of the great expulsion. Before turning to the poet and his poetry, however, some background is in order.

Solomon Simḥah bar Eleazar, a descendant of the great exegete "Rashi" (R. Solomon b. Isaac – d. 1105), was born and lived in Troyes. Until 1284, the Jews of the County of Champagne, including the city of Troyes, lay largely beyond the reach of French kings and their quest for Jewish credit and conversion. In 1284 the young Philip IV married the heiress to Champagne, and in 1285 he assumed the throne (Chazan 1973; Jordan 1989; Strayer 1971 and 1980). The new king quickly exploited available methods for tapping Jewish credit in the region, while local officials intensified pressures of their own. In Troyes, famed throughout the twelfth century as a seat of Jewish learning, the competing interests of local, Dominican, and royal officials converged on the Jews memorably in the spring of 1288. That year, thirteen local Jews were burned at the stake following an accusation of ritual murder. Of five surviving laments for the victims, one mentions the royal *bailli* and several refer to Dominican (and possibly Franciscan) clerics who pressed the doomed Jews to convert. All of the victims—even one who fled and was recaptured—died loyal to their faith (Einbinder 1999 and 2002). Solomon Simḥah wrote two laments for the Troyes martyrs. They are unusual compositions, demonstrating familiarity with both Eastern and Sephardic models, and perhaps also with vernacular ones. Equally striking is their mystical imagery, some of it ignored by scholars and some of it dismissed as "obscure."[1] Nine other poems, several embedded in a theosophical treatise called the *Sefer haMaskil*, enrich our sense of his repertoire.[2] To date, only four of the eleven known poems have been published; the rest are still in manuscript. In the following pages, I explore some of their motifs: images of the human body, both as a microcosm and in partition; cultic metaphors for writing poetry; and allusions to riding on clouds. A blend of inherited and contemporary elements, these motifs express a dialectic of competing intellectual traditions, both Tosafist and Pietist as well as Jewish and Christian.

First, what do we know about the historical Solomon Simḥah? Relying on his comments in the *Sefer haMaskil*, he was fifty-three or so at the time of the Troyes incident. The *Sefer haMaskil* was written between 1294 and 1296, the year the author believed would launch the End of Days (Freudenthal 1994, 187; Ta-Shma 1982–1983, 418; Kanarfogel 2000, 152). Significantly, contemporary Jewish legal texts, which frequently cite the inquiries, rulings, and (even dissident) opinions of

---

[1] The better-known lament, *"Shaḥar avi' todah"* ("At dawn let me bring an offering"), was published in Darmesteter 1881, and see the review in *HeAsif* 4 (1888): 113-19; S. Bernfeld included the poem also in his anthology of persecution poetry (Bernfeld 1923, 1: 335-39). As early as the first of these publications, the manuscript source for the poem was lost. According to Darmesteter, he was supplied a transcription by Zunz, "qui ne désigne pas le ms. d'où il l'a tirée" (227). The lament *"El erekh appayyim"* ("O Long-Suffering God") appears in Goldschmidt and Fraenkel 1993, 2: 632-36.

[2] To date, I can identify the poetic corpus as follows: (1) *Shaḥar avi' todah*, manuscript source unknown, published in Darmesteter 1881, and in Bernfeld 1923, 1: 335-39. Five poems by Solomon appear in MS. Bern 228, a fourteenth-century *maḥzor* (festival liturgy). Three of these five poems were published by Goldschmidt and Fraenkel 1993: (2) *El erekh appayyim*, in vol. 2: 632-36; (3) *Shaddai dumah shakhnah*, 2: 636-38; (4) *Shuvi limenuḥaiekhi*, 2: 638-40. The two unpublished poems are (5) *El bameh akhabedekha;* and (6) *Shammah bein dumah.* In Moscow, Russian State Library MS. Günzburg 508 (henceforth MS Moscow 508), containing the unique text of the *Sefer haMaskil*, I have identified the following poems: (7) *Shaviti adonai lenegdi*, a four-line introductory poem constituted of biblical verse citations, fol. 1r; (8) *Lehaskil maskilim*, following the preceding poem, fol. 1r; (9) *Titbarakh elohei ha-ᵓelohim*, fol. 16rv; followed by (10) *Sharshei levavi keᶜal mayyim*, fol. 16v; and (11) *Shaᶜarei libbi*, fol. 16v. On the *Sefer haMaskil*, see Ta-Shma 1982-1983; and Freudenthal 1994 and 1995; Kanarfogel 2000, 239-43.

local scholars, do not preserve a single reference to Solomon; their silence suggests that he was not precisely a luminary on the halakhic scene. Nonetheless, Solomon tells us that he studied with two well-known figures, R. Meir of Rothenburg and R. Pereẓ of Corbeil. Both men were great halakhic scholars and Tosafists who were also interested in esoteric practices.[3] R. Meir died in prison in 1293, and R. Pereẓ died about the same time, certainly by 1294. Thus when he wrote his metaphysical treatise, Solomon was newly bereft of his beloved teachers, a factor that may have enhanced the sense of isolation and persecution that finds expression in that work.[4]

He was also living in a time of increasing instability for northern French Jews. Solomon may have lived to see the expulsion of 1306, and if he did not, his poetry engages the imagery of exile in ways that suggests he knew of some of the local expulsions that preceded the 1306 decree. These included the expulsion of the Jews of Gascony (1287), Anjou and Maine (1289), England (1290), and Nevers (1294) (Jordan 1989, 181–85; Mundill 1998, 276). Many of the refugees from England and Gascony headed for royal France, where fragmentary evidence suggests some of the difficulties local communities faced in absorbing them. According to William Jordan, as many as twenty percent of Parisian Jewry at the end of the thirteenth century came from England; similarly, seventy-six percent of the Jews in Paris in 1297 were not listed as "taxable heads of households" in 1291 (Jordan 1989, 183). Moreover, Philip the Fair was at war with Edward I of England, and their forces were fighting in Flanders and in the Franche-Comté directly to the southeast of Troyes (Morey 1883; Redoutey 1997). The Franche-Comté was also the trade route between Champagne and Italy, and Champenois Jews must have felt the effects of the conflict between 1296 and 1301 (Redoutey 1977, 208). Philip taxed all of his subjects heavily to finance these wars, and administrative reforms during this period sought to streamline the process of collecting money from the Jews.[5] Indeed, the crippling tallages of the mid-1290s

---

[3] If Solomon studied with R. Meir, this implies that he spent some time in Germany, as Meir of Rothenburg left Paris not long after the burning of the Talmud there in 1242. See Kanarfogel 1992-1993; Einbinder 2000 and 2002.

[4] The acrostic to the opening poem in the *Sefer haMaskil* spells out "Solomon Simḥah bar Eleazar mi-Troyes the persecuted" (*hanirdaf*). As Ta-Shma has observed, given some of the author's ideas, it is no wonder he felt himself persecuted. Nonetheless, I am suggesting—gently, because such psychological reconstruction is hazardous—that an adult man who already finds himself marginalized by his opinions and beliefs may have felt the loss of revered childood teachers deeply.

[5] Notice the new role of "procureur général" among the Jews, held by Kalot of Rouen from 1297. Kalot worked with two other assigned Jewish intermediaries, Joucet de Pontoise and Vivant de Troyes for Champagne, and Hagins de Provins and Vivant de Godemar in Troyes. See Lazard 1887, 239-40.

imply "financial ruin" for Jewish communities, and rampant inflation through the 1290s—near 300%—could not have helped.[6]

Surely the ongoing and debilitating pressures of these years had an impact on intellectual attitudes as well as on daily Jewish life. The situation with respect to the composition of martyrological poetry is telling: through the mid-century, a sharply defined set of conventions characterizes this poetry, most of it of To-safist authorship, but the latter decades bring a number of dissonant features to the fore. Some of this dissonance emerges in motifs that emphasize the moment of the martyr's death as a moment of personal, often mystical, transfiguration. These depictions stand in sharp contrast to the Tosafist imagery of martyrdom as a moment of covenantal renewal and collective revelation, embodied in the figure of an idealized scholar-martyr (Einbinder 2002).

Some of the motifs enlisted by Solomon Simḥah fall very much into the category of the newer, mystical, repertoire. In *Shaḥar avi' todah*, for instance, written for the Troyes martyrs, Solomon explicitly portrays the martyrs' fiery deaths as a mystical quest that demands an offering of "blood and flesh and souls." The same idea is expressed, more cryptically, in *El erekh appayyim*, in which the martyrs "stream forth" with radiant faces, the culmination of their search for wisdom and of their willingness to face God's ultimate test.

The luminescence of the enlightened is described in Jewish liturgical poetry from Late Antiquity, as well as in the classical text of Jewish mysticism, the *Zohar*.[7] It is a motif found also in medieval Christian writing, where the holy ones appear frequently as "creatures of light" (Vauchez 1997, 436). The radiance of enlightenment also opens Solomon's prefatory poem to the *Sefer haMaskil*. There he explains his purpose in writing this work as "to enlighten the wise, that they may shine like stars."[8] Solomon explains that the soul is like the seven-branched candelabra of the biblical Sanctuary. Why did God command that the Israelites install candelabra in the Sanctuary? After all, God Himself does not need light.

---

[6] Jordan 1989, 98; and 1998, 11. In 1305-1306, the sudden devaluation of the currency jolted the economy. Jordan argues that Philip IV's desperate need for cash in the wake of these ruinous policies was the main impetus for the 1306 expulsion.

[7] See Swartz 1997, 150. Poetic descriptions of the officiation of the biblical priests on Yom Kippur often mentioned the "unearthly radiance" of the priest's face. In the medieval *Zohar*, the enlightened companions of R. Shimᶜon ben Yoḥai have "faces illuminated like the light of the sun . . . for each day they see the light of Torah . . . " See Wolfson 1993, 168 and notes 87- 88.

[8] להשכיל משכילים יזהירו / ככוכבים תמוך ידי יעוררו

עשות נוגה להאיר עין חשוכים / יחוו סוד ואיש איש יעזורו

MS. Moscow 508, fol. 1r. The poem conforms to Sephardic prosody, yet another indication of Solomon Simḥah's Tosafist training and broad interests. The allusion is to Daniel 12:3.

Rather, the candelabra are an image of the soul, which has seven "servants": the mouth to speak, the tongue to form words, the eyes to see, the ears to hear, the hands to work, the legs to walk, and the nose to take in "the breath of life" and to smell (MS Moscow 508, fol. 1r). These body parts are ruled by the heart, which houses the "breath" of divinity that animates human life in the form of an all-pervasive "air" or cosmic ether, which we experience as light.[9]

The human body animated by God's spirit is thus a microcosm, reflecting the plan of the biblical Temple and of the heavens. Solomon's descriptions of the martyrs make vivid use of cultic language, reflecting both his personal metaphysics and a contemporary fascination with images of dismemberment and suffering. One martyr declares:

I bow on my knee, to confess my transgressions.
To illumine my darkness, I offer my head and my face,
And my hands and my feet – for in Him is my Source.
I shall make libation with blood and tears.
On the fiery altar my heart is laid out, my soul is my offering.
My pain is nectar to my palate, and the fire of my foes has no power [over me].[10]

The language of cultic sacrifice had entered Hebrew martyrological poetry in the wake of the First Crusade; it continued to serve later poets commemorating victims of judicial as well as mob violence. In heart-wrenching ways, it offered both mourners and the rabbi-poets a theological framework that encompassed senseless violence. Exceeding even the rigors of their biblical ancestors, medieval Jews did not offer God the flesh and blood of rams or goats, the tender bodies of doves, or grain and wine. In laments for victims of crusade violence,

---

[9] Solomon "proves" this by rearranging the letters of God's biblical utterance, "Let there be light" (יהי אור) to read "God is air" (יה אויר). Freudenthal 1994, 198, cites the passage, which can also be found in Freudenthal 1995, 94. As Ta-Shma and Freudenthal note, the concept of the divine pneuma, or cosmic ether, has a long history in Jewish thought. Solomon Simḥah's sources, beginning with his misunderstanding of Saadia Gaon's commentary to the *Sefer Yezirah*, are discussed in detail by both scholars. As Ta-Shma observes, however, unlike the formulations of Saadia, Shabbetai Donnolo, Judah of Barcelona, and others, Solomon's idiosyncratic understanding of the cosmic ether, as well as other strange views he develops in the *Sefer haMaskil*, "were bound to arouse serious criticism" (Ta-Shma 1982-1983, 428).

[10] From stanza 4; see Darmesteter 1881, 229. The image of the fireproof martyr is evidence of the longevity of another esoteric tradition, which first surfaces in the descriptions of the Blois martyrs (1171). See Einbinder 2002 for a treatment of the derivation of this motif, which relies on Daniel 3:25-27 but evolves in remarkable ways in medieval Jewish writing.

Jewish parents offer up their children, husbands their wives, and teachers their students. In laments for victims of judicial violence, the martyrs are burnt offerings for the sins of the community. In Solomon Simḥah's laments, the martyrs offer up themselves.

Solomon's descriptions of martyrdom tap a number of extra-martyrological traditions, some certainly present in the vernacular world around him. Scholars of medieval Christian piety have noted that the late thirteenth century witnessed a great interest in images of bodily partition (Bynum 1995, 309–22; Vauchez 1997, 427–31). The cult of relics is only one example. As Bynum has observed, late thirteenth-century hagiographical conventions frequently feature saints who resist partition and saints, as it were, in pieces. In the Golden Legend, for instance, St. Catherine offers her mutilated "flesh and blood to Christ as He offered Himself for me" (Bynum 1995, 314–16; Jacobus of Voragine, 1:17 and 2:338). Vernacular analogues of this language must have confronted medieval Jews as well as their intended Christian audiences; the visual iconography of the saints, often bearing disembodied heads, breasts, or eyes, was also pervasive and not confined to the interior of churches. Saints' plays were a common feature at fairs, where the presence of Jews is well attested.

The degree to which this general cultural preoccupation was reflected in Jewish life is visible in the lyrics of Solomon's contemporary in Provence, the Hebrew troubadour Isaac haGorni. Among Isaac's works is a parodic "last will and testament" in which he bequeaths various accoutrements ("contact relics") to former lovers and friends:

> From afar they will bring the dust of my tomb to be peddled as cosmetics to beautiful girls,
> And the planks of my coffin shall go to barren women, to give birth to sons and daughters.
> They shall grind up my lice for stutterers and mutes, that they may speak in seventy tongues,
> And my hair shall turn into instruments' strings, to please those who can't play tunes.
> My sash shall become an adulterer's girdle, that he may cease whoring and adultery,
> And all my instruments shall become sacred relics, and my clothes guarded like treasure!
> Oh, who shall pulverize my bones before they make them into icons?[11]

---

[11] Isaac haGorni, "Le ḥishqi hineni holekh letannot," in Schirmann 1960, 2: 483-84, vv. 11-17. For another secular example, see the later (fifteenth-century) rhymed-prose saga of the "war of the limbs" (milḥemet haʾeivarim) published by Habermann 1936a. According to Habermann (1936a, 135), the story draws on a legend found in a midrashic collection on the Psalms called the Shoḥar ṭov, mizmor 39b.

Still, writers like Solomon and Isaac did not draw exclusively on Christian imagery. They had Jewish fields to harvest as well. "When you awaken from sleep," writes the author of the Pietist compendium known as the *Sefer Ḥasidim*, "take to heart your crafting and your needs." The writer continues,

> When a man leaves prison he should thank the Holy One Blessed Be He. There is no one confined more than one asleep, and therefore you must bless the Holy One Blessed Be He because you were powerless and had no control over your body. Bless Him for each and every limb and organ,[12] for they were bound and now they are released to meet your needs . . . There once was a pious man who would bless each and every limb and organ . . . pray[ing]that they work for the One who created them and for His glory, and not cause him [the supplicant] to sin.[13]

The *Sefer Ḥasidim* refers to an ancient tradition known as the *toᶜelet ʾeivarim*. This listing of body parts and functions had roots in medical texts beginning with Galen, and quickly acquired metaphysical resonance in Neoplatonic traditions that treated the human body as a microcosm of the universe. This perspective found expression in Jewish sources in the ninth-century writings of Shabbetai Donnolo, which were known to the German Pietists and perhaps to Solomon Simḥah as well (Abramson 1977 and 1978; Donnolo 1880). Donnolo's commentary was also revered by less familiar branches of Jewish esoterics, some of them flourishing in northern France.[14] Indeed, the tradition of ascribing metaphysical significance to the parts of the human body flourished not only in theosophical and poetic genres but also in the works of Tosafist scholars like Moses of Coucy and Isaac of Corbeil.[15]

---

[12] על כל אבר ואבר (literally, each and every limb). But it is clear from the context that the word refers to internal organs as well as to external appendages. See the examples further on.

[13] *Sefer Ḥasidim* Parma, sec. 2 (= Bologna, sec. 155). See the discussion in Kanarfogel 2000, 74-75.

[14] See Dan 1966; Wolfson 1995. As Dan notes, one of the characteristic beliefs of the non-Pietist esoteric circles, also expressed in Donnolo's writing, is of the "hidden" or unrevealed nature of the divinity, who is accessible only in derivative emanations or forms. Solomon Simh.ah also articulates this view, once in a gentle analogy to a king who wraps his infant son in his robe and hugs him; the son cannot see the king's head or lower body, and "knows" only his experience of being cradled at the king's breast. See Freudenthal 1995, 98.

[15] Abramson 1977. Abramson cites the poet Falaquera, who refers to a (lost) work on this topic written in rhymed prose (*be-ma'amarim shequlim*) (1977, 216). On Isaac of Corbeil, whose *Sefer Mitzvot Qatan* ordered the commandments according to parts of the body, see Kanarfogel 2000, 89. Moses of Coucy and Isaac of Corbeil may have been influenced by the German Pietists, who arguably authored the "blessings of the limbs"

The *Sefer haMaskil* unfolds Solomon's reading of this tradition, emphasizing, as noted, the primacy of the heart, which he likens to a king who commands his servants (the parts of the body) to serve him.[16] The heart thus contains a whiff of the cosmic ether that is present in all creation.[17] The heart is also the locus of knowledge and wisdom, which vary from person to person depending upon whether the heart's chambers are open or clogged to the circulation of the divine ether. Still, if the body offers a home to God's Presence, it is merely a window through which that Presence passes freely, unperturbed by human corporeality and sin.[18] Solomon returns to his metaphor of the soul as a light, or lamp. The lamp requires four "helpers"—an instrument to hold oil; the oil itself; a wick; and fire.

> As long as the fire ignites the wick, the wick draws oil, and the oil
> is held in the container, then the lamp functions well. But if one of them is
> impaired, the lamp cannot burn and goes out. Analogously, the human
> body is the container, the oil is the blood which carries the soul . . . and
> the wick is the strand of the spirit of life that reaches from the Hand of
> God into the heart of all that lives . . . (Freudenthal 1995, 123–24).

Thus on some level the cultic ritual of dismemberment, echoed in the descriptions of martyrdom, suggests a sacred reversal of the process by which life is formed (compare Freudenthal 1994, 202). It is a gesture that liberates the Divine

---

preserved in a Bodleian manuscript; see Beit-Arié 1987, and Kanarfogel 2000, 74-75. R. Joseph Qara', a student of Rashi's and a prominent exegete in his own right, interpreted the Kallir's verse "איבריה מפאריך קול אזון" to refer to the *"Shema^c,"* a benediction whose full form "contains 248 words, equal to the number of limbs in the human body." See Grossman 1994, 301.

[16] Solomon may have gleaned this analogy from a work called the *Midrash Temurah ha-shalem*. See Wertheimer 1953-1955, especially the selection beginning on p. 190, *la-mah ha-guf domeh le-melekh*. Let me follow Ta-Shma's gracious lead and note that the article was elided from the volume's table of contents.

[17] Three degrees ("spirits") of the cosmic ether govern the created world: the *ruaḥ ha-tzimḥi*, which pervades inanimate and vegetative matter; the *ruaḥ ha-hehemot*, which animates living creatures; and the *ruaḥ ha-sikhli*, which is uniquely human (Freudenthal 1994, 201).

[18] For the Pietist misreading of Saadia's words on this point, see Dan 1968, 174. One of Dan's examples comes from the writings of Elḥanan b. Yaqar, whose name is frequently associated with the diffusion of esoteric practices to northern France (Kanarfogel 2000). In the *Sod ha-sodot*, Elḥanan compares God's presence to the sun, which shines on all things and is unaffected by their impurity, "כי זריחתו בכל מקום אשר יבחר לשכן שמו שם" (179). Solomon Simḥah's peculiar form of sun-worship may owe something to his reading of Elḥanan.

Spirit from its corporeal boundaries, and restores it to the "air" that is its origin. Indeed, in Donnolo's explanation, the "spirit of life" is intact in its human body only as long as the body is intact, too. If any part of the body is sick or damaged, the animating spirit is distressed, and if it is sufficiently distressed, it will depart from the body and return to God.[19] Solomon's imagery of dismemberment thus represents a far leap from anything imagined by the martyrological poets of the First Crusade. On the contrary, and apparently drawing upon a number of mainstream and marginal currents, his use of sacrificial motifs points to a mystical notion of immanence in which the body both houses and liberates its divine source. At the same time, Solomon's use of cultic imagery as a metaphor for the act of composing poetry and prayer is noteworthy.[20]

The medieval Jews of Christian Europe have left us almost no information about how they understood the art of making poetry or how they taught this craft to one another. Nor, despite the abundant evidence for their fascination with complex and allusive verse forms, do we know much about the aesthetic criteria by which they judged the compositions of their ancestors and peers. One small and curious treatise by Solomon's Provençal Jewish contemporary, Yedaʿiah Penini (haBedersi), discusses the art of "rhetoric and poetry" (Yedaʿiah 1515; Dukes 1853; Luzzatto and Lass 1890). Although Yedaʿiah devotes many of his aphoristic observations in the *Shaʿar bimeliẓah ve-shir* to the social function and status of the poet, he offers some interesting recommendations for excellence in poetic language and style.[21] Yedaʿiah describes a cultural environment in which the poet, however poor in wealth, commands respect for his power with words and his mastery of Hebrew grammar.[22] It is not clear that the social status of the Hebrew poet was so revered in the north. His training, if we are to judge from the grammatical peculiarities of northern Jewish writers, may have been acquired in different venues. The love of grammar and clean style endorsed (although not illustrated) by Yedaʿiah testifies to an aesthetic shared by the Jews of Provence and Spain; this aesthetic made only partial inroads into the north,

---

[19] Donnolo 1880, 13: תצא הרוח מרוב המצוק מן הגוף הוא הגולם ותשוב אל האלהים אשר נתנה

[20] It should be considered along with the anti-allegorical positions expounded by the author in the *Sefer haMaskil.* See Wolfson 2001.

[21] See Schirmann/Fleischer 1997, 501-2. There is no modern edition of this little document.

[22] Note Yedaʿiah's remarkable comment: "Language is sick, and clean grammar will heal it . . . Were it not for lordship, men would devour one another; were it not for the wicked, we would not recognize the qualities of the pious; were it not for the pious we would not recognize the Creator; and were it not for the Creator's compassion for us in bestowing grammar upon us, language would be destroyed and the Torah (or Law) lost" (Luzzatto and Lass, 13).

and was either imperfectly understood or rejected when it came to grammatical purity and prosody.

Significantly, Yedaʿiah lived in Perpignan, where he was exposed to poetic traditions and genres, including the poetic treatise, found in Provence and in Spain. The situation in the north was different. There, the survival of lengthy commentaries on liturgical verse, many still in manuscript, does suggest who and what the educated medieval (male) Jewish audience admired. But for the most part, it remains unclear how these dense exegetical writings could have offered practical instruction. Certainly, Joseph Qaraʾ's work endorses thematic progression and an enthusiasm for rich allusions (Grossman 1994). Another, anonymous, author offers a detailed commentary on the liturgical sequence known as the *qerovah*, interspersing numerological explanations with statements concerning the number of constituent poems in the cycle and their invariant stanza lengths and rhymes (Habermann 1936b). None of this seems terribly helpful when compared with the detailed and opinionated guidance available in Provençal or in Latin, not to mention the Arabic treatises authored by Muslim and Jewish poets in Andalusia.

Solomon's allusions to writing, largely cultic, are rare, if not unique, among the Hebrew poets from northern Europe. Jews had described their liturgy as a substitute for the Temple offerings since the destruction of 70 C.E. But Solomon expresses this notion with unusual literalness. His richest poem in this regard is undoubtedly "*Shuvi li-menuḥaikhi*" (Rest once more, my soul), which opens with this arresting image:

> Rest once more, my soul, afflicted in fasting.
> Make an altar of song, to joyfully offer [your] heart.
> Bless God, saying "I will give [Him] glory."
> If you stride mightily in song, alighting high upon a cloud,
> *Weeping will tarry for the evening, but joy [will come] at dawn.* [Ps. 30:6 = 30:5 RSV] [23]

---

[23] Goldschmidt and Fraenkel 2:638-40; MS. Bern 228, fol. 264r. In Hebrew:

שובי למנוחיכי / נפשי בצום נענה
מזבח שיר תערוכי / לב הקריב ברננה
ולאל ברך תברכי / לאמר כבוד אתנה
אם עז שירים תדרכי / על במות עב חונה
ולערב ילין בכי / לבקר רנה

The fourth line of the stanza is not easy to translate. "If you stride mightily in song" might be "you will stride *by means of* the power of song," although the more usual preposition would be ʿim and not ʾim. The second half of the verse concludes with a participial form of the verb "to rest" or "to alight." *Bamot ʿav* is attested in Isa.14:14 and translated in the RSV as "the heights of the clouds."

Later in this poem, the poet returns to this cultic metaphor and asks that his "mouth's offering" act like incense to arrange his words (v. 14). Another small poem enlists a more familiar topos:

> The roots of my heart opened as if watered;
>   they grew fine and their branches extended.
> Birds spread their wings at the top of the tree
>   and hop back and forth to the Living God.
> They will utter a song of praise throughout the world
>   and offer thanksgiving to God in song.[24]

In both extended metaphors, music is the vehicle for a carefully ordered verbal creation whose inspiration comes from the heart.[25] Thus the divine breath that is housed by the heart inspires thought that is arranged in words and then carried by melody ultimately to dissolve into the cosmic ether.[26]

It is not only songs that sail the divine ether, however. A final example of Solomon's motifs also derives from esoteric traditions. In "At dawn let me bring an offering," Solomon describes the martyr Barukh as saying (Darmesteter 1881, 230–31):

> . . . I shall ascend on a cloud, acceptable [to God].
> My head is revealed in the fire, and all my blood is extracted.
> Are these [Christians] a people of God? They do not come from His land.

---

[24] "*Sharshei levavi*," MS. Moscow 508, fol. 16rv:

שרשי לבבי כעל מים נפתחו / גבהו עד דוק פארותיו נמתחו
כנפי רננות בראש אמיר פרחו / ושתי סעפיו עבור לאל חי פסחו
שיר עם תהלה בכל עולם יפצחו / ובשיר לאלהים זבחי תודה יזבחו

Another poem, found in MS. Moscow 508, fol. 16v, begins with a kindred image:

שערי לבי יום פקחי אשא / עיני בם [?] חדרי אולם
עם משכית לבב ארא / ואשאל מי הבין כללם

When the gates of my heart open, my eyes will see the inner portals.
I will see with the heart's veil, and ask who understands their workings.

[25] Compare the verses "My innermost soul will glorify You / In the chamber of my heart . . ." after which the heart's praises then rise to God's heavenly dwelling place. "*El, bameh akhabedekha*," MS. Bern 228, vv. 2-6.

[26] Conversely, two poems state that despair leads to silence, a psychosomatic connection that implies it takes some temerity to inscribe suffering in verse. See "*Shammah bein dumah*," v. 9; "*Shaddai dumah*," v. 20. Both poems are found in Bern, Burgerbibliothek MS. Bern 228 (henceforth MS. Bern 228); the second is also published in Goldschmidt and Fraenkel 1993, 2:636-38. Both opening verses also refer to silence, or desolation, in the first poem Israel's and in the second poem God's.

The description of Barukh clearly seeks to transform the terrible spectacle of his death into a scene of (equally terrible) transfiguration. The man who is surrounded by faggots, smoke, and flame so that only his head is visible appears to sail aloft on a mystical sky journey; his incinerated ashes, like those of the ancient sacrifices, rise to heaven on clouds of smoke. This description is reinforced by the vignette preserved in another Troyes lament, by Jacob b. Judah, who describes Barukh surrounded by flames (Darmesteter 1874 and 1881; Einbinder 1999). Yet we recall that the opening stanza of "Rest once more, my soul," which called to the soul to make "an altar of song," added:

If you stride mightily in song, alighting high upon the cloud,
Weeping will tarry for the evening, but joy [will come] at dawn. [Ps. 30:6]

Clearly, the cloud-rider is not just a martyrological convention.[27] In fact, a number of Solomon's contemporaries also referred to riding clouds—and not as mere "symbols" but as fact.

Solomon Simḥah alludes to this practice in the *Sefer haMaskil*:

[W]hen Moses our Teacher ascended to heaven . . . the Holy One Blessed Be He said to him, "Come up to Me on the mountain" [Exod. 24:12], [and] the cloud gathered him and bore him aloft. He said, where is the place of His Glory? Then Hadraniel came.and led him . . .[28]

How did Moses engineer this cloud ascent? According to a number of medieval Pietist sources, the feat was accomplished with the proper manipulation of Divine Names. The rabbis vouched for the procedure, which some of them had tried. A certain R. Meshullam, about whom little is known, reported that the Rokeaḥ frequently had resort to a Name of God to "transport himself on a

---

[27] Solomon may intend the same image to echo behind a verse in the poem *"Shaddai dummah shakhnah,"* cited in the preceding note. In v. 23, the poet says:

ועננים לא ישאו / מים כבות אהבה.

Goldschmidt and Fraenkel 1993 (2: 637) try to read the line as referring (in the plural!) to "the descendants of Anah," i.e., Christianity. This seems to me quite a stretch. The surrounding verses list the sufferings of Israel and ask how they can be reconciled with the prophets' promise of redemption. In that context, perhaps the poet is asking:
Did the prophets not prophesy / that there would be no more sorrow ?
And that the clouds would no more bear waters to extinguish [Israel's] love?

[28] Freudenthal 1995, 102, citing from fols. 15b-16a. The story goes on to describe the angel Hadraniel touring Moses through three terrifying sites, each of which elicits a new cry of *"Qadosh"* from the biblical hero, explaining the threefold liturgical recitation *"qadosh qadosh qadosh"* (citing Isa.6:3).

cloud."[29] With or without a cloud, R. Isaac of Dampierre, a well-known Tosafist, also "ascended to Heaven to receive information from the ministering angels" (Kanarfogel 2000, 192; Marx 1921, 195). According to a curious thirteenth-century commentary to the Mishnah Avot, largely eschatological in tone, the same journey was undertaken by R. Ezra of Moncontour.[30] Solomon Simḥah cites this story, too, to bolster his own calculations for an imminent End of Days (Ta-Shma 1982–1983, 432).

Like the other motifs found in medieval Jewish poetry from northern Europe, the motif of heavenly ascents was old. Some of the ascent traditions of the Hekhalot mystics survived among the German Pietists, and apparently influenced northern French Jews as well (Marcus 1981; Schäfer 1990). The transfer of this motif to a martyrological context is an unusual choice, however, and it tells us a great deal about what was feeding the production of martyrological conventions in the late thirteenth century. The proud image of the scholar-martyr, immortalized in the earlier poetry with the prophetic language of Sinai, had faltered much as had his real-life counterpart and creator. In the context of general social disruption, demoralization, and fear that characterized the years preceding the 1306 expulsion, mystical, apocalyptic, and even magical teachings held obvious appeal. Magic, said Malinowski, is a "ritualization of human optimism," a means for coping with the frustration and failures of the world (Harari 2000, 37). Certainly, medieval French Jews had enough of those. But not until the middle to late thirteenth century did magic and mysticism make deep inroads into their communities. The forces that held their world and faith together had to shatter first.[31]

---

[29] See Kanarfogel 2000, 243, and n. 65 there, citing MS. Milan, Ambrosiana 62, fol. 109v. In Kanarfogel's translation: "Meshullam the Zadokite from Brittany [Treport] transcribed a Name from the Sefer Hekhalot found by R. Neḥunyah b. Ha-Qanah: R. Eleazar conjured this Name . . . when he rode a a cloud, as he did frequently." As the citation documents, R. Meshullam is also transmitting Hekhalot traditions. As Elliot Wolfson has shown, the Rokeaḥ's own mystical writings refer to flights upon the great cherub whose image (identified with Jacob) is affixed to God's throne of Glory. In the Rokeaḥ's description, "this was the cherub upon which He rose and came to Egypt, as it is written, 'He rode upon a cherub and flew' [2 Sam. 22:11; Ps. 18:11] (Wolfson 1995, 37, 160-61).

[30] Marx 1921, 195, citing R. Eleazar b. Solomon. And on 197: "And a further proof of my statements: The prophet of Moncontour ascended to heaven and asked Haggai, Zachariah, and Malachi about the End of Days, and each one of them wrote him three ~~rhymes using his name and a Name~~ of God." See also Kanarfogel 2000, 244.

[31] Kanarfogel several times makes the point that esoteric beliefs and practices take real root in French soil only in the thirteenth century, but he does not ask why that was. The historical context offers a fairly strong explanation. See, e.g., Kanarfogel 2000, 59, 81.

And here, in that shattered world, I place Solomon Simḥah. His esoteric traditions reflect a blend of "mainstream" Pietist teachings and other, less well-known schools. His interests demonstrate familiarity with a wide range of literature, and his way of expressing himself suggests how much vernacular cultural norms were shared by French Jews. He declares himself "persecuted," a statement Israel Ta-Shma took to refer to his treatment by fellow Jews (Ta-Shma 1982–1983, 426). Perhaps. Even in a troubled time, all strange views do not fare equally well. And yet, neither theological rigor nor Aristotelian logic can guarantee good poetry, and Solomon Simḥah wrote good verse. Moreover, known or unknown to modern scholars, a lot of what he wrote has survived. This cannot be said for the work of many of his Jewish contemporaries, and may not be entirely a matter of chance.[32] Rather, I would guess that the haunting images of these verses, sometimes translucent, sometimes enigmatically dense, conveyed some hope to listeners for whom hope was very dear. And who can blame them? After all, it was a time when cherished faces rose heavenward in smoke and ashes, and in their shadow a beloved landscape was irrevocably transformed. Perhaps, just perhaps, those who rode the clouds with their shining faces offered in verse what had been savagely ripped from history: a small place of consolation.

---

[32] At least one poet from the southern end of the kingdom fared better, as we have approximately fifty liturgical poems by the otherwise unknown Reuven b. Isaac, which survive in the liturgical traditions both of Algerian and Comtadin Jews. In my talk, "Hebrew Poetry and the Expulsion from France," International Medieval Congress at the University of Leeds, July 9-12, 2002, I offered an introductory treatment of this poet; I have continued to develop this material for forthcoming work.

Works Cited

Manuscripts

Bern, Switzerland, Burgerbibliothek MS. 228 (Heb.).
Moscow, Russian State Library, MS. Günzburg 508.

Printed works

Abramson, Shraga. 1978. "On the *toᶜelet haʾeivarim*" [in Hebrew]. *Sinai* 82: 7–11.

―――. 1977. "A Close Look at the *Sefer Mitzvot Gadol*" [in Hebrew]. *Sinai* 80: 207–16.

Beit-Arié, Malachi. 1987. "Birkat haʾeivarim" [in Hebrew]. *Tarbiz* 56: 265–72.

Bernfeld, Simon. 1923. *Sefer haDemaᶜot*. 1: 335–339. Berlin: Eshkol.

Bynum, Caroline. 1995. *The Resurrection of the Body in Western Christianity, 200–1336*. New York: Columbia University Press.

Chazan, Robert. 1973. *Medieval Jewry in Northern France*. Baltimore: Johns Hopkins University Press.

Dan, Joseph. 1968. *Torat ha-Sod shel Ḥasidei-Ashkenaz*. Jerusalem: Mosad Bialik.

―――. 1966. "The 'Circle of the Unique Cherub' in the German Pietist Movement" [in Hebrew]. *Tarbiz* 35: 349–72.

Darmesteter, Arsène. 1881. "L'auto da fé de Troyes." *Revue des Études Juives* 2: 199–247.

―――. 1874. "Deux Elégies du Vatican." *Romania* 3: 1–46.

Donnolo, Shabbetai. 1880. *Sefer Ḥakhkemoni*. Ed. David Castelli. Firenze: Successori Le Monnier.

Dukes, Y. L. 1853. "Transcriptions from the *Sefer haPardes* of Yedaᶜiah haBedersi" [in Hebrew]. *Naḥal Qadmonim*, 21–23. Hanover.

Einbinder, Susan L. 2002. *Beautiful Death: Jewish Poetry and Martyrdom in Medieval France*. Princeton: Princeton University Press.

―――. 2000. *Trial by Fire: Burning Jewish Books*. Lectures on Medieval Judaism at Trinity University, Occasional Papers, 3. Kalamazoo: Medieval Institute Publications.

―――. 1999. "The Troyes Laments: Hebrew Martyrology in Hebrew and Old French." *Viator* 30: 201–30.

Fraenkel, Abraham, and Daniel Goldschmidt. 1993. *Leqet Piyyutei-Seliḥot*. Jerusalem: Meqitzei-nirdamim.

Freudenthal, Gad. 1994. "*Ha-avir barukh hu uvarukh shemo* in the *Sefer haMaskil* of R. Solomon Simḥah of Troyes – Toward a Portrait of an Aggadic-scientific Cosmology of Stoic Inspiration from the Thirteenth Century" [in Hebrew]. *Daᶜat* 32–33: 187–234.

————. 1995. Sequel to above, consisting of transcribed excerpts of the *Sefer haMaskil. Daᶜat* 33: 89–129.

Grossman, Abraham. 1994. "Praise for R. Eleazar berabbi Qallir in the Piyyut Commentary of R. J. Qara" [in Hebrew]. In *Keneset ᶜEzra: Sifrut ve-Ḥayyim beveit ha-keneset: asufat maʾamarim musseget le-Ezra Fleischer*, ed. Shulamit Elitzur et al., 293–308. Jerusalem: Makhon Ben-Zvi.

Habermann, Abraham. 1936a. "The 'War of the Limbs' of Yom Tov Soriano" [in Hebrew]. *Yediᶜot ha-makhon le-ḥeqer ha-shirah haᶜivrit* 3: 135–51.

————. 1936b. "Sefer Qerovah" [in Hebrew]. *Yediᶜot haMakhon le-ḥeqer ha-shirah haᶜivrit* 3: 93–131.

Harari, Yuval. 2000. "Power and Money: Economic Aspects to the Use of Magic by Jews" [in Hebrew]. *Peᶜamim* 85: 14–42.

Jacobus of Voragine. 1993. *The Golden Legend.* Trans. William Granger Ryan. 2 vols. Princeton: Princeton University Press.

Jordan, William C. 1998. "Jews, Regalian Rights, and the Constitution." *Association for Jewish Studies Review* 23: 1–16.

————. 1989. *The French Monarchy and the Jews.* Philadelphia: University of Pennsylvania Press.

Kanarfogel, Ephraim. 2000. *Peering through the Lattices: Mystical, Magical and Pietistic Dimensions in the Tosafist Period.* Detroit: Wayne State University Press.

————. 1992–1993. "Preservation, Creativity, and Courage: The Life and Works of Rabbi Meir of Rothenburg." *Jewish Book Annual* 50: 249–59.

Lazard, L. 1887. "Les revenues tirées des juifs dans le domaine royal." *Revue des Études Juives* 15: 233–61.

Luzzatto, Y. and A. Lass, 1890. "Lights from the Shadows: The *Sefer haPardes*" [in Hebrew]. *Otzar hasifrut* 3: 1–13.

Marcus, Ivan. 1981. *Piety and Society: The Jewish Pietists of Medieval Germany.* Leiden: Brill.

Marx, Alexander. 1921. "An Essay on the Year of Redemption found in a Manuscript Commentary to *Pirqei Avot*" [in Hebrew]. *Ha-Tzofeh le Ḥakhmat Yisrael* 5: 194–202.

Morey, J. 1883. "Les Juifs en Franche-Comté au XIVe siècle." *Revue des Études Juives* 7: 1–39.

Mundill, Robin. 1998. *England's Jewish Solution.* Cambridge: Cambridge University Press.

Redoutey, J.P. 1977. "Philippe le Bel et la Franche-Comté au XIVe siècle." In *Provinces et états dans la France de l'Est*, 207–32. Cahiers de l'Association interuniversitaire de l'Est 19.

Schäfer, Peter. 1990. "Jewish Magic Literature in Late Antiquity and the Early Middle Ages." *Journal of Jewish Studies* 41: 75–91.

Schirmann, Hayyim (Jefim). 1960. *Ha-shirah haᶜivrit bisefarad uveprovans.* Jerusalem and Tel-Aviv: Mosad Bialik and Dvir.

———. 1997. *Toldot ha-Shirah haᶜivrit bisefarad ha-notzrit uvedrom tẓarfat,* ed. and completed by Ezra Fleischer. Jerusalem: Magnes.

Sefer Ḥasidim of Judah heḤasid. 1995 repr. of 1891 edition of the Parma MS. by Judah Wistenitzki. Jerusalem: Meqitzei-nirdamim.

Strayer, Joseph. 1980. *The Reign of Philip the Fair.* Princeton: Princeton University Press.

———. 1971. "France: The Holy Land, the Chosen People, and the Most Christian King." In *Medieval Statecraft and the Perspectives of History,* ed. J. Benton and T. Bisson, 300–15. Princeton: Princeton University Press.

Swartz, Michael. 1997. "Ritual about Myth about Ritual: Towards an Understanding of the Avodah in the Rabbinic Period." *Journal of Jewish Thought and Philosophy* 6: 135–55.

Ta-Shma, Israel. 1982–1983. "The *Sefer haMaskil* – an unknown French Jewish composition from the late thirteenth century" [in Hebrew]. *Meḥqerei-yerushalayyim bemaḥshevet yisrael* 2: 416–38.

Vauchez, André. 1997. *Sainthood in the Later Middle Ages.* Cambridge: Cambridge University Press.

Wertheimer, S. 1953–1955. "Midrash Temurah ha-Shalem" [in Hebrew]. *Batei-midrashot* 2: 187–201.

Wolfson, Elliot. 2001. "Phantasmagoria: The Image of the Image in Jewish Magic from Late Antiquity to the Early Middle Ages." *Review of Rabbinic Judaism: Ancient, Medieval and Modern* 4: 78–120.

———. 1995. "The Image of Jacob Engraved upon the Throne: Further Reflections on the Esoteric Doctrine of the German Pietists." In idem, *Along the Path: Studies in Kabbalistic Myth, Symbolism, and Hermeneutics,* 1–62. Albany: State University of New York Press.

———. 1993. "Beautiful Maiden without Eyes: *Peshat* and *Sod* in Zoharic Hermeneutics." In *The Midrashic Imagination: Jewish Exegesis, Thought, and History,* ed. Michael Fishbane, 155–204. Albany: State University of New York Press.

Yedaᶜiah haBedersi. 1515. *Sefer haPardes.* Constantinople.

Ubi Sunt? Three Lost (and Found) Ladies in Troubadour Lyric

Roy Rosenstein

This exercise in textual and interpretive criticism seeks to build on current research in the troubadours to categorize three types of lost (and happily, found) ladies in troubadour lyric. *Ubi sunt?* What remains of such "dames du temps jadis," as Villon already labeled them? Although their names are concealed deep in troubadour lyric, these three women can nevertheless be made visible for all to see.

The present paper recovers one unknown woman, one forgotten woman, and one legendary woman, all of them historical players behind the genesis of texts by as many and more troubadours: Guiraudo lo Ros, Jaufre Rudel, Uc de Mataplana, Raimon de Miraval, Uc de Saint-Circ. Of each of the three subjects' lives, we know little, if anything: *De vita sua pauca scimus.* The biographical cliché could serve as epitaph to our unknown soldier of troubadour lyric. For countless such figures, whether major or lesser, we know precious little of his and generally still less of her life. Even the vast majority of the very few well-known—that is, well-documented—women of medieval Occitania have remained largely unknown, as if they modestly were particularly resistant to biographical criticism (but now see Evergates 1999, Cheyette 2001, and others). That unobtrusiveness characterizes the women and perhaps especially the women poets or trobairitz (see Bruckner 1995, "Introduction"). Gerald Bond (1992, 1–5, 57–59) tracked down and identified the documented historical ladies Agnes of Gimel and Arsen of Niol expressly named by the first known troubadour, the Count of Poitiers, William IX, in his song comparing the two horses in his stable. We now have the spadework of Angelica Rieger (1995, 183–92) in exhuming the probable identity of trobairitz Alamanda. I say "exhuming" because Rieger chased down the tombstone and epitaph of this woman buried on 27 December 1223. An Alamanda had been a partner of the master of the troubadours, Guiraut de Bornelh, in a poetic debate preserved with his other lyrics in some fourteen manuscripts. Despite these two recent successes, it has remained exceedingly difficult to attach a genuinely personal physiognomy to the women in the circle of the troubadours. Their private lives remain largely closed to us and their public lyrics have come down to us in small numbers. With Agnes and Arsen, we now have a historical and personal context for understanding the Count of Poitiers's outlandish, loutish boasting song or *gap.* For Alamanda, we recognize a true poet and a genuine woman, at once a lyric voice and a historical figure. In the cases of too many of her sister trobairitz, little of their works has survived while fewer traces still of their extra-poetic identities have reached us. Still other women are all but anonymous: we have their names and no more.

In looking at three other cases we will recognize some of the commonalities and categories they invite us to develop. Small players in the lyric corpus, they have long been awaiting resurrection, these three unsung ladies of troubadour lyric.

1. Alis

I begin with a woman whose identity is unknown because it is concealed beneath a codename or *senhal*, used by a troubadour to refer to his Lady without betraying her identity. Some of these labels may have been more or less transparent to contemporaries. In many other cases, when the pen-name was not used reciprocally by two interlocutors in their exchanges, we have no means of identifying the person lurking just behind the cryptonym. This is the case for the recipient of an indeterminate number of lyrics by Guiraudo lo Ros, the fifth and least known of the first generation of troubadours of Toulouse, those born before the Albigensian Crusade of 1209 (Anglade 1928; Rosenstein 1995a). Among the seven songs and one debate attributable to him, two songs address in their final stanzas either one Alixandres or Belhs Alixandres:

> Alixandres, de cor hi entendi
> Dieus quan formet vostre gen cors ioyos
> (Finoli 1974, 1056)

> (Alexander, God understood the matter well
> when he created your noble, joyful body)

> Belhs Alixandres, l'enveya
> que neguna res vos fai
> es adreitz pretz covinens
> (Finoli 1974, 1064)

> (Dear Alexander, that you need be
> envious of no living thing
> is your just and appropriate recognition)

Despite the negligible orthographic variants in some manuscripts and the semantically empty epithet *belhs*, the same recipient is obviously intended in the two lyrics. But the identity of the Lady designated by the traditionally masculine name Alexander (of Macedon, frequently cited in the troubadours: Chambers 1971, 42–43) is unknown. Was she one of several ladies sung by Guiraudo? His five other lyrics initially seem nowhere to mention the intended recipient of his songs. Indeed, two others have neither *envoy* (a named recipient on the envelope, as it were) nor even a *tornada* (a shorter, concluding partial stanza recapping the metrics and often including the *envoy* with the poet's name and the *senhal* of his lady, whether as beloved or sponsor or both). The early troubadour scholar Count Giovanni Galvani first noted this absence of *envoy* and *tornada* long ago, and it has remained unexplained (Galvani 1829, 42). But that does not mean we will be unable to authenticate the attribution to Guiraudo of those two songs without *envoy*. Even in the absence of apparent dedications, we can do so by noting to what Lady—indeed, the same Lady—he voices his sentiments.

> Ai, belhs cors francx ab honor,
> la genser qu'el mon remanh,
> ieu muer si cum fetz el banh
> Serena, lo vielh autor.
>   (Finoli 1974, 1071)

> (Ah, beautiful one, with your grace and honor
> you are the most noble to be found in the world:
> I am dying, as surely as old Seneca
> the writer died in his bath)

If there is no *envoy* or *tornada*, the recipient is nevertheless named plainly for all to see—if we notice, as the late Aurelio Roncaglia (1975, 276) did, that the first letters of these four Occitan lines spell out *A L I S*. Here then is a late twelfth- or early thirteenth-century example of the name *Alis* as an acrostic concealing but also revealing the female equivalent of the masculine *senhal Alixandres*.

But there is more, that neither Anna Maria Finoli, our poet's most recent editor, nor Aurelio Roncaglia in reviewing her edition had noticed. In this second song without *tornada*, the same Lady's name is incorporated into the song, not as acrostic at the beginning of the lines, but as equivocal rhyme at the end, if the corrupt text is written and punctuated as I propose here:

> Don', ayssi cum selh qu'es conquis
> e cuy vostr'amors agensa
> vostre belh cors blanc e lis,
> per merce, merce vos prenda
> de me que.us am e.us servis,
> qu'autra e.l mon no m'agensa
> ni nulh'autra no conquis,
> ni farai, sol no.s desmenta
> lo vostre cors, belh' Elis.
>   (Finoli 1974, 1068: lo vostre cors belh e lis)

> (Lady, as one who is conquered
> and whose love for you embellishes
> your sweet, sleek, white body,
> I beg you to take pity
> on me, who love and serve you,

for none other in the world so pleases me,
nor have I won any other, nor will I seek to,
provided you do not go back
on your word, dear Elis.)

As the late Frank M. Chambers (1971, 43) reminds us from other examples, *Elis* is indeed the same name as *Alis*. In this song in which Guiraudo twice re-affirms his ritual dedication to his Lady and no other but her (*autra . . . no, ni nulh'autra*), the song not inappropriately includes a concealed but named dedication to his one and only. The formal device of the equivocal rhyme is cousin to the *figura etymologica* and the polyptoton: poetic law banned the rhyming of one word with itself. That is, *e lis* 'and sleek' (end of line 3) cannot rhyme with a second *e lis* (last words of the song) because they would be identical. The reading *Elis* as name is the only poetically acceptable one because it makes the rhyme words different. Similarly, *conquis* (lines 1 and 7) and *agensa* (lines 2 and 6) do not rhyme with themselves because each pair differs in function or nature: *conquis* is first a past participle, then a preterite, while transitive *agensar* first means 'to embellish', then as intransitive *agensar* 'to please'. The same distinction might be observed to apply internally to the two *merce* in line 4 ('please' and 'pity') and the two *cors* of lines 3 and 9 ('body' and 'person').

The last three *cansos* attributable to Guiraudo do not indicate recipients in any form that I have been able to determine, explicit or encoded, named directly or through wordplay. But in noting the acrostic *Alis* and the equivocal rhyme *Elis* we have already confirmed the attribution to him of two additional songs and thereby doubled the number of songs intended for one Alis. We can now affirm that the majority of attributed lovesongs were written for her. From the occasional object of his poetry or his desires in two songs where she is *Alixandres*, we can justifiably promote her to his full-time Lady in a total of four songs of now certain attribution.

Because her name appears nowhere in the other attributed lyrics, we have no way of authenticating their attribution. But with four songs of certain attribution, where she alone is sung, Alis in guaranteeing his authorship is in one crucial sense more present than the unnamed poet himself. They become his songs precisely because they are doubly dedicated to her. The poetic specificity of his oeuvre is thus determined by the continuity not so much in his familiar poetic inspiration, which is classical and derivative, but by its singular, furtive, affective object. In this case, *cherchez la femme!* leads to the heart of his poetic individuality. The concealed lady's name, his *femme cachée*, gives his work its poetic cachet. The Lady here is now no longer so invisible, because her perhaps real name gives shape and continuity and meaning ultimately to his scattered songs since she alone unites them as their subject and recipient. Guiraudo is a classic poet, but one mocked by Peire d'Alvernhe and fellow troubadours for resembling other poets to the point of being undistinguished, indistinguishable from them: "sol viure d'autrui cansos," that is, he made a living from other people's songs (Rosenstein 1995a, 196). Yet here his poetic identity, so to speak, is re-established by the reader's identification of her, of Alis. And like Poe's purloined letter, her presence is concealed in full view of everyone.

More than the male name *Alixandres*, *Alis* is a common name in Old French, where it is attested notably in the popular *chanson de toile* about another "Belle Aeliz" (Poulaille 1946, 96–97; Hunt 1983). In Occitan it more commonly takes the form *Elis*. Like all names, this gynonym in several forms (it is ultimately related etymologically to *Adelaide*) rises and falls in popularity. It seems to have been quite common in the period that concerns us. For the final years of the twelfth and the first years of the thirteenth centuries when Guiraudo flourished, Ulysse Chevalier lists at least eight contemporary examples (Chevalier 1905–1907, 156). There are enough candidates to hope that one of them might someday allow us to identify our—Guiraudo's—Alis or Elis. Or we might assimilate her to the otherwise unattested Lady Aldenai and to his famous protector Dalfi d'Alvernha, both named in Guiraudo's one debate poem and both curiously sharing several letters and phonemes with *Alis* in what may well be a partial anagram (text in Finoli 1974, 1095; Alis, Elis, and Aldenai in Bergert 1913, 18–19; Rosenstein 1995a, 207). In any event, and whatever her name, that poetic identity is hers, not his: we know little to nothing about the poet Guiraudo lo Ros. *Pauca scimus*, or *poco si conosce*, as his editor puts it (Finoli 1974, 1051). One day we may know just a bit more about his Lady. If *Alixandres* is a typically male covername visible to all and concealing here a female recipient, the name of the Lady apparently named *Elis /Alis /Aldenai* at the court of Dalfi is hidden precisely because the common woman's name, unlike the artificial *senhal*, is perhaps genuine. Why encode that female name unless it is not a substitute name (like the substitute lady in Dante's *Vita nuova*) at all but one concealing the Lady's identity? In that case her naming is no longer an impenetrable codename like *Alixandres*, but in the form *Elis* or *Alis* it perhaps becomes a transparent identification, a positive sighting of a woman whose own name may be known. No one has yet looked for an Elis or Alis at the court of Dalfi d'Alvernha and others frequented by Guiraudo. We have only to establish her identity, if we can—and as is already possible for our remaining two examples.

2. Sarrazina

From a common name, *Alis* or *Elis*, we move to a common noun that is also a proper name, *Sarrazina*. This second example is drawn from one of the best-known and most influential troubadours, Jaufre Rudel. Here a name is also encoded, but this time not as *senhal* or acrostic or equivocal rhyme as were Alis's several sightings. This time the person of another historical lady, not the recipient this time, is folded into the lyric only as common noun, yet in this case it is possible to establish her identity. Since she is the wife of this crusade song's recipient, it is pertinent to posit her presence in the poem alongside that of her devoted husband of thirty years, also inscribed by name in the song. All the more so since this oblique reference to her conceals and reveals the only historical woman to surface in the hermetic lyrics of the famous poet of distant love.

Was Jaufre's love object in this and his other songs the Church, the Bride of Christ, the Virgin Mary, the Holy Land itself? All are plausible readings that have been advocated by past generations of scholars, given how Jaufre Rudel melds secular and sacred poetic registers (Paden 1979, 77–79). This song, "Quan lo rius," has a recipient made explicit in the *tornado/envoy*: Hugh Brown or Uc Bru, that is, Hugh VII of Lusignan, whom we know from Abbot Suger's report to have been present when St. Bernard preached the Second Crusade at Vezelay in the presence of Eleanor and countless others on 31 March 1146:

> tramet lo vers que chantam . . .
> a.N Hugon Brun per Fillol;
> bon m'es car gens Peitavina,
> de Beiriu et de Guiana
> s'esgau per lui, e Bretaigna.
>   (Rosenstein 1990: 226)

> (I send the song we sing . . .
> to Lord Hugh Brown, via Godson;
> I am glad, for the people of Poitou,
> Berry, Guyenne, and Brittany
> rejoice for him)

Hugh had recently been widowed of his spouse of some thirty years. On her grave, in the presence of their five sons, he had sworn to set out on the disastrous crusade from which he, like his friend and companion Jaufre Rudel, would not return. This stirring song seems to have been the theme song of the Second Crusade: it is preserved in seventeen manuscripts, fully as many as his most famous "When the days are long in May." Jaufre here congratulates his old friend and neighbor Hugh of Lusignan on his turning aside from petty local quarrels like the one that had earlier set Jaufre's father and Hugh's father against the first troubadour, William IX. Jaufre especially congratulates Hugh on his pursuit on crusade of a feminine ideal that surpasses all other women, even Hugh's beloved Sarrazina. When Jaufre says his own beloved is unsurpassed among all earthly women, he affirms hyperbolically that there never was a nobler Christian woman, neither Jewess nor Saracen. The common noun for Saracen woman is *Sarrazina*, which was also as proper name the wife of Hugh Brown, or Uc Bru:

car anc genser Crestiana
non fo, que Dieus non la vol,
Juzeva ni Sarrazina
(Rosenstein 1990, 226)

(There never was a nobler Christian woman,
for God does not wish there to be
neither Jewess nor Saracen woman/Sarrazina)

Jaufre deliberately places Hugh's wife's name in the marked final position after the negative conjunctions and at the rhyme. In a song addressed to the loving husband who survived her, "ni Sarrazina" must first have meant to Hugh "not even Sarrazina herself." That is, "not even your own Sarrazina" can equal my noble, distant love in the Holy Land, says Jaufre to Hugh Brown. In saluting Hugh, who had recently pledged on his wife's grave to join the Second Crusade, Jaufre appeals first to the memory of Hugh's late wife and congratulates him on turning away from profane ambitions in local land quarrels and reorienting instead his longings now in a sacred direction, toward the Holy Land and a distant love evidently like Jaufre's own. In what might otherwise seem a standard, purely hyperbolic periphrasis, the troubadour encodes the name of the recently deceased wife of the song's recipient. The formulaic here takes on a personal dimension that could be known only to those happy few, beginning with the poet himself, who were aware of Hugh's recent widowerhood and new vows—and the name of his beloved late wife.

Here is what we can say for certain about the woman bearing the name Sarrazina (Rosenstein 1990, 230). We know that Hugh had married her sometime before 1118. In the course of a long and devoted marriage she apparently bore him two daughters and certainly the five sons who in the mid-1140s would mourn with their father "at the tomb of our beloved Sarrazina": *ad sepulchrum dilectae nostrae Sarracenae* (Champollion 1843, 2:27–29). Hugh and Sarrazina, as husband and wife, and sometimes in conjunction with their numerous offspring, together signed a variety of charters which span the thirty years which the couple spent together and which in effect conclude on this charter signed by her husband and sons shortly after her death in 1144–1145. Likely she was responsible for exercising some positive control over her husband, known for voicing the blasphemy and sacrilege that defined the lords of Lusignan and led to Hugh's excommunication. Indeed, her father-in-law was early labeled Hugh the Devil, and her husband seems to have resembled him: both were excommunicated for their words and deeds. Yet by 1120, at Bonnevaux, six miles from Lusignan, perhaps at Sarrazina's insistence (she co-signs the charter), Hugh founded a daughter house for the Cistercian abbey of Cadouin in the Perigord (Sainte-Marthe 1715, cols. 375–76; Painter 1957, 38). As Sharon Farmer and Jean Leclercq have shown, monks document many examples, starting with the daughter-in-law of Charlemagne, of donations made by nobles under the inspiration or at the exhortation or following the specific request of their spouses.

Consequently even this oblique cameo of a woman named Sarrazina is of interest to us, just as she was significant to Jaufre Rudel and especially to the husband whose mourning is here evoked obliquely in the context of his new quest for an immortal, enduring, upper-case Spouse precisely in the land of the Saracens—and of the Sarrazinas.

3. Gaudairenca

From the unknown Alis and the largely forgotten Sarrazina, we advance finally to a woman troubadour or trobairitz, Gaudairenca. Her name appears in four texts. She is a unique case as the sole trobairitz about whose person we know a little—but for whom, alas, no works have come down to us (Bruckner 1995, xi, xxxiii). *Pauca scimus*, but this is a time a little must go far because we have nothing else to go on.

Gaudairenca, the only known trobairitz from the Aude region in Southern France, was also the perhaps estranged wife of the troubadour Raimon de Miraval (fl.1191–1229), a poor knight but prolific and popular poet from near Carcassonne. Little is known of her life, and no works attributed to her have survived. That she lived and composed at all is confirmed only through the distorting prism of three literary sources, the work of as many male authors, including her husband. Early in the thirteenth century, the Catalan troubadour Uc de Mataplana (fl.1185–1213) composed a *sirventes* directed at Miraval on the subject of his marriage and naming Gaudairenca in the *envoy* (Riquer 1972, 488). As recipient Miraval replied with his own *sirventes* citing Mataplana's wife in its *envoy* and responding to the accusations as made in his song, whose metrics and rhymes it adopts (Topsfield 1971, 330–36, esp. 333; Riquer 1972, 492). Finally and most elaborately, several fourteenth-century manuscripts include two *razos* recounting (and no doubt embellishing) events behind the exchange of *sirventes* (Boutière Schutz 1964, 380, 394–99, Burgwinkle 1990, 235, 259). Since Lacurne de Sainte-Palaye (1775, 396–423) the story of Gaudairenca and Miraval's relations with her has wisely been taken *cum grano*. Accusations of gross unfaithfulness and willful deception are as much applicable to the narration as they are rife in the narrative. But even Sainte-Palaye himself (1775, 407), who finds the story "suspect d'infidélité ou d'erreur," concludes that "il y a sans doute un fond de vrai." No doubt he was accurate in this assessment: "hay un punto de verdad," says also but exactly two hundred years later the senior modern scholar Martín de Riquer (1975, 985). Where the historical *fond* ends and the narrative *forme* begins is less clear, as will be shown.

According to the story developed in the *razos*, Lord Raimon de Miraval went courting a lady named Aimengarda de Castras and nicknamed "la belle Albigeoise," from modern-day Castres in the region around Albi. Albigensian heretical doctrine authorized a husband to repudiate his wife for another, and to do so was apparently not uncommon. Aimengarda maintained she would surrender to Miraval only if he abandoned his wife to marry her. That was supposedly reason enough for Gaudairenca to be turned out by Miraval, who justified himself with the claim that "he did not want a wife who knew how to compose poetry." When he, *fort alegres*, gaily instructed Gaudairenca to return to her parents, she pretended to be quite angry, *feis se fort irada*, while wisely summoning instead Lord Guillem Bremon, her own suitor. Rather than go home to mother, she was given by her husband to Bremon in marriage, and with Miraval's blessing. He thus not only abandoned his wife but married her off to another: *sa moiller avia laisada e maridada*. Bremon was delighted (*molt alegres*) with the arrangement, and so was Miraval (*fort alegres*), but his wife—now Bremon's wife— most of all (*e sa moiller plus*). This hierarchy in the escalating degrees of happiness is worth noting. In an imaginative inversion of the paraclausithyron theme, the wife is locked out . . . and she is glad to go!

The story does not end there, of course: the many repetitions of *alegres* are clearly preparing us for a *nessun maggior dolore*. Aimengarda now congratulated Miraval and told him to prepare their marriage celebrations. Meanwhile, she also summoned her own suitor, Lord Olivier de Saisac, and took him as her husband instead the very next day, making him now the happiest man alive (*fo lo plus alegres hom del mon*). Thus the would-be deceiver Miraval was himself doubly deceived, for only he was left alone and miserable (*fort fo dolens et tristz*). He naturally lamented the doublecross and with it the double loss of lady and wife, regretted by him in that order. According to one *razo*, he went about like a madman for fully two years.

Internal evidence from the songs as much confirms as infirms the historicity of these events. Mataplana's accusation, as echoed in the *razos*, is that Miraval spurned his courtly wife because of her worthy conduct and praiseworthy poetry.

Car per sos bels captenemens
e per son bel trobar parti
sa cortesa moiller de si:
ben par qe.l conseilles sirvens.
   (Riquer 1975, 1000–02)

(Indeed, it was because of her fine manners
and because of her fine songs that he dissociated
from himself his courtly wife:
it seems a servant advised him to do so.)

While his *sirventes* accuses Miraval of turning out Gaudairenca, he intimates that husband and wife may yet be reconciled. Probably for that reason,
René Nelli and others presume that Miraval could and would eventually have
taken Gaudairenca back—if indeed he had ever totally repudiated her. Miraval
in his reply does not deny that he dismissed Gaudairenca in the first place, but
only that he did so on the advice of a servant, which was indeed another criticism
leveled at him by Mataplana in his *sirventes*.

> Ni moiller non longiei de mi
> per conseill de menudas gens.
> (Riquer 1975, 1090–93)

> (Nor did I drive out my wife
> on the advice of servants)

Miraval counters Mataplana's reproaches by justifying marital separation in
unspecified cases and by insisting that he has always supported the dual causes
of love and poetry. Thus Miraval cautiously separates cause and effect: his professed support for poetry on the one hand, and the acknowledged rejection of
Gaudairenca on the other. The marital status of the other participants in this
episode has not been confirmed, nor even their identities positively estabished
(*pace* Nelli). Consequently, as is so often the case with *vidas* and *razos*, it remains
uncertain how much of the detail to Miraval's married life and extra-marital adventures lies in the realm of history and how much is legend.

In either case, the songs and especially the *razos* are charged with meaning
as a result of the strong role they award to Gaudairenca, concurrently Miraval's
discarded wife and his fellow poet. According to several parallel troubadour *vidas*, a pledge of compensation or reward (*esmenda*) from a lady also lured poets
Gaucelm Faidit and Uc de Saint-Circ into renouncing their current loves (but
not wives). In these variations on essentially the same story, these two other poets and would-be lovers find themselves jilted and mocked by the first lady, who
perfidiously does not keep to her word. The novel element in the Gaudairenca
episode and especially in the courtly career of Miraval, however, is the character
strength attributed to his decisive wife. In contradistinction to Griselda in the
novella popularized by Boccaccio, also in the fourteenth century, this proto-fem-
inist *razo* version of the jettisoned wife shows that she need not patiently await
her husband's beck and recall (or *rebec* and call, as we might say in the case of
a troubadour). Rather, this wife promptly and wisely contracts a new marriage
with her long-standing lover, who is more noble, in both senses of aristocracy
and *noblesse de coeur*, and certainly more devoted than her doubly poor now ex-
husband. Miraval's sorry plight may be read as a tongue-in-cheek resolution of
the many troubadour *tensos* or debates in which poets weigh the relative virtues

(and no less attractive vices) of distant ladies (who give little or nothing, Jaufre Rudel notwithstanding) and near-at-hand women (who grant their all). To the more familiar such oppositions of *domna* (lady) vs. *femna* (woman) and *domna* vs. *piucella* (maid) is now added the more obvious one juxtaposing *domna* vs. *moiller* (wife) (for these related debates, see Rosenstein 1995b, 51–53). Unfortunately for Miraval, according to the *razos*, in renouncing his wife and proposing to his lady he relinquishes the company of one but fails to win the favor — or favors — of the other. In sum, he enjoys neither his *domna* nor his *moiller*. Like the model wife "patient Grisel," it is the husband now who has been tested and tried; but unlike Griselda and Gaudairenca, Miraval is found wanting. As one *razo* notes, after the ladies made fun of Raimon came the mockery of "many troubadour knights," including perhaps Uc de Saint-Circ, himself a candidate for authorship of this very *razo*.

Marriage and especially wives are not usually so flattered by the *vidas* and *razos*. Gaucelm Faidit's *régulière* may have been a reformed bawd, or just a jongleresse. Gausbert de Puycibot's jilted *légitime* is said to have turned to prostitution (Poe 1993, 362). In the lyrics themselves, marriage is twice scorned. In the 2700 Old Occitan lyrics preserved, not one seems to sing on a positive note the joys of marriage. When it is at issue at all, which is rarely, some troubadours poke fun at the hypocrisy of marriage, while the Gascon satirists in particular bewail the widespread abuse of a sanctified union (Paden 1975, 39–40). In Old French lyric, when a single trouvère, Jacques d'Autun, claims to be married, his song is nothing less than a calculated attempt by a later performer or copyist to legitimize the child born out of wedlock to the trouvère and his mistress (Rosenberg 1975). In sum, the *maritalis affectio* or harmonious marital contract on which the medieval institution of marriage reposes seems entirely lacking here.

Still, the example of Gaudairenca as wife triumphant is richer and more complex than her wife-swapping, *échangiste* fabliau situation suggests, not simply because she is yet another medieval woman who has the last laugh over her foolhardy, wayward spouse, but principally because she is herself a poet. In this sense, her story is not only a social statement by virtue of the uncommon issues it raises and a literary artefact given its architectonic balance and mirror composition. It is above all a rare document attesting the reception of the trobairitz. According to the story, precisely the very poetic and musical skills that Raimon should appreciate in his wife serve him instead as a pretext for rejecting her.

The Chinese ideogram for 'discord' plainly depicts two women under one roof. No less revealing is Gaudairenca's case as an example of two singers in one household. Lady Gaudairenca (like other trobairitz, she is labeled *Na* in one of the *razos*) may have been a "mujer intelectual" (Riquer 1975, 1090) or a "fine mouche" (Nelli 1941, 179). As such, she must have been more than a match for her husband, like Sarrazina for Uc Bru. Apparently no double standard reigned in this household. The *razo* specifies that Raimon praised his lady in story and song (*en contan et en cantan*), much as Gaudairenca had a talent for *coblas* and particularly *dansas* about her suitor. A strict parallelism is thus maintained: each sings the charms of her or his lover. Thus far, husband and wife would seem to have achieved parity and to practice courtly love on an equal footing. We know from his *vida* that Miraval owned a part of a small castle; there Gaudairenca would have held a modest court, exactly as Mataplana's *sirventes* intimates. However, when the moment of truth and its consequences arrives, the greater wisdom of the trobairitz is made abundantly clear in the *razo*. Miraval is tricked into renouncing his wife in vain hopes of marrying a lady who ultimately will neither satisfy his desires nor make good on her marriage proposal to him. Concurrently but contrastively, Gaudairenca, when renounced by her husband, at once finds fulfillment and marriage in the arms of her lover. That is, she rewrites the end of *Cligès*, about whose protagonist Chrétien says that he made of his lover his wife: "de s'amie a feite sa dame." That would become, in Gaudairenca's case, "she made of her lover her husband."

What little we know of Gaudairenca says nothing if it does not confirm her personal *virtù*, or manly strength of character. She is the strongest of the principal players for she alone controls her emotions: *feis se fort irada*. Indeed, her very name is significant. The one that posterity has accepted for Raimon de Miraval's wife is not one of the medieval variants *Caudairenca* (commonest in the *razos*) or *Caudaiga* (ms. R) or *Gaudierna* (unicum in ms. A) but most often until recently *Gaudairenca* (Boutière even proposes to read *Gaudaira* for a parent's name). The preferred gynonym marries the local Occitan suffix *-enc(a)* and a reflex of Late Latin **gaudire*. It suggests an undead metaphor for the storytellers who recognize its meaning as 'she who enjoys herself', as Jaufre Rudel would have appreciated: he signed his own songs with wordplay on *jauzir*, the Occitan reflex of the same root. Gaudairenca's generalized joy rings loud and clear, in stark contrast to her unhappy husband; he is no longer so *jauzens* after his initial enthusiasm, for now he enjoys neither his lady nor his wife. In this and other episodes, Miraval is simply reduced to the role of *mari berné*. *Totas l'enganeren*, says his *vida*, that is, all the ladies deceived him, including both Aimengarda and Gaudairenca, both *domna* and *moiller*.

It is sometimes mistakenly asserted that there are no references to *dansas* or dancesongs in the *vidas* and *razos*, or that wives among the troubadours are never portrayed in a positive light. The case of Gaudairenca disproves both rules. Through this fabliau-type reversal, we glimpse one woman who comes out on top of her ridiculous and ridiculed husband. Unfortunately, the two women, Aimengarda and Gaudairenca, triumph more by their trickery than by their talents, not what we might have preferred, especially in the case of a trobairitz. It is this same trickery that is highlighted by William Burgwinkle (1997, 218–19, 223) in his study of the *razos*. René Nelli said, "Je crois que la vérité, c'est que les troubadours étaient plutôt hostiles au fait que les femmes, comme eux, écrivent. [. . .] D'abord, ça lui [Raimon] faisait concurrence" (cited in Rieger 1991, 104). If it was awkward for Miraval to compete with his wife, it is frustrating for us that Gaudairenca should be the only trobairitz for whom we may reconstruct a perhaps historical face but can unfortunately hear no poetic voice, just as if she were now become precisely as Miraval may have wished her, silenced in her own house and expelled from the troubadour corpus.

This then is all that we have to attach to Gaudairenca's name and persona. It is precious little, but it is a great deal. *Pauca scimus*, to be sure, but that very absence of data is in her case particularly telling, a speaking silence, as it were.

4. Conclusion

From the lost and found department of troubadour ladies we have resurrected three distinct examples. With a little verbal slight of hand on the part of the poets, now you see them, now you don't. Or rather the opposite, it is to be hoped: at first we did not see them, but now we do, even if not yet quite clearly. Alis, Sarrazina, and Gaudairenca—like the three blessed ladies who are evoked but not yet seen in *Inferno 2*—represent three degrees of invisibility or visibility. *Alis/Elis* is only a name hidden in an acrostic and an equivocal rhyme. But that name in its several forms not only directs our attention to the object and recipient of the bulk of Guiraudo lo Ros's love poetry but also gives it a poetic individuality and thematic continuity that his pale persona and his uninspired corpus otherwise lack. Sarrazina's name, concealed in another paronomastic device, introduces a traceable historical figure who is forever wedded to her grieving husband, recipient of a crusade song from troubadour Jaufre Rudel. In it Rudel wishes godspeed to Hugh on the Second Crusade and concurrently on his new Bride quest (with an upper-case *B*) in the Holy Land, among the Saracens and the Sarrazinas. Named only obliquely in a troubadour's song, she comes with a full and documented life "not without incident," as Lady Bracknell used to say, and which we can and must recover because it was certainly known to the poet, a long-standing companion to her husband, recipient of this song. Her role thus becomes significant not only in the genesis of the song itself but for our understanding of one of the most important troubadours. And then comes Gaudairenca, whose own name, buried this time in an *envoy*, leads us to a historical woman and what is more a woman poet, a trobairitz finally, whose works have been lost, perhaps to the advantage of her local legend.

So, must we say then she is "lost" to us? A lost lady perhaps, but certainly not in Willa Cather's negative sense. Gauidairenca's outspokenness, perhaps censored by her husband and like-minded troubadours, nevertheless shines through the scant mentions of her in male troubadour poetry and the subsequent *vida* and *razo* pseudo-biographical commentary tradition. Gaudairenca's poetry has not come down to us, but her name at least is not lost, not to history or to literature, only perhaps to us post-medieval readers who cannot recover her works. Certainly the names and perhaps the identities of these three ladies are still present, encoded in the poetry and not totally forgotten, as if dormant, waiting to be recovered. These sleeping beauties, from Alis to Sarrazina to Gaudairenca, from the most invisible woman to the most visible and audible and even outspoken one, from the simplest to the most complex example, from the least instructive to the most meaningful case history, from the near-anonymous Alis to the silenced Gaudairenca, these three women are not unsung. Their three names are there, buried in a male-dominated discourse perhaps but awaiting our full attention. *Ubi sunt*? No, these ladies may not be irrecoverable but simply hidden, by poets, scribes, even editors. Yet they are still there for all readers to glimpse, if we care to look for them.

Works Cited

Anglade, Joseph. 1928. *Les troubadours de Toulouse.* Toulouse: Privat.

Bergert, Fritz. 1913. *Die von den Trobadors gennanten oder gefeierten Damen.* Halle: Niemeyer.

Bond, Gerald Albert. 1982. *The Poetry of William VII, Count of Poitiers, IX Duke of Aquitaine.* New York: Garland.

Boutière, Jean, and A. H. Schutz, 1964. *Biographies des troubadours.* Paris: Nizet.

Bruckner, Matilda T., Laurie Shepard, and Sarah White. 1995. *Songs of the Women Troubadours.* New York: Garland.

Burgwinkle, William E. 1990. *Razos and Troubadour Songs.* New York: Garland.

————. 1997. *Love for Sale*: *Materialist Readings of the Troubadour Razo Corpus.* New York: Garland.

Chambers, Frank M. 1971. *Proper Names in the Lyrics of the Troubadours.* Chapel Hill: University of North Carolina Press.

Champollion Figeac, [Aimé]. 1843. *Documents historiques inédits tirés des collections manuscrites de la Bibliothèque royale.* Paris: Archives Nationales.

Chevalier, Ulysse. 1905–1907. *Répertoire des sources historiques du Moyen Age: Bio-bibliographie.* Paris: Picard.

Cheyette, Fredric L. 2001. *Ermengard of Narbonne and the World of the Troubadours.* Ithaca: Cornell University Press.

Evergates, Theodore. 1999. *Aristocratic Women in Medieval France.* Philadelphia: University of Pennsylvania Press.

Farmer, Sharon. 1986. "Persuasive Wives: Clerical Images of Medieval Wives." *Speculum* 61: 517–43.

Finoli, Anna Maria. 1974. "Le poesie di Guiraudo lo Ros." *Studi Medievali* 15: 1051–97.

Galvani, Giovanni. 1829. *Osservazioni sulla poesia dei trovatori.* Modena: Soliani.

Hunt, Tony. 1983. "De la chanson au sermon: 'Bele Aalis' et 'Sur la rive de la mer'." *Romania* 104: 433–56.

Leclercq, Jean. 1990. "Rôle et pouvoir des épouses au Moyen Age." In Georges Duby et al., *La femme au Moyen Age*, 87–98. Maubeuge: Touzot.

Nelli, René. 1941. "De quelques 'Poetae minores': Gaudairenca." In *Actualité des troubadours (Les troubadours de l'Aude)*, special number of *Pyrénées* 1.2: 179–81.

Paden, William D. et al. 1975. "The Troubadour's Lady: Her Marital Status and Social Rank." *Studies in Philology* 72: 28–50.

————. 1979. "*Utrum copularentur*: Of *Cors*." *L'Esprit Créateur* 19: 70–83.

Painter, Sydney. 1957. "The Lords of Lusignan in the Eleventh and Twelfth Centuries." *Speculum* 32: 27–47. Repr. in *Feudalism and Liberty: Articles and Addresses of Sydney Painter*, ed. Fred Cazel, Jr., 41–72. Baltimore: Johns Hopkins University Press, 1961.

Poe, Elizabeth W. 1993. "Strange Bedfellows: Giraut de Bornelh and Bertran de Born." In *Studies in Honor of Hans-Erich Keller*, ed. Rupert T. Pickens, 359–81. Kalamazoo: Medieval Institute.

Poulaille, Henry, and Régine Pernoud. 1946. *Les chansons de toile*. Bondy: Presses-Eclair.

Rieger, Angelica. 1991. *Trobairitz. Der Beitrag der Frau in der altokzitanischen höfischen Lyrik*. Tübingen: Niemeyer.

———. 1995. "Alamanda de Castelnau, une trobairitz dans l'entourage des comtes de Toulouse?" In *Les troubadours et l'état toulousain avant la Croisade (1209)*, ed. Arno Krispin, 183–92. Bordes: Centre d'Etude de la littérature occitane.

Riquer, Martín de. 1972. "El trovador Huguet de Mataplana." In *Studia Hispanica in Honorem Rafael Lapesa*, 1: 455–94. Madrid: Cátedra-Seminario Menéndez Pidal.

———. 1975. *Los trovadores: historia literaria y textos*. 3 vols. Barcelona: Planeta.

Roncaglia, Aurelio. 1975. Review of Finoli 1974. *Cultura Neolatina* 35: 276.

Rosenberg, Samuel. 1975. "Observations on the Chanson of Jacques d'Autun (R. 350/51)." *Romania* 96: 552–60.

Rosenstein, Roy. 1990. "New Perspectives on Distant Love." *Modern Philology* 87: 225–38.

———. 1995a. "Guiraudo lo Ros ou le conventionnalisme littéraire." In *Les troubadours et l'état toulousain avant la Croisade (1209)*, ed. Arno Krispin, 193–210. Bordes: Centre d'Etude de la littérature occitane.

———. 1995b. "Dans le sillage de Marcabru." In *Etudes Georges Bonifassi*, special number of *La France latine* n.s. 120: 39–62.

———. 2004. "Gaudairenca." In *Women in the Middle Ages: An Encyclopedia*, ed. Katharina M. Wilson and Nadia Margolis, 355–58. Westport, Conn. and London: Greenwood.

Sainte-Marthe, Denys de. 1715. *Gallia Christiana in Provincias ecclesiasticas distributa*. Paris.

[Sainte Palaye, Lacurne de.] 1774. *Histoire littéraire des troubadours*. 3 vols. Paris: Durand.

Topsfield, Leslie. 1971. *Les poésies du troubadour Raimon de Miraval*. Paris: Nizet.

Wolf, George and Roy Rosenstein. 1983. *The Poetry of Cercamon and Jaufre Rudel*. New York and London: Garland.

LIVES AND WORKS: CHAUCER AND THE COMPILERS OF THE TROUBADOUR SONGBOOKS

LAURA KENDRICK

As scholars have long recognized, there is no single model for Chaucer's *General Prologue* to the *Canterbury Tales*.[1] Partly for lack of a convincing source, some have believed, with John M. Manly (1926, 76), that Chaucer drew the portraits "from life," that he set down his observations of individual contemporaries "familiar to every member of the audience." Such thoroughgoing mimetic realism would be very precocious, and it does not explain the necessity for a series of portraits as an introduction to a series of stories.

The standard collection of sources and analogues to Chaucer's works, Bryan and Dempster (1941), proposes the literary analogue of Benoît de Sainte-Maure's series of portraits of Trojan and Greek heroes and heroines in his twelfth-century *Roman de Troie*, a series of rhetorical descriptions of physical features and manners or moral character that does not begin until line 5093 of the narrative. However, Robert Pratt and Karl Young (1941, 5) conclude that this portrait series is "much too limited in social variety and in realistic detail" to serve as a convincing analogue for Chaucer, and they add for good measure: "Neither in this group . . . nor in the whole range of earlier portraiture, do we find anything that could be exhibited in the present volume as a source or appropriate analogue for Chaucer's miscellaneous company of vivid and living personalities."

R. M. Lumiansky (1956, 434–37) pointed out that Benoit's portraits do have several features in common with Chaucer's. Even though they begin at line 5093, they serve as a "prologue to the coming action" by calling attention in some cases to moral traits that foreshadow the later behavior of the characters, such as Briseïda's "changing heart." The portraits are also set in a conversational framework by a narrator who intersperses among the sketches comments to his audience stated in the first person. Yet Benoît is no first-hand observer; he claims to be merely reporting what his author, Dares, had observed and written of these characters; furthermore, as Lumiansky remarks, "Benoît does not make use in his portraits of the past experiences of his personages, material which Chaucer regularly employs."

In *Chaucer and Medieval Estates Satire* (1973), Jill Mann suggested that Chaucer's series of portraits may have been modeled on the medieval genre of estates satire, which criticized the faults of the different estates of society in a

---

[1] Benson's edition of *The Riverside Chaucer* (1987) will be the source for all quotations from Chaucer's *Canterbury Tales*; in parenthetical references *General Prologue* will be abbreviated *GP*, followed by line numbers.

hierarchical order. Such a model would help to explain the broad social sweep of Chaucer's portrait series (as compared to Benoît's), although the higher echelons of both clergy and nobility (pope, bishops, king, dukes . . .), with which estates satire conventionally begins, are absent from Chaucer's descriptions. Nor is the intent of Chaucer's portrait series entirely critical, even though the moral foibles and faults the narrator manages to suggest in an individual belonging to a partic-ular estate (the taste for worldly luxuries of a particular monk, for instance) often correspond closely to those criticized in estates satire as belonging to the whole estate (for example, the luxurious lifestyle of monks in general).

Whereas the purpose of estates satire is to blame, that of rhetorical *descriptio personae* can be either to praise or to blame. For earlier examples of uncertainty about the intention behind the narrator's description, as in many of Chaucer's pilgrim portraits, Mann turns, not to estates satire, but to occasional instances in the *Roman de Troie*. Sometimes Benoît seems to be trying to praise a blamewor-thy feature, such as when he says that Hector surpassed all other men in worth ("pris") — but then adds that he stammered ("baubeoit") a bit, and that both his eyes were crossed ("d'andous les ieux borgnes esteit")—before assuring us that this did not in the least make him unattractive ("mais point ne li mesaveneit"). Mann remarked (1973, 179–80) that Benoît's *"mais"* works like Chaucer's "but" to complicate our response by introducing unattractive features sympathetically. For example, in the Cook's portrait, after praising his skill at sauce-making, Chaucer's narrator adds, "But greet harm was it, as it thoughte me, / That on his shyne a mormal hadde he" (*GP* 385–386). Such contradictions create an equivo-cal effect, an uncertainty concerning the narrator's intention or his values, which is not characteristic of estates satire.

In short, although Chaucer certainly knew Benoît's portrait series, it cannot have been his sole source of inspiration for the portraits of the *General Prologue*. Nor can estates satire, whose criticism is focused upon the sins and turpitudes of whole estates treated in hierarchical order, not individuals treated in more ran-dom groupings. There is yet another partial model possible for Chaucer's *General Prologue* portraits. This written model is neither a specific literary text (as in the case of Benoît's portrait series in the *Roman de Troie*) nor a whole literary genre (such as estates satire), but rather a material artifact, a concrete way of present-ing medieval literary texts developed in the fourteenth century: the manuscript compilation of vernacular poets accompanied, sometimes even prefaced, by the authorizing *accessus* of a compilation of their "lives." I will talk about extant ex-amples of such manuscripts, but I can propose none as a model that Chaucer might have seen. Surviving compilations are likely to be only a small sample of those that once existed; furthermore, the new phenomenon of compilations that treated vernacular poets as authors by providing biographical sketches of them may well have been widely known among literary men, so that Chaucer would not have had to see such a compilation in order to know about it.

In *Medieval Theory of Authorship* (1984, 203), A. J. Minnis suggested that Chaucer in his *Canterbury Tales* deliberately assumed the role of compiler and used the conventional compilers' technique of "authenticating sources"; that is, in his *General Prologue*, he claimed to be reporting the very words of his sources:

Whoso shal telle a tale after a man,
He moot reherce as ny as evere he kan
Everich a word, if it be in his charge,
Al speke he never so rudeliche and large,
Or ellis he moot telle his tale untrewe,
Or feyne thyng, or fynde wordes newe.
He may nat spare, althogh he were his brother;
He moot as wel seye o word as another. (*GP* 731–738)

Minnis concluded that "Chaucer treats his fictional characters with the re-spect that the Latin compilers had reserved for their *auctores*. The 'lewd compila-tor' has become the compiler of the 'lewd'." To present himself as the mere com-piler of various English verse narratives and a prose exemplum is, as Minnis put it, a "self-deprecating" role. Indeed, it may even be a comic parody of the sort of ambitious vernacular compilation that had been undertaken on the continent.

Although he discussed at some length the different types of academic pro-logues to *auctores* which, along with the name of the author, might include a short life (*vita auctoris*), Minnis did not go so far as to suggest that Chaucer intended the portrait series of his *General Prologue* to be understood as a parodic compila-tion of "lives of the authors" introducing and authorizing a compilation of their works. Perhaps this reticence to extend the comparison may be due to the rela-tive rarity of medieval Latin *accessus ad auctores* collected into a series apart from the poets' works. In only one surviving Latin codex does this collection head the whole compilation, and in two others it forms a separate section in the middle of the codex (Huygens 1970, 5).[2]

Nevertheless, in the late thirteenth- and fourteenth-century compilations of troubadour verse that we now call "songbooks," there is ample precedent for col-lecting vernacular poets' "lives" and presenting them as an aid to understanding, an *accessus* to their works. These prose lives or *vidas*, often supplemented by *ra-zos*, or prose interpretations of the poets' reasons for composing particular songs, survive in about twenty manuscripts. Two fine thirteenth-century songbooks written in the region of Venice but now in the Bibliothèque Nationale de France (MS. fr. 854, known as the I songbook, and MS. fr. 12473, known as the K

---

[2] A twelfth-century codex from the monastery of Tegernsee (Munich, Bayerische Staatsbibliothek, MS. Clm 19475, fols. 1–16) presents the only example of a Latin *accessus ad auctores* collected at the beginning of a codex.

songbook) present the largest number of *vidas*—eighty-seven each—and do so in a scholarly format. The collected songs of each troubadour are prefaced by his or her rubricated name, often by a *vida* in red letters, and by a large initial containing a pictorial representation of the poet either on horseback or afoot, usually turned toward the text of his or her lyrics in the opposite column. Chaucerians familiar with the Ellesmere manuscript of the *Canterbury Tales* will, of course, think of the pilgrim-storytellers represented on horseback in the margins (rather than within initial letters) at the beginning of their tales.[3]

In a comparative study of Latin *accessus ad auctores* and Occitan *vidas*, Margarita Egan (1983) has shown that both belong to the tradition of scholarly commentary and that they were originally presented visually in similar ways, that is, in red ink to signal a gloss, in contrast to the black ink in which the text itself was inscribed. She remarks as well (1983, 37) that "in later MS traditions both Latin and Old Provençal 'lives' gain autonomy. Two *chansonniers* from the 14th c. [MSS. Paris, B. N. Fr. 22543 and 1949] group *vidas* and *razos* together, apart from the troubadour poems. For the *accessus* we find a parallel development. Two 12th-c. codices [MSS. Munich Clm 19475 and 19474] also contain collections of *accessus* only."

In a single surviving fourteenth-century codex (B.N.F. MS. fr. 22543), a manuscript known as the R songbook, written in the region of Toulouse[4] in the fourteenth century, a collection of *vidas* and *razos* is gathered together and presented as a prologue (fols. 1–4) or *accessus* to the following compilation of troubadour lyrics (fols. 5–114), and of narrative, didactic texts in verse and prose (fols. 115–142). Three other late songbooks compile *vidas* and *razos* together in a separate section placed somewhere in the middle of the codex. For example, in the E songbook (B.N.F. MS. fr. 1749), written in the region of Montpellier in the fourteenth century, this collection of *vidas* and *razos* for twenty-three troubadours occupies folios 189–210, immediately following a collection of *cansos* and *sirventes* organized by author, and immediately preceding a collection of debate poems on folios 221–226.

When *vidas* are compiled separately, their order does not correspond to that in which, in the same codex, the lyric anthologies of the different troubadours are presented. Nor does every troubadour who appears in the "lives" section reappear in the compilation of "works," and vice versa. Likewise, the collected lives of the pilgrim-storytellers in Chaucer's *General Prologue* are not presented in the same order as their stories: the *General Prologue* order of "lives" begins with Knight, Squire, and Yeoman, while the order of tales begins with Knight's, Mill-

---

[3] For color reproductions, see *The New Ellesmere Chaucer Facsimile* (1995).
[4] For the provenance of the troubadour songbooks, see Zufferey 1987.

er's, Reeve's. Some pilgrims are given a place in the *General Prologue*, but have no tale in the following anthology, while others, like the Canon's Yeoman, have a tale but no "life" in the *General Prologue*. The two compilations—of lives and of works—must have been separate in Chaucer's late-fourteenth-century manuscript of the *Canterbury Tales*, just as they are in certain troubadour songbooks.

The ordinary social hierarchy plays little part in the order of compilation of these collected troubadour *vidas*, for the order of poets is, at best, a meritocracy.[5] The R songbook begins its introductory collection of *vidas* with that of the "master of the troubadours," Guiraut de Borneill, while its subsequent poetry anthology begins with a crusade song by Marcabru, one of the earliest troubadours. The E songbook's *vida* compilation begins with Peire d'Alvergne because, according to his *vida*, "he was considered to be the best troubadour in the world prior to Guiraut de Borneill" (Boutière and Schutz 1964, 263).[6] The poetry anthology of the E songbook begins, on the other hand, with the *cansos* of Folquet de Marseilla, perhaps because he rose to become a bishop; after a few other poets reputed for their excellence, including Guiraut de Borneill, this songbook reverts to an approximately alphabetical order of presentation of poets and their verse.

One might well argue that Chaucer's collection of "lives" of the storytellers (like the R and E songbook compilations of *vidas*) gives pride of place to the most consummate artist, for the Knight's *roman antique* is the highest literary genre in the anthology. However, according to Chaucer's framing fiction, the Knight's tale begins the compilation of stories solely due to the luck of the draw (*GP* 845).

But how do Chaucer's pilgrim portraits—which, as I am suggesting, might more appropriately be called "lives"—compare thematically with the troubadour *vidas*? Egan has defined the content of the *vidas* as unvarying (1983, 45): "Troubadours are characterized by moral character (generosity, social acceptability, wit, eloquence, lady service, valor), social status, place of origin, parentage, and, more rarely, physical appearance. The poets perform similar actions. Specific sequences in a troubadour's 'life' recur in many texts; usually, the troubadour loves, sings, retires to a monastery, and dies." This definition is not entirely unfair, but the search for a common pattern has led Egan to disregard a great deal of individualizing detail.

The description in the *vidas* is indeed more formulaic than in Chaucer's pilgrim "lives," especially as regards the troubadour's outward appearance, which is

---

[5] Whereas women invariably come at the tail end of the hierarchy of estates satire, the *vidas* of women troubadours, like the "lives" of Chaucer's female pilgrims, are mixed in with those of the men.

[6] E, I, K, R manuscript versions, among others; orthography of I: "era tengutz per lo meillor trobador del mon, tro que venc Guirautz de Borneill."

often passed over in silence. An attractive man is almost invariably, in romance vocabulary, "bels et avinens . . . de la persona" (handsome and charming in physique). Exceptions to the rule, such as the portly Gaucelm Faidit, receive more unusual treatment: "He was a generous [big] man and very gluttonous in eating and drinking, which is why he grew extremely fat" (Boutière and Schutz 1964, 167).[7] We learn, in fact, that the woman of low repute Gaucelm eventually took to wife, although very beautiful and well taught ("fort fo bella e fort enseingnada"), eventually became as big and fat as he was ("e si venc si grossa e si grassa com era el"). The *vidas* are by no means devoid of individualizing detail, even with respect to personal appearance. Still, we are a long way from the minutiae concerning physical appearance—the red bristles sprouting from the wart on the very tip of the Miller's nose (*GP* 554–556)—called to our attention in the "lives" of Chaucer's *General Prologue*.

One of the most striking themes the troubadour *vidas* share with the pilgrim "lives" is precisely what, according to Lumiansky, we do *not* find in Benoît de Sainte-Maure's portraits: "past experiences" or events of personal history. The *vidas* tend to treat personal history as a record of mobility, both social (in the sense of improving one's status, for poetic prowess was a way into and up in courtly society) and physical (in the sense of travel, which widened reputation, so that the names of patrons and courts are listed, as well as noteworthy pilgrimages and voyages). Perdigon's *vida*, for example, identifies him as the son of a fisherman from the small town of Lesperon in the bishopric of Gévaudan, a man who was good at playing the viol and at inventing lyrics. Because of his "sense" and his poetic composition, he won admiration and honor until the Dauphin d'Auvergne took him for his knight, giving him arms, land, and rents (Boutière and Schutz 1964, 408).[8] The *vida* of the troubadour Aimeric de Peguillan, son of a cloth merchant from Toulouse, stresses his widening reputation and social ascension. After falling in love with a bourgeois neighbor's wife and learning to compose love songs for her, he avenged her shaming by her jealous husband with a sword blow to the man's head. Forced to flee Toulouse, he went to Catalonia to the court of Guillem de Berguedan, who made him a *jongleur*, gave him a horse and clothing, and presented him to King Alfonso of Castile, "who gave him arms

---

[7] E, I, K, R manuscript versions, among others; orthography of I: "Hom fo que ac gran larguesa; e fo molt glotz de manjar et de beure; per so venc gros oltra mesura."

[8] E, I, K, R manuscript versions, among others; orthography of I: "Perdigons si fo joglars e saup trop ben violar e trobar. E fo de l'evesquat de Javadan, d'un borget que a nom Lesperon. E fo fils d'un paubre home que era pescaire. E per so sen e per son trobar montet en gran pretz et en gran honor, que.l Dalfins d'Alverne lo tenc per son cavallier e.l vesti e l'arma ab si lonc temps, e.ill det terra et renda. Et tuit li prince e.ill gran baron li fasian fort gran honor. E de grans bonas venturas ac lonc temps."

and honors." Finally Aimeric went to Lombardy where "all the important men honored him" (Boutière and Schutz 1964, 425–26).[9]

According to their *vidas*, a few troubadours were black sheep who used their poetic talents, not to move up in courtly society, but to entertain in taverns. Such was the case with Guillem Figueira, son of a tailor from Toulouse, who "knew how to compose and sing very well and became an entertainer (*jongleur*) in Lombardy among the townspeople. But he was not a man who enjoyed the company of lords and good society; rather he was much appreciated by rascals and prostitutes and innkeepers and tavernkeepers" (Boutière and Schutz 1964, 434).[10] Like the occasional troubadour black sheep, some of the Canterbury pilgrims frequent taverns to make their social reputations. The ambitious Friar, for example, finds more lucrative contacts there than among the poor and sick:

> He knew the tavernes wel in every toun
> And everich hostiler and tappestere
> Bet than a lazar or a beggestere,
> For unto swich a worthy man as he
> Accorded nat, as by his facultee,
> To have with sike lazars aqueyntaunce
> It is nat honest; it may nat avaunce,
> For to deelen with no swich poraille,
> But al with riche and selleres of vitaille. (*GP* 240–248)

The travels of some of Chaucer's pilgrims are also featured in their "lives" as evidence of their characters, or more precisely, of how they have achieved reputations of one sort or another: the Knight's international fame is proven by the surprisingly long list of places where he has fought and won (*GP* 51–66); the Squire's

---

[9] E, I, K, R manuscript versions, among others; orthography of I: "N'Aimerics de Peguillan si fo de Tolosa, fils d'un borges qu'era mercadiers, que tenia draps a vendre . . . Et enamoret se d'una borgesa, soa visina. Et aquella amors li mostret trobar. E fetz de leis maintas bonas cansos. Et mesclet se ab lui lo marritz de la domna e fetz li desonor. E 'N Aimerics si s'en venget, qu'el lo feri d'una espaza per la testa. Per que.l convenc ad issir de Tollosa e faidir. Et anet s'en en Cataloingna. E'N Guillems de Berguedan si l'acuilli; et enansset lui en son trobar. . .E fetz lo joglar, qu'el li det son pallafre e sos vestirs. E presentet lo al rei Anfos de Castella, que.l crec d'arnes e d'onor. Et estet en aquellas encontradas lonc temps. Puois s'en venc en Lombardia, on tuich li bon ome li feron gran honor."

[10] I and K manuscript versions, among others; orthography of I: "Guillems Figuera si fo de Tolosa, fils d'un sartor, et el fo sartres. E quant li Franses aguen Tolosa, si s'en venc en Lombardia. E saup ben trobar e cantar; e fez se joglars entre los ciutadis. Non fo hom que saubes caber entre.ls baros ni entre la bona gen; mas mout se fez grazir als arlotz et als putans et als hostes et als taverniers."

foreign engagements also receive mention (*GP* 85–86); the Shipman's reputation as navigator is upheld by the list of harbors he knew (*GP* 407–409); and the Wife of Bath's reputation as a woman of the world is evoked by the list of places she has visited on pilgrimage: Jerusalem three times, Rome, Bologne-sur-Mer, St. James of Compostela, Cologne (*GP* 463–466).

Identity in the troubadour *vidas* is defined in terms of where one comes from and where one goes or has gone. The *vidas* almost invariably identify a place of origin for each poet: a region, a bishopric, a town, a castle, or some combination of all of these. This physical point of origin is then completed with the troubadour's social origin (his father's profession or estate) and his own acquired status in life; taken together, the troubadours cover nearly the whole social spectrum (king, count, viscount, castellan, knight, bishop, monk, canon, cleric, judge, bourgeois, merchant, tailor, metalsmith, fisherman, kitchen servant, noble and non-noble women, *jongleur* or entertainer — every estate except agricultural laborer).

The collected "lives" of Chaucer's pilgrim storytellers also cover a great range of late medieval English society, with the exception of the upper ranks of the nobility and clergy (no storyteller being a king, a count, or a bishop). Each pilgrim's "life" identifies his or her current estate or profession, but never a parental one. Furthermore, most of the Canterbury pilgrims remain nameless, with only their profession or estate to identify them. Sometimes a pilgrim is localized: the Clerk is from Oxford; the Shipman is apparently from Dartmouth; the Wife is from near Bath; the Reeve is from Norfolk, near Bawdeswell (*GP* 285, 389, 445, 619–620). However, these localities — Oxford, Dartmouth, near Bath, near Bawdeswell — are not necessarily birthplaces, as they are in the troubadour *vidas*. Thus, even though most of the Canterbury pilgrims' "lives" are full of detail that we might consider personal or individualizing, the pilgrim storytellers remain more anonymous than do the troubadours.

The troubadour *vidas* treat individuals from nearly all the classes and groups of late medieval society, a highly mixed company having in common a certain poetic expertise. This expertise receives evaluation in every *vida*; the troubadour is considered as a composer of lyrics and of music, as a singer, as an instrumentalist, as an explainer of his own verse or that of others, even as a scribe or recorder. Thus for Elias Cairel, born in Sarlat in Périgord, a metalsmith and designer of armor by trade, we learn that he became a *jongleur* and travelled widely, spending a long time in "Romania" before returning to Sarlat to die. Of his talents, the judgment is categorical: "he sang badly and composed badly and played the viol badly and spoke even worse, but he wrote down the words and music of his songs very well" (Boutière and Schutz 1964, 252).[11] The talents of the Canterbury pilgrims are also assessed in their *General Prologue* "lives," even though these talents have little to do with storytelling ability and more to do with the "special qualifications demanded by the profession or estate of each pilgrim," as Mann has ar- gued (1973, 12). For example, the Wife of Bath was an excellent clothmaker; the Yeoman took good care of his arrows; the Prioress sang the liturgy becomingly through her nose (*GP* 447–448, 106–107, 122–123).

In the compilations of troubadour *vidas*, as in the collected "lives" of the *General Prologue*, a first-person narrator unifies the different accounts and ad- dresses an audience of readers imagined, most of the time, as a live audience of listeners. Whereas Chaucer's pilgrim narrator describes himself and becomes a character in his own right, the narrators of the troubadour *vida* compilations call attention to themselves chiefly through direct admonitions.

For example, in the R songbook, the only one prefaced by a collection of *vidas*, the narrator frequently addresses the audience to recollect what he has already said: "Peire Vidal, just as I told you, courted all the noble ladies . . ." (Boutière and Schutz 1964, 361).[12] Likewise, he addresses the audience to point out that they will find a sample of Peire Vidal's poetic work "here" (that is, in the manuscript compilation at hand): "And here you will find some of his works" (Boutière and Schutz 1964, 353).[13] The compilation of *vidas* sandwiched into the E manuscript presents a slightly different version; the narrator of Peire Vidal's *vida* announces directly to an audience of readers imagined also as listeners that they will now be able to read and hear his songs: "And here are written a large number of his songs, as you will be able to hear" (Boutière and Schutz 1964, 353).[14] In other cases, the phrase used is "as you will be able to hear and see" ("auzir et vezer").[15]

In his *General Prologue* compilation of lives of the pilgrims, Chaucer's nar- rator maintains the fiction of orality—of speaking to us—although he also in- troduces the notion that he is writing by using the word "space" in the lines an- nouncing these lives:

---

[11] I and K manuscript versions, among others; orthography of I: "Elias Cairels si fo de Sarlat, d'un borc de Peiregorc, et era laboraire d'aur e d'argent e deseingnaire d'armas. E fetz se joglars e anet gran temps per lo mon. Mal cantava e mal trobava e mal violava e peichs parlava, e ben escrivia motz e sons. En Romania estet lonc temps; e quant el s'en parti, si s'en tornet a Sarlat, e lai el moric."

[12] E and R manuscript versions, among others; orthography of E: "Peyre Vidal—si com ieu vos ai dig—s'entendia en totas las bonas dona . . ."

[13] R manuscript version: "Et aysi trobares de sa obra."

[14] E manuscript version: "Et aqui son escriutas de las soas chansos gran re si com vos poiretz auzir."

[15] See Schutz 1939, 568, for further examples of such mixed references in the *vidas* to both hearing and reading the poetry that followed.

But natheless, whil I have tyme and space,
Er that I ferther in this tale pace,
Me thynketh it acordaunt to resoun
To telle yow al the condicioun
Of ech of hem, so as it semed me,
And whiche they weren, and of what degree,
And eek in what array that they were inne. (*GP* 35–41)

Because he has enough time and space (suggestive of writing space in a manuscript), the narrator-recorder promises us a series of biographical sketches of the
pilgrim storytellers as a "reasonable" introduction to the tales that will follow. In
the interlude between the Knight's and Miller's tales, Chaucer's narrator addresses us suddenly and quite clearly as readers by referring to the stories he retells as
already written in the book before us:

. . . but for I moot reherce
Hir tales alle, be they bettre or werse,
Or elles falsen som of my mateere.
And therfore, whoso list it nat yheere,
Turne over the leef and chese another tale. (A 3173–3177)

Here we have a situation comparable to that at the end of many a troubadour *vida* in the E and R songbook compilations, where the narrator explicitly
refers to the written poetry that will follow in the manuscript. The information
Chaucer's narrator here gives us about certain pilgrims ("The Millere is a cherl;
ye knowe wel this") (A 3182) recollects what he has already told us in the *accessus*
formed by their collected "lives," which should better enable us to approach and
appreciate — or to avoid — their recorded works.

The judgments in the *vidas* concern troubadour lives that are finished; the
judgments of the *General Prologue* — considerably more equivocal — concern the
ongoing lives of Chaucer's fictional storytellers. The narrators of *vida* compilations inevitably characterize themselves, as does the narrator of the pilgrims'
"lives," by the values they express and the judgments they pronounce. However,
they do not often present themselves as friends or acquaintances of troubadours
or eyewitnesses to their lives in the way that Chaucer's narrator-observer claims
familiarity with the pilgrim storytellers: "So hadde I spoken with hem everichon
/ That I was of hir felaweshipe anon" (*GP* 31–32).

In the *vida* compilation heading the R songbook, the man who collected
and wrote down the *vidas* does, however, claim personal acquaintance with one
troubadour. In a lengthy *vida* of the troubadour Savaric de Malleo which incor-
porates commentaries on his verse (*razos* explaining the motivations or reasons
behind certain poems), the narrator, who has addressed an imagined listening

audience with phrases such as "as I told you"("be.us dis"), eventually names himself as writer and claims insider status, for he was the messenger who carried Savaric's written messages: "And know in truth that it is I, Uc de Saint-Circ, the writer of these commentaries, who was the messenger that went there carrying all the missives and writings" (Boutière and Schutz 1964, 224).[16]

The narrators of *vidas* in late thirteenth-century songbooks, such as I and K, more frequently claim firsthand knowledge, but in these songbooks there is no sense of a unifying commentatorial voice, in part simply because the *vidas* are not collected in one place, but rather each *vida* is presented separately at the head of the anthology of a particular troubadour's verse. At the end of Savaric de Malleo's *vida* in the I and K songbooks, for example, the anonymous narrator testifies that, of all the men "he has ever seen or heard," Savaric was the best, so that a large book could be made of his good deeds (Boutière and Schutz 1964, 220).[17] At the end of Cadenet's *vida*, too, an anonymous narrator calls attention to himself as an eyewitness: "And all his deeds I know from having seen and heard them" (Boutière and Schutz 1964, 500).[18] As a conclusion to the *vida* of Peire Cardenal, who lived to the remarkable age of "around a hundred," the narrator names himself, "master Miquel de la Tor," and his occupation: he is the scribe who, in the city of Nimes, wrote down in the manuscript at hand the *sirventes* of Peire Cardenal (Boutière and Schutz 1964, 335–36).[19]

Analogies between Chaucer's *General Prologue* "lives" of the pilgrim storytellers and the collected *vidas* of the troubadours should not be pressed too hard. After all, if anything, Chaucer is burlesquing this relatively new phenomenon of treating vernacular poets as authors by providing commentary in the form of an explanatory *accessus* to their work. As their *vidas* show, the troubadours came from all walks of life. So do Chaucer's vernacular storytellers. For each tale in his compilation of the *Canterbury Tales*, he has invented a vernacular voice and a life.

---

[16] R manuscript version: "E sapias per ver que ieu, Uc de San Sirc, que ay escrichas estas razos, fuy lo mesatje que lay aniey e.l portey totz los mans e.ls escrisz."

[17] I and K manuscript versions, among others; orthography of I: "E dels sieus bons faichs se poria far un gran libre, qui lo volgues escrire, con d'aquellui que ac plus en si d'umelitat e de merce e de franquessa, e que mais fez de bons faichs d'ome qu'eu anc vis ni auzis, e plus n'avia voluntat de far."

[18] I and K manuscript versions, among others; orthography of I: "E tot lo sieu faig eu saubi per auzir et per vezer."

[19] I and K manuscript versions, among others; orthography of I: "Et ieu, maistre Miquel de la Tor, escrivan, fauc asaber qu'En Peire Cardinal, quan passet d'aquesta vida, qu'el avia ben entor sent ans. Et ieu, sobredig Miquel, ai aquestz sirventes escrit en la ciutat de Nemze. Et aqui son escritz de los sieus sirventes."

But whereas the troubadours really existed, and their *vidas* may contain some small nugget of truth, Chaucer's "lives" are as fictive as his pilgrim storytellers. Nor do the things we learn from their lives necessarily enhance our understanding of their stories. Some lives might even warn us to skip certain stories, or so Chaucer's narrator suggests. An *accessus* that warns the reader away: can this be anything but comic parody?[20]

---

[20] An earlier version of this essay appeared under the title "Chaucer's *General Prologue* and the *Lives* of the Troubadours" (Kendrick 2001).

Works Cited

Boutière, Jean, and A. H. Schutz, eds. 1964. *Biographies des troubadours: textes provençaux des XIIIe et XIVe siècles*. Paris: Nizet.

Bryan, W. F., and Germaine Dempster, eds. 1941. *Sources and Analogues of Chaucer's* Canterbury Tales. Repr. Atlantic Highlands, NJ: Humanities Press, 1958.

Chaucer, Geoffrey. 1987. *The Riverside Chaucer*. 3d ed., ed. Larry D. Benson et al. Boston: Houghton Mifflin.

Egan, Margarita. 1983. "Commentary, *vita poetae*, and *vida*: Latin and Old Provençal 'Lives of Poets'." *Romance Philology* 37:36–48.

Huygens. R. B. C. 1970. *Accessus ad auctores: Bernard d'Utrecht, Conrad d'Hirsau, Dialogus super auctores*. Leiden: Brill.

Kendrick, Laura. 2001. "Chaucer's *General Prologue* and the *Lives* of the Troubadours." In *Prologues et épilogues dans la littérature anglaise au Moyen Age*, ed. Leo Carruthers and Adrian Papahagi, Publications de l'Association des Médiévistes Anglicistes de l'Enseignement Supérieur 24. Paris: A.M.A.E.S.

Lumiansky, R. M. 1956. "Benoît's Portraits and Chaucer's *General Prologue*." *Journal of English and Germanic Philology* 55:431–38.

Manly, John M. 1926. *Some New Light on Chaucer*. New York: Holt.

Mann, Jill. 1973. *Chaucer and Medieval Estates Satire: The Literature of Social Classes and the* General Prologue *to the* Canterbury Tales. Cambridge: Cambridge University Press.

Minnis, Alistair J. 1984. *Medieval Theory of Authorship: Scholastic Literary Attitudes in the Later Middle Ages*. London: Scolar Press.

Pratt, Robert, and Karl Young. 1941. "The Literary Framework of the *Canterbury Tales*." In *Sources and Analogues of Chaucer's* Canterbury Tales, 1–81.

Schutz, A. H. 1939. "Were the *Vidas* and *Razos* Recited?" *Studies in Philology* 36:564–70.

Woodward, Daniel, and Martin Stevens, eds. 1995. *The Canterbury Tales by Geoffrey Chaucer: The New Ellesmere Chaucer Facsimile* (of Huntington Library MS. EL 26.C.9). San Marino, Calif.: Huntington Library; Tokyo: Yushodo.

Zufferey, François. 1987. *Recherches linguistiques sur les chansonniers provençaux*. Geneva: Droz.

Following Instructions: Remaking Dante's *Vita Nova* in the Fourteenth Century

H. Wayne Storey

for Joan,
for her passion for precision,
her passion for questions others are too timid to ask,
for the passion for literature she taught me,
with sincere and everlasting gratitude

The development of book production and the book trade in general in thirteenth- and fourteenth-century Tuscany has for some time been the subject of a scholarly investigation which has led overall to a much clearer picture of the history of Tuscan books and registers and more precisely to improved codicological tools for further inquiry.[1] The once difficult terrain of late thirteenth- and early fourteenth-century production of vernacular works has been greatly clarified by studies of the material composition and organization of these books from the primary building blocks of the medieval codex, the bifolium, to the construction and ordering of quires.[2] This kind of material inquiry has been particularly important in assessing the most typical forms of the medieval book, the miscellany and the composite manuscript.

In the light of these studies Dante's *Vita Nova* stands as one of the more problematic puzzles, not only in the history of manuscript production but also

---

[1] Of particular bibliographic note are the collective contributions of Lombardi and Nebbiai Dalla Guarda 2000, and the essays dedicated to the three principal anthologies of early Italian literature (MSS. Vaticano Latino 3793, Laurenziano Rediano 9, and BNCF Banco Rari 217) contained in Leonardi 2001.

[2] In addition to Léon Gillissen's work on the construction of quires (especially Gillissen 1977) and Avalle's introduction to what he dubs the primary construction material of the genre of the anthology, the *quaderno*, or the quire (1985, 363–82), we should recall also Robinson 1980 and Hanna 1986 on the role of the fascicle as an intermediary material between the individual work which might have circulated in some sort of wrapper which contained one or two quires and the larger, repository volume in which the work ultimately came to rest. As both have pointed out, while we can occasionally trace the direct transfer of the smaller work's fascicles, few are the medieval compositions which have survived in the fragile state of their original material circulation. Particularly useful for its methodological considerations is the analysis of the material construction of the early manuscript fragment Escorial e.III.23 in Capelli 2004. For additional methodological and analytical considerations in the construction and reconstruction of medieval fascicles, see Ornato 2000.

in the development of Italian literary history in the fourteenth century. Indeed in the case of the *Vita Nova* these are not separate issues. Rather the reception and growing significance of Dante's so-called *libello* in the fourteenth century as a biographical monument and stylistic icon of *stilnovismo* depend very much upon significant changes in the ways the *Vita Nova* was copied and passed along from reader to reader. As we shall see, Dante himself was wholly conscious of the work's transcription and the problems it would potentially pose to future copyists. Within the prose of the *Vita Nova*, Dante carefully integrates instructions for copying his little book designed to guarantee its compilational strategies of diverse and co-dependent genres and the ordering of its compositions. However, by the 1350s and '60s these same instructions were superseded by the scribal and literary-historical recasting of the *libello* as a *liber*, a fully-fledged icon of the status afforded Dante through his *Commedia* and subsequently applied to his youthful *Vita Nova*. To understand this material shift, we should first re-examine briefly the form of the *libello* itself.

As we know from late thirteenth-century correspondence, the most popular vehicle for sending individual compositions, such as poems, was the prose letter.[3] These letters took several forms, from simple private greetings attached to short compositions such as sonnets or ballads, to elaborate public pronouncements which provided explanatory glosses and a kind of material frame for their short compositions. Limited examples show that the letter consisted of a single folio or two, probably folded after transcription.[4] While the letter sufficed for exchanges of occasional poetry, it seems that longer, more elaborate poetic cycles sent from poet to poet or from poet to patron took the shape of individual gatherings of parchment or paper of varying lengths. These small cycles did not require the production of a book per se, but of a little book, which consisted of one or two quires notably destined for a limited circulation, a *libellus*.

Before Dante, instances of the lexical distinction between *libello* and *libro* appear in poems by Monte Andrea and a certain Terino da Castelfiorentino, one

---

[3] In epistolary correspondence with Meo Abracciavacca, Dotto Reali di Lucca announces that he is sending the enclosed sonnet (*Similimente canoscensa move*) in the letter so that Meo can show the sonnet to two other friars, Gaddo and Finfo (MS. Laurenziano, Rediano 9, c. 32r). Similar evidence is found in Guittone d'Arezzo's letters from the second half of the thirteenth century (see Margueron 1994).

[4] Some of the best evidence of the letter's material form is supplied by Petrarch's mid-fourteenth-century autograph letters collected by Moggio de' Moggi da Parma and now in MS. Laurenziano, Pluteo LIII 35. Though these letters do not contain poems, they do demonstrate the physical construction of the medieval letter sent by messenger. Historically more relevant are the examples of letters from the second half of the thirteenth century found in Castellani 1982, examples 31, 36, 43, and 45.

of Dante's early correspondents. In *Non t'à donato, Amor, piciola partte* (MS. Vaticano Latino 3793, c. 147r [#683]) Terino asks for a copy of Monte's book (*libro*). In Monte's response, *Bene m'à messo, Amore, in gran partte* (MS. Vaticano Latino 3793, c. 147r [#684]), it is clear that the book to which Terino refers is, in fact, not for circulation among friends and poets; it is not a *libellus*, but part of a larger book, or *libro*.⁵ Around 1301, the Spiritual Franciscan Jacopone da Todi refers to a work sent to his nemesis, Pope Boniface VIII, as part of a *libello* ("Scrissite nel meo libello, de quel non fui essaudito," v. 8 of *Lo pastor per meo peccato*).⁶ Without knowing the exact contents of the collection, it is impossible to define the material nature of Jacopone's *libello*. But what should strike us here is the application of the term to designate a possibly small work for an apparently very limited audience: Pope Boniface VIII.

Problematically curious is the later attestation of the word's use by the learned Bolognese jurist Cino da Pistoia in his sonnet supposedly critical of two passages in the second and third canticles of Dante's *Commedia* (*Infra gli altri difetti del libello*). Written between 1320 and 1336, it seems clear that the sonnet does not refer to a shorter work by Dante that would have been contained in one or two fascicles. It seems equally unlikely that the *Purgatorio* and the *Paradiso* would have circulated together in a material form small enough to be called a *libello*. But does the diminutive *-ello* simply serve to disparage the poetic accomplishment of Cino's dear friend? Later witnesses to the term's usage would suggest such a reading.⁷ But given the material circumstances of the early circulation of the *Commedia*'s canticles in the regions of Bologna and Padua, one can also speculate that Cino might have been identifying a personal copy of limited circulation and in a "poor" material form, perhaps in paper rather than parchment.⁸

However, the best evidence of the term's technical significance comes from Salimbene's *Chronica*, written between 1283 and 1288. In his discussions of Gerard of Borgo San Donnino's Introduction to three of Joachim of Fiore's commentaries (an introduction which landed Gerard in prison for life in 1254), Salimbene observes that once in Paris Gerard "thought out the foolish plan of writing a

---

⁵ At issue here is the possible presence of a multi-author, but assuredly unauthorized, anthology (*libro*) in which Monte's poems would have appeared. For a discussion of this exchange, see Storey 2004, 273-79.

⁶ Jacopone's poem is contained in Contini 1960, 112.

⁷ Remembering Boccaccio's use of *libellus* in his epistle IX to Zanobi da Strada, see especially Rizzo 1973 and Grübmuller 1986.

⁸ In addition to Papka 1999, which posits a production of early copies of the *Comedy* in paper manuscripts, evidence of the circulation of popular vernacularizations, such as Andrea Lancia's translation of the *Aeneid*, in paper manuscripts appears early in the fourteenth century. See also Dolbeau 1989.

little book, a *libellus*, and he showed his foolishness by *publishing that book among some ignorant brothers*" (emphasis added) ("excogitavit fatuitatem componendo libellum et divulgavit stultitiam suam propalando ipsum ignorantibus fratribus" [¶ 341, 16–18]).[9] Salimbene's lexical insistence on describing Gerardino's work as a *libellus* is consistent throughout the *Chronica*. By the same token, materially more substantial volumes, such as the complete works of Joachim of Fiore owned by Brother Hugo, are designated as *libri* ("omnes libros abbatis Ioachim de grossa littera habebat" [¶ 339, 11–12]).

We believe that probably around 1293 Dante sent to Guido Cavalcanti, his friend and an influential literary figure in Florence, a copy of a work of poetry and prose entitled in Latin *Vita Nova*. If the earliest copies of the work are reliable for their layout of the *libello*, the little book would have consisted materially of no more than two quinternions (10 bifolia / 20 *chartae*), or perhaps even two quaternions (8 bifolia or 16 *chartae*). In the first two sentences of the introductory prose, Dante draws a sharp contrast between the metaphorical *libro della memoria* and the product of his transcription, his *libello*. The passage reflects a remarkably notarial attention to the material details and vocabulary of scribal production, referencing the rubricated title (*la rubrica*) and the written text (*parole scripte*) found below that title in red ink that Dante intends to transcribe (*asemplare*) in this little book:

> In quella parte del libro della mia memoria dinanzi alla quale poco si potrebbe leggere, si trova una rubrica la quale dice incipit VITA NOVA. Sotto la quale rubrica io trovo scripte le parole le quali è mio intendimento d'asemplare in questo libello . . . [1.1] [10]

> (In that part of the book of my memory before which little can be read is found the rubric which says here begins THE NEW LIFE, under which I find words written which it is my intention to transcribe in this little book . . .)

---

[9] Citations from Salimbene's *Chronica* are from ed. Scalia 1998.

[10] Citations from Dante's *Vita Nova* are indicated from ed. Gorni 1996 when taken from a printed source. Otherwise manuscript sources are noted according to collocation and manuscript *charta*. The primary paragraph numbers are Gorni's; Barbi's now superseded *paragrafazioni* are indicated in brackets. Translations are my own. Gorni argues that *libello* represents an "affectionate suffix" reminiscent of Ovid's "titulum nomenque libelli" in the first verse of the *Remedia Amoris*. Nevertheless editors of the *Remedia* have convincingly demonstrated that *libellus* was a technical term among the elegiac poets for a work containing erotic poetry, a usage which a philologically attentive Dante would have, in my estimation, been unwilling to apply to a collection of praise poems for the now deceased and venerated Beatrice. Rather, as we shall see, the conscious use of scribal technical terms was a motif drawing copyist and literary creator ever closer together in Dante's artistic expression.

Dante's *libello* is not the first in early Italian literature. While we have re-constituted several poetic collections by individual authors that would qualify as *Liederbücher*, or song books organized around a single theme, none has survived materially except Guittone d'Arezzo's *libello* on the nature of love, infelicitously dubbed the *Trattato d'amore*, or *Treatise on love*, by an early twentieth-century critic. This collection of thirteen lyric poems composed by Guittone centers on the figure of love depicted in an accompanying illumination. Today the *libello* with its accompanying *titoli* is crammed into the recto and verso of an early fourteenth-century manuscript from the southern Veneto-northern Emilia (MS. Escorial e.III.23).[11] The minuscule space in which the illustration should have gone contains the compiler's instructions to the illuminator. But I'm convinced that the limited space simply did not allow for the illustration's execution.[12] Con-temporary manuscripts such as the illuminated Banco Rari 217 or Banco Rari 69 suggest that an illustration with such a central role in the interpretation of the poetic texts would have taken up at least half of one side of a *charta* if not a full recto with the poetic cycle's descriptive title ("Here is the depiction of the fig-ure of love and and all its aspects as you will be able to understand and from the figure see") and introductory poem: "Dear friend, look at the figure / of carnal love in this picture" ("Caro amico, guarda la figura / 'n esta pinctura del carnale amore" [vv. 1–2]). Calculating, as was then common, four compositions per side of each *charta* for the remaining twelve poems by Guittone, the *libello* would have consisted of a simple duernion: two bifolia; hardly a *libro*, but because of its orga-nizing frame of the glossed illustration, Guittone's cycle would not have circulat-ed simply as loose leaves (or *chartae*). Given the critical response of Dante's con-temporaries, especially Guido Cavalcanti, to Guittone's *libello*, there is little doubt that Dante himself knew Guittone's little book. He certainly learned from it.

    If there is an organizing principle at the core of Dante's *Vita Nova*, it is, as we saw in the work's opening prose lines, the motif of little book production itself. Throughout the *Vita Nova*, in passages usually overlooked for their seemingly mundane technical instructions and *divisiones*, we find Dante the copyist guid-ing what he knew would be other copyists of his work on *how* to transcribe his *libello*. Why? I believe there are several reasons.

    The first reason has to do with the little book's intended audience. Dante conceived of the *Vita Nova* as a "private publication" for a few poet friends. In the *libello*, Dante confesses to Guido Cavalcanti that he has already erred by perhaps revealing too much of the meaning of one of his songs to a wider public; a public,

---

[11] For comprehensive material studies of the codex, see Capelli 2003.
[12] Capelli's research (2004, 84-100) demonstrates as well that the codex served as a service copy and that the illumination was never intended to be carried out in the minus-cule space of c. 74r. See also Storey 1993, 171-92.

unlike his close circle of friends, incapable of understanding the poem's true significance (10.33 [XIX.22]). Consequently Dante's instructions on the layout and transcription of the *libello* would have been intended for the private, non-professional copyist-friend who simply wanted to make a personal copy. Nevertheless, and here we are onto reason number two, Dante would also have been very familiar with the fate of other small books, such as Guittone's, whose individual poems were dispersed because of the casual material nature of the poetic *libello* in its unbound quire or two. Dante's elaborate narrative frame might well have been designed not only to elucidate the poems' reconstructed compositional contexts and hidden meanings but also, as in the tradition of the *trobar clus*, to protect materially the little book's lyrics which could have otherwise been reordered outside the poet's narrative or even scattered from their collected form in disparate copies. Yet not even Dante's elaborate scribal instructions and narrative devices were able to keep some scribes from simply lifting the poetry from the *Vita Nova* and assembling newly ordered copies of the *libello*'s poems, as evidenced by numerous fourteenth- and fifteenth-century manuscripts. One explanation for such a poems-only manuscript tradition and for the difficulties of subsequent scribes in following Dante's instructions serves as the third reason for the young poet's insistent didactic repetitions: the complicated resurrection of the prose/poetry structure of the work, for which there might have been only distant models among the *vidas* and *razos* of his Occitan predecessors.

While I will not review all of Dante's copy instructions in the *Vita Nova*, it will be helpful to recognize two of the distinctive forms of instruction we find in the prose. The first we encounter throughout the *libello*. In its repeated formula, it constitutes what should have been a reliable means of suturing the transitions between prose and poetry while guaranteeing the order and the inclusion of the correct poems. Before each poem Dante always notes in the prose the poetic genre of the composition that will follow and either its partial or complete first verse. In the prose which immediately follows the poem, Dante reiterates the genre and then often interpretatively divides the poem ("e dissi questo sonetto, lo quale comincia *Gentile pensero*" [27.4 (XXXVIII.4)] . . . "In questo sonetto fo due parti" [27.5]). This essentially scribal system of reiteration establishes both linkage and framing devices for the physical act of copying the poems. From this repeated instruction alone the compiler would have been able to plan the manuscript's ruling and layout, and the copyist would always have been able to check that he was about to copy the correct poem in the correct transcriptional format (sonnet/*ballata*/canzone).

The second type of instruction concerns a unique moment in the prose of the *Vita Nova*, in which Dante explains why he has altered the position of the *divisione*, or the prose explanation, for the canzone *Gli occhi dolenti per pietà del core* from its usual place after the poem to before its presentation in the macrotext. We recall that the canzone is the first poem after the revelation of Beatrice's death: "And so that this canzone will seem more widowed after its conclusion, I will divide it before I write it down; and I will maintain this mode of presenting [poems and their explanations] from here on" (20.2 [XXXI.2]: "E acciò che questa canzone paia rimanere più vedova dopo lo suo fine, la dividerò prima ch'io la scriva; e cotale modo terrò da qui innançi"). Again the scribal nature of Dante's language dominates the instruction: interpretations will precede transcription (obviously not composition [*scrivere*]). But the instruction also serves two additional functions. The first is that it clearly reverses the scribal formula established in the preceding paragraphs of the *Vita Nova* and fixes this change as permanent throughout the rest of the *libello*. The instruction also intersects the interpretative plane of the *Vita Nova*, reinforcing the "loneliness" of the poem at the completion of its reading since there will be no commentary to follow. Dante has now designed the scribal apparatus to reflect the theme and tone of the lonely sorrow caused by Beatrice's absence.

When we turn to the manuscripts of the *Vita Nova*, we must admit that there is little external evidence that the *Vita Nova* even circulated until 1308, perhaps fifteen years after its composition and six years after Dante's exile from Florence, when we have a mere report that a reader had seen a copy of the *libello*, a little codex (*codicetto*) that has not survived. Rather our earliest and, I believe, best copies come from the 1340s and '50s and are all miscellanies of differing lengths and textual focus (MSS. Martelli 12, Chigiano L.VIII.305, and Magliabechiano Cl. VI, 143 [named the Strozziano, or S copy, due to its earlier provenance]; the last comes the closest to the material shape of a little book in the Middle Ages but ironically identifies Dante's work in both the incipit and the explicit as a *libro* ["Incipit illibro della nuova vita di dante"] and *liber* ["Explicit liber nove vite dantis"]). Boccaccio's two, but not identical, copies (MSS. Toledo, Archivo y Biblioteca Capitolares 104.6, and Vaticano Chigiano L.V.176) change our critical and material orientation to the work with editorial interventions that, in the words of Boccaccio's introduction, "correct" Dante's youthful errors as a copyist of his own work: errors of which the more mature Dante was "ashamed" and would have wanted to amend.[13] These so-called artistic "errors" committed by the young Dante amounted to the inclusion of his instructions in the text of his *libello* rather than in marginal glosses as the protohumanist copyists of the

---

[13] Boccaccio's copies are famous for, not to mention identified by, their material treatment of Dante's prose explanations of the divisions of the poems into interpretative parts, which are placed by the illustrious scribe outside the main body of the text in the margins. Boccaccio's own editorial premise, repeated in both copies, occupies the same editorial space as Dante's marginalia. In a longer study on Boccaccio's editorial methods (in preparation), I translate Boccaccio's editorial preamble from the Toledo codex and

1350s and '60s would have preferred. As we shall see below, Boccaccio renders the editorial favor of virtually destroying the *Vita Nova*'s unique and often intricate narratives which interweave episodes with notes on *how* and *why* the poems were composed, *how* they should be read, and *how* they should be copied and ordered by the private reader.

Perhaps the most extraordinary moment of scribal explanation within the dramatic and realistic movements of the *libello*'s narrative occurs when the poet's announced canzone *Sì lungiamente m'à tenuto Amore* is interrupted by the plaintive declamation of the Lamentations of Jeremiah, the opening of the service of Tenebrae, to announce Beatrice's death: "Quomodo sedet sola civitas plena populo! facta est quasi vidua domina gentium" ["How lonely she sits, the city once filled with people as if she were made a widow, she that ruled nations"]. The mournful interjection leaves only the fragment of the first 14-line stanza of what we presume would have been the canzone's multiple stanzas. If it is Dante the poet who expresses his grief through this dramatic interruption of his own poem by the opening of Lamentations, it is surely Dante the copyist who intervenes immediately after to remind his fellow copyist of the genre, and thus transcriptional layout, of the albeit fragmented composition: "I was working on this canzone and had finished the stanza written above, when the Lord of Justice called this most noble woman to her glory under the insignia of that blessed queen Maria" (19.1 [XXVIII.1]). But is Dante the copyist successful in clarifying the complicated thematic and material relationships among these pieces of text? When we analyze the complex systems of initials, paragraph markers, and textual layout in each of

reproduce it here: "Many will be amazed by what I recommend, that is that I have not placed in the body of the text the 'divisions' of the songs as the author of the present little book placed them. I answer that there are two reasons for this. The first is that the 'divisions' of the sonnets are clearly explanations ('declarations') of the sonnets since they appear to be glosses rather than text. And for that reason I have placed them as glosses, not as text, the one not to be mixed with the other. If perhaps here someone were commenting or there were themes of the sonnets and canzoni written by him, these could similarly be called glosses since they are no less of an explanation than those of the 'divisions'. I say that even if they are explanations, they are not explanations to explain but demonstrations of the reasons which brought him to write the sonnets and canzoni. And it appears that these demonstrations were a primary intention because they are rightfully text and not gloss. The second reason is that many times I have heard people worthy of trust say that Dante, having composed this little book in his youth and then with time having grown in his understanding of learning and the arts, was ashamed of having written this, for it seemed to him too juvenile. And among the things he had done which pained him, he regretted having included the 'divisions' in the text perhaps for the same reason that moves me. Therefore I, being unable to emend this in others [copies], wanted to satisfy the desire of the author in these (copies) that I have transcribed."

the seven oldest copies of the *Vita Nova* (Martelli, Strozzi, Chigi L.VIII.305, Laurenziano Acquisti e Doni 224, the Trespiano fragment, Toledo 104.6, and Chigi L.V.176), we can tentatively answer yes, maybe, but not for long.[14]

The early codex Martelli 12 (Fig. 1; c. 41r), produced between 1330 and 1350, follows Dante's directions, treating the initial S of S*ì lungiamente* as any complete poem in the *Vita Nova* and copying the canzone in the standard prose format that has been used throughout the manuscript. The interruptive interjection from Lamentations is distinguished with a paragraph marker and a slight left indentation, as are most Latin citations in the Martelli copy. Notably, the same marker is used with an initial the same height as the Q of Q*uomodo* to indicate the T of T*uctavia* (the actual beginning, I believe, of Paragraph 19]). This separation is reinforced thematically by the text itself, as immediately above Dante consigns the discussion of Beatrice's death to another glossator ("and for that reason I leave this topic to another glossator" ["e però lascio cotale tractato ad altro chiosatore" [19.2]).

The Strozziano copyist (MS. BNCF Magliabechiano Cl. VI.143 [Fig. 2; c. 11r]), who avails himself of little marginal punctuation, seems to interpret the importance of the Latin from Lamentations, separating the verses from the text of S*ì lungiamente* and the prose explanation that follows ("Io ero nel proponimento . . . " [I was working on this canzone]). But the shared grade of the initial Q and I[o era nel proponimento] leave the status of the paragraph uncertain. This is, possibly, the same uncertainty that pervades the transcription of the fragmented stanza S*ì lungiamente*. The scribe has interpreted the 14-line composition as a sonnet and adopted the sonnet's conventional scribal format of two verses per written line. The canzone form allows for the shorter, seven-syllable verse (*settenario*) we find in the stanza's v. 11 ("ed escon for chiamando"). However the sonnet is always composed of the hendecasyllables our copyist was expecting to find. In line 6 of the transcription (v. 11), the scribe finds himself a few syllables short of a hendecasyllable and borrows four syllables (la donna mia) from v. 12, leaving it the awkward *settenario*. The beginning of the next paragraph's *Tuttavia* is left unmarked.

The virtually unpunctuated transcription in MS. Chigiano L.VIII.305 codex (Fig. 3; c. 21v) perhaps best punctuates the relationship among the interrupted stanza, the Latin citation, and the prose explanation of the poet-copyist.

---

[14] Of the three fragments from the first half of the fourteenth century, Laurenziano Acquisti e Doni 224, the so-called Trespiano fragment, and BNCF Tordi 339, only the Laurentian and the Trespiano manuscripts contain the sequence of the interrupted canzone S*ì lungiamente* to the explanation of Dante's reasons for leaving the discussion of Beatrice's death to another commentator (*chiosatore*). For the Trespiano codex, see Tamburrino 1967.

There is no dramatic structural shift and the paragraph is uninterrupted. It is, rather, Boccaccio's uniquely invested handling of the *Vita Nova* and this passage which altered not only the fourteenth-century textual transmission of the *libello*, but also six hundred years of literary interpretation. For Boccaccio the *Vita Nova* is a biographical key to interpreting Dante's works. In both copies of the *Vita Nova* produced by Boccaccio's hand, the sole stanza of *Sì lungiamente m'à tenuto Amore* is interrupted by the lament, whose initial Q (Fig. 4 [detail of c. 24r of Chigiano L.V.176]) dwarfs all the other initials in the *libello* except the initial I with which the *Vita Nova* begins ("In quella parte del libro della mia memoria"). This Q*uomodo*, writ particularly large, is essential to Boccaccio's interpretation of the episode which now constitutes the beginning of the second part of the *libello*. In the first part Beatrice is alive; in the second she is dead: a neat partition, but completely unjustified by Dante's careful instructions. By the close of the fourteenth century, most copyists, like the scribe of MS. Laurenziano Pluteo XC sup. 136, follow Boccaccio's editorial creation. I presume it will surprise few that it is an interpretation still alive and well today. Instead, the non-Boccaccian manuscript tradition of the *Vita Nova*, which goes back to earlier fourteenth-century exemplars and is represented by the manuscripts Martelli, Strozzi, Acquisti e Doni, Trespiano, and Chigiano L.VIII.305, supports an interpretative trajectory in which the narrative movement from the canzone *Sì lungiamente*, the biblical citation, and the brief treatment of Beatrice's death constitute a single, episodic unit whose dramatic intensity concludes only when Dante definitively refers further commentary to another glossator ("lascio cotale tractato ad altro chiosatore" [19.2; XXVIII.2]).[15] The narrative's turn toward the separate metaphoric considerations of Beatrice and the number nine is announced by the conjunction "*Tuctavia* però che molte volte lo numero del nove" (emphasis added), a usage not dissimilar from the beginning of other paragraphs ("Poi che," "Avenne poi che," and the often repeated "Apresso ciò").

As the *libello* entered a wider and progressively more humanist circulation, the quaint medieval devices of the young copyist were deemed less and less representative of a poet of Dante's stature and certainly less necessary given the mechanics of book production. But mercifully in its historical progression from *libello* to *libro*, the author's concerns in the early production of little books in medieval Florence were preserved in the copyist's instructions in the text of the *Vita Nova*.

---

[15] With this revised episodic construction, the section from "Apresso ciò, cominciai a pensare un giorno" (18.1), which introduces the canzone *Sì lungiamente*, to "però lascio cotale tractato ad altro chiosatore" would make up a longer Paragraph 18.1-7.

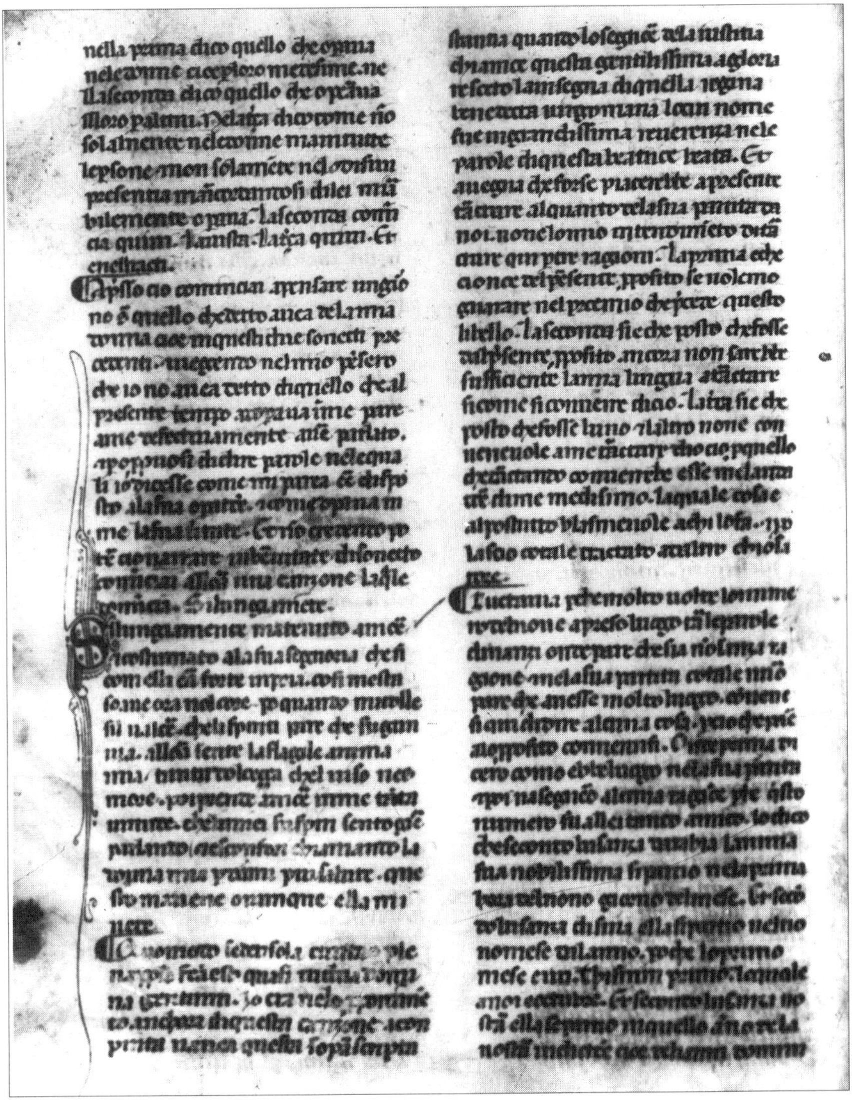

Fig. 1
Firenze, Laurenziano Martelli 12, c. 41r

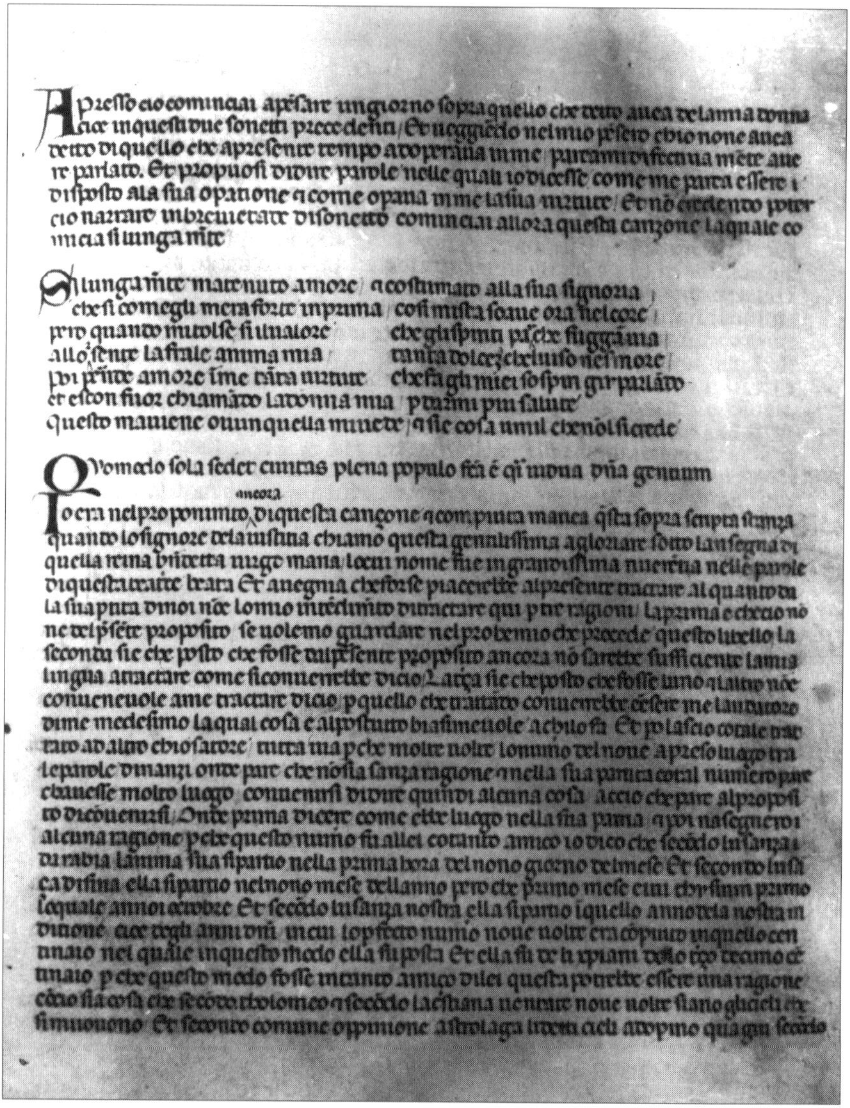

Fig. 2

Firenze, Biblioteca Nazionale Centrale, Magliabechiano Cl. VI.143, c. 11r

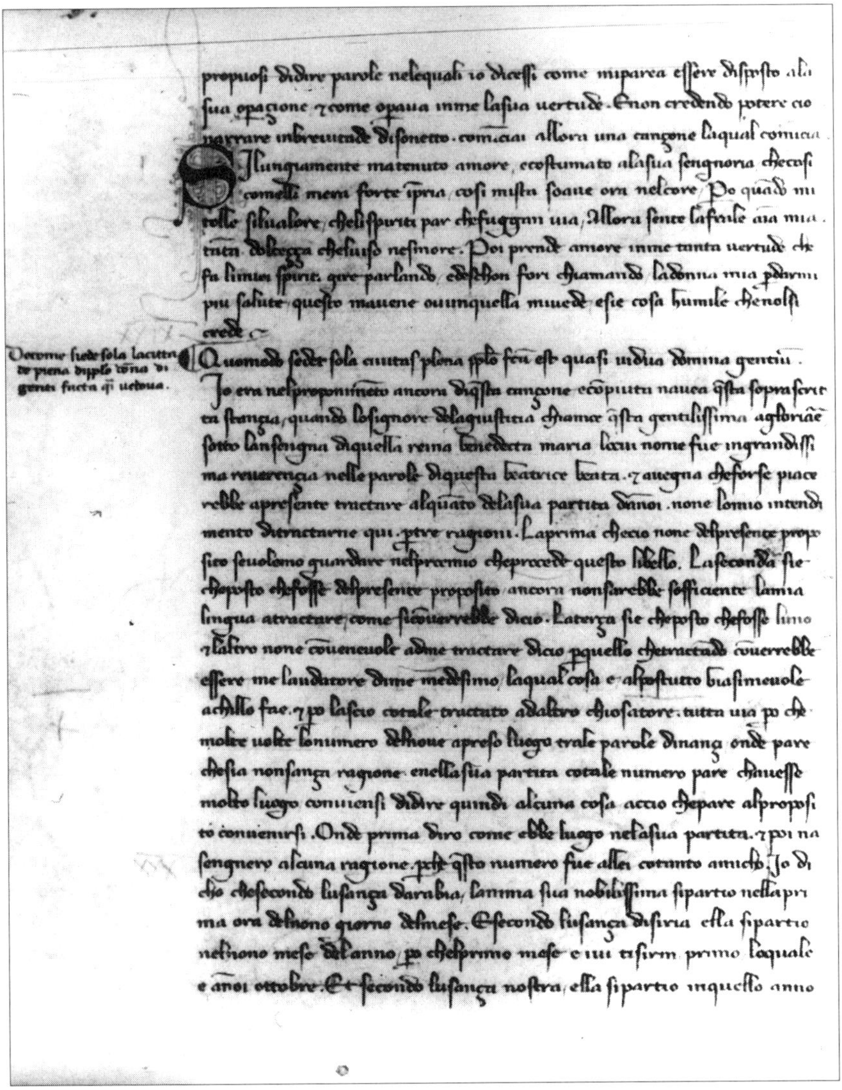

Fig. 3
Vaticano, Biblioteca Apostolica, Chigiano L.VIII.305, c. 21v

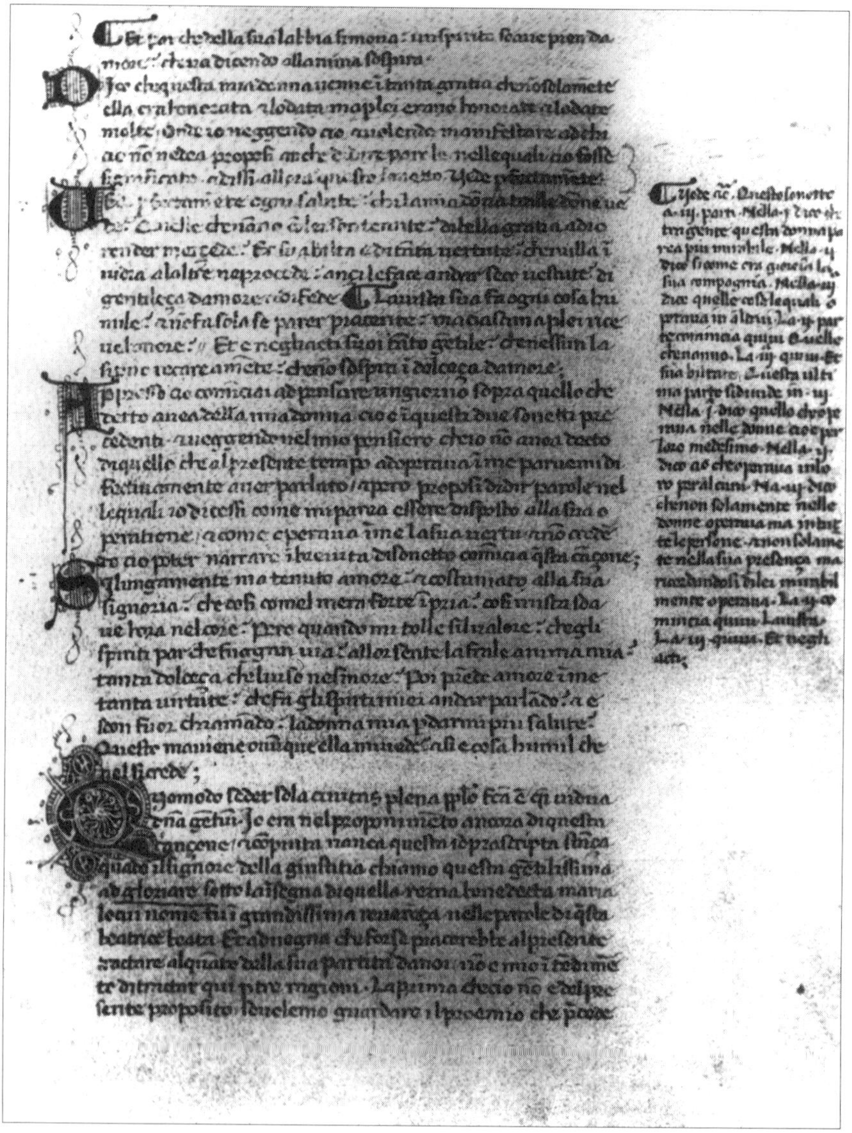

FIG. 4
Vaticano, Biblioteca Apostolica, Chigiano L.V.176, c. 24r (detail)

Works Cited

Alighieri, Dante. 1996. *Vita Nova*, ed. Guglielmo Gorni. Turin: Einaudi.

Avalle, D'Arco Silvio. 1985. "I canzonieri: definizione di genere e problemi di edizione." In *La critica del testo: problemi di metodo ed esperienze di lavoro. Atti del Convegno di Lecce, 22–26 Ottobre 1984*, 363–82. Rome: Salerno.

Capelli, Roberta. 2003. "Materiali dell'Escorialense e.III.23: Contesti di produzione e àmbiti di circolazione di un'antologia poetica delle origini." Università di Firenze, tesi di dottorato di ricerca.

———. 2004. "Nuove indagini sulla raccolta di rime italiane del MS. Escorial e.III.23." *Medioevo letterario d'Italia* 1: 73–113.

Castellani, Arrigo. 1982. *Prosa italiana delle origini*. Bologna: Commissione per i Testi di Lingua.

Contini, Gianfranco, ed. 1960. *Poeti del Duecento*. Vol. 2. Milan-Naples: Ricciardi.

Dolbeau, François. 1989. "Noms de livres." In *Vocabulaire du livre et de l'écriture au moyen âge: Actes de la table ronde, Paris, 24–26 septembre 1987*, ed. Olga Weijers, pp. 79–99. Turnhout: Brepols.

Gillissen, Léon. 1977. *Prolégomènes à la Codicologie. Recherches sur la construction des cahiers et la mise en page des manuscrits médiévaux*. Publications de Scriptorium 7. Gand: Éditions Scientifiques Story-Scientia.

Grübmuller, Konrad. 1986. "'Liber a libertate legencium.' Vokabularien als Instrument von Kontinuität und Wandel." In *The Role of the Book in Medieval Culture*, ed. Peter Ganz, 2: 95–114. Turnhout: Brepols.

Hanna III, Ralph. 1986. "Booklets in Medieval Manuscripts: Further Considerations." *Studies in Bibliography* 39: 100–11.

Leonardi, Lino, ed. 2001. *I canzonieri della lirica italiana delle origini*. Idem, *Studi critici* 4. Florence: SISMEL.

Lombardi, Giuseppe and Donatella Nebbiai Dalla Guarda, eds. 2000. *Libri lettori e biblioteche dell'Italia medievale*. Rome: ICCU and Paris: CNRS.

Margueron, Claude, ed. 1994. *Lettere di Guittone d'Arezzo*. Bologna: Commissione per i Testi di lingua.

Ornato, Ezio. 2000. *Apologia dell'apogeo*. Rome: Viella.

Papka, Claudia. 1999. "'Tra feltro e feltro' (*Inf.* I.105)." *Dante Studies* 117: 35–44.

Rizzo, Silvia. 1973. *Lessico filologico degli umanisti*. Rome: Edizioni di Storia e Letteratura.

Robinson, Pamela. 1980. "The 'Booklet': a Self-Contained Unit in Composite Manuscripts." *Codicologia* 3: 46–69.

Salimbene. 1998. *Chronica*, ed. Giuseppe Scalia. Turnhout: Brepols.

Storey, H. Wayne. 1993. *Transcription and Visual Poetics in the Early Italian Lyric*. New York: Garland.

————. 2004. "Di libello in libro: problemi materiali nella poetica di Monte Andrea e Dante." In *Da Guido Guinizzelli a Dante: Nuove prospettive sulla lirica del Duecento*, ed Furio Brugnolo and Gianfelice Peron, pp. 271–90. Padua: Poligrafo.

Tamburrino, Giuseppe. 1967. "Un antico frammento della *Vita Nuova*." *Italia medioevale e umanistica* 10: 377–83.

THE STRAITS OF EMPIRE:
SICILY IN VERGIL AND DANTE

SARAH SPENCE

for Joan

In "Bryn Glas" Terence Hawkes offers a powerful reading of Shakespeare's *Henry V* through an interpretation of the roles played by Wales, France, and England. In this "construction of a new identity called Britain" (2002, 36-37), Hawkes argues, France and Wales serve two distinct purposes. On the one hand, France is a place that has become "sufficiently referential to be joked at." "We are what we oppose," he says. "[T]hat, to speak broadly, is what the French . . . are traditionally for." The Welsh, according to Hawkes, serve a different function. Like the Irish and the Scots they are not foreign but, rather, evidence of a culture that is "native and true." Shakespeare's play chronicles not so much the imposition "of a culture on a society that pre-exists it . . . as [a] discovery and lay[ing] bare [of] a substratum that" has been obscured. Wales, Hawkes argues, provides the "underpinnings of the new [British] identity" (2002, 31).

Both France and Wales serve to define Britain, though in different ways: France by opposition, Wales by dependence. It will be my argument that Sicily, in both Vergil's *Aeneid* and Dante's *Purgatorio*, serves a role comparable to that of Wales in Hawkes's reading of *Henry V*. In particular, I want to examine the role of Sicily as an example of what I will call the "poetics of empire," or the ways in which poets draw literary and rhetorical constructions from the political landscape. This can be the land itself, or treatises and tracts about that land. It can be more abstract than that: a conceptual sense of a political term that is translated into the poetic. But in each case the poetics of empire asserts that the poetic and the political intersect in the geographic: the ground of this poetry is in the real, in the land. The perception of that land, in this case Sicily, may be shaped by political decisions that then, in turn, shape poetic ones. Politics feeds poetry even as the poetry offers a means for grasping the political; the language of political vision is found embedded in tropes that are themselves drawn from the geopolitical realia.

In *Landscape and Power* W. J. T. Mitchell argues that "[e]mpires move outward in space as a way of moving forward in time; the 'prospect' that opens up is not just a spatial scene but a projected future of 'development'" (1994, 17). This movement, Mitchell argues, "is not confined to the external, foreign fields toward which empire directs itself; it is typically accompanied by a renewed interest in the re-presentation of the home landscape" (1994, 17). For both Vergil and

Dante, the island of Sicily and its relationship to the mainland of Italy serve as just such a focus for conceptualizing empire. Sicily enables Vergil and Dante to "re-present the home landscape," to articulate a poetic vision that redefines empire through tropes drawn from geographical reality. This vision, in both cases, is not limited to the reigning political ideology; it is neither pro- nor anti-imperialist. Instead, I will argue that Vergil and Dante both use Sicily as a way to transcend the dichotomy between nationalism and imperialism.

Sicily in the *Aeneid*

Sicily is rarely presented as critical to Aeneas', or Vergil's, purpose. Yet the action of the *Aeneid* begins off Sicily ("vix e conspectu Siculae telluris" [1.34]) and the setting of the entire poem is limited to that part of the Mediterranean dominated by Sicily: only in flashbacks does Aeneas travel east of Italy. Sicily provides the setting for the end of Book 3 and for all of Book 5, stops on Aeneas' journey from Troy to Rome; Aeneas' father dies there; it is the last land Aeneas sees before his encounter with Dido and the first he sees after he leaves her; it is the place where many of the older Trojan women and men decide to settle. Sicily, as we shall see, is mentioned repeatedly in the prophecies of *Aeneid* 3 and is, of course, the place where, at the end of that book, Aeneas' father Anchises dies. In the fifth book, where the funeral games for Anchises are played, Sicily provides scope for Vergil's prowess, perhaps, in his reworking of Homer, but it doesn't compare to the drama that surrounds it in Book 4 with Dido or Book 6 in the Underworld. It is indeed, as Galinsky (1969, chap.1) has pointed out, a significant factor in Vergil's and Augustus' formulation of elements necessary to the *pax Augusta* and it is the location most associated with Trojan *pietas* in the poem. It is also the spot where, as Nugent (1992, 255-92) and Miller (1995, 225-40) have argued, Trojan *furor* explodes and is, at least partially, contained. What I want to focus on, however, are its geographic, literary, and historic roles in the grand project of constructing Rome—what Quint in *Epic and Empire* (1993, chap. 2) calls the "narrative of political foundation"—that the poem engages in.

Sicily, the text suggests, is important: It is the first place we see Aeneas and his men as well as the last stop before Aeneas reaches the "antiquam . . . matrem," the "ancient mother" of Italy, as prophesied to Anchises in 3.96. In *Aen.* 3, Sicily, like the majority of locations where Aeneas and his men land, is a land of terror: through the story of Achaemenides they hear the tale of the Cyclops, and, at the very end of the book, Aeneas witnesses the death of his father. Nevertheless, it is also the land associated even here with Trojan *pietas*: Anchises' embrace of Achaemenides at the end of 3 reminds the reader of the disastrously naïve acceptance of the comparable figure of Sinon in 2 even as it insists on the unchanging quality of the Trojan character. This is the theme rung most loudly again in 5 as Anchises' death is celebrated through the *lusus Troiae*, the games played among the Trojans. Emphasis throughout these games, as through the fifth book at large, is placed on interaction between the men, and on father-son relationships — all of which reinforce a message of *pietas* — as well as on the apparent necessity of sacrifice.[1] Aeneas assumes the role of *pater*; Ascanius at the end of the book takes on the role of leader; the competition between the men is often framed by discussion of filial relations.

When, in Book 3, Helenus describes Sicily to Aeneas and his men he states:

> ast ubi digressum Siculae te admoverit orae
> ventus, et angusti rarescent claustra Pelori,
> laeva tibi tellus et longo laeva petantur
> aequora circuitu; dextram fuge litus et undas.
> haec loca vi quondam et vasta convulsa ruina
> (tantum aevi loginqua valet mutare vetustas)
> dissiluisse ferunt; cum protinus utraque tellus
> una foret, venit medio vi pontus et undis
> Hesperium Siculo latus abscidit, arvaque et urbes
> litore diductas angusto interluit aestu. (*Aen.* 3.410-419)

> (But when, after you depart, the wind shall have brought you to the Sicilian shore and the headlands of narrow Pelorus close in, the land and the waters on your left are to be sought by you, the long way around; flee the right-hand shore and waves. These lands, they say, at one time, torn by violence and great upheaval (a great lapse of time can produce such changes), leapt apart; when both lands were one continuously, the sea came through the middle with its force; it cut the Italian side off from the Sicilian with its waves and washed fields and towns — separated by their narrow shore — with its waters.)[2]

---

[1] In contrast to the *Iliad*, where filial relations do not provide the focus for the games. For a brilliant review of the father-son issues in *Aen.* 5 see Farrell 1999, chap. 5. In this chapter Farrell, quite rightly to my mind, balances the emphasis placed on *pietas* and filial relations with the observation that Venus, too, plays an important part in the book. The emphasis placed here on Anchises' death tends to obscure the fact that his wife's shrine at Eryx is there too. Didorus Siculus 4.83.2-6 says Aeneas embellished the sanctuary on his way to Italy; Vergil overwrites this with the celebration of Anchises' death, reducing the overt presence of Venus in 5. Nonetheless, as Farrell points out, motherhood is not forgotten in this book. The feminine is certainly present, if unintegrated. On sacrifice see Putnam 1965, chap. 2.

[2] Ed. Mynors 1972. Translations are my own.

Once joined, now separated, Sicily was but is no longer a part of the mainland, a sentiment shared by many including Diodorus Siculus 4.85.3-4:

> The ancient mythographers, that is, say that Sicily was originally a penin-
> sula, and that afterwards it became an island, the cause being somewhat as
> follows. The isthmus at its narrowest point was subjected to the dash of the
> waves of the sea on its two sides and so a gap was made . . . Some men say,
> however, that mighty earthquakes took place and the neck of what was the
> mainland was broken through.[3]

But this passage has a literary history as well. In the *De rerum natura* Lucretius uses Sicily to rewrite and undermine his predecessor Empedocles:

> quorum Acragantinus cum primis Empedocles est,
> insula quem triquetris terrarum gessit in oris,
> quam fluitans circum magnis anfractibus aequor
> Ionium glaucis aspergit virus ab undis,
> angustoque fretu rapidum mare dividit undis
> Aeoliae terrarum oras a finibus eius.
> hic est vasta Charybdis et hic Aetnaea minantur
> murmura flammarum rursum se colligere iras,
> faucibus eruptos iterum vis ut vomat ignis
> ad caelumque ferat flammai fulgura rursum. (*DRN* 1.716-725)

> (Of them in the forefront comes Empedocles of Acragas; him that island
> bore within the three-cornered coasts of its lands, around which flows the
> Ionian ocean, with many a winding inlet, splashing salt foam from its green
> waves, while with narrow strait a tearing sea sunders with its waves the
> coasts of Aeolia's lands from its island-borders. Here is devastating Cha-
> rybdis, and here the rumblings of Aetna threaten to gather once more the
> flames of its wrath, that again in its might it may belch forth the fires burst-
> ing from its throat, and once more dash to the sky its flashing flames.)[4]

As Bailey notes: "[Empedocles] held that the 'four roots,' as he called them
. . . themselves remained permanent and unchanged, but produced the world of

---

[3] Trans. Oldfather 1936. So also Strabo 6.1.6 where he cites Aeschylus as source
and again 6.2.7-8: "The island is a part of Italy, as it were." Pliny reiterates this belief:
"Namque et hoc modo insulas rerum natura fecit: avellit Siciliam Italiae" (Pliny, *N.H.*
2.204; see also 3.86-87) as does Ovid: "Zancle quoque iuncta fuisse / dicitur Italiae,
donec confinia pontus / abstulit et media tellurem reppulit unda" (Ovid, *Metamorphoses*
15.290-292).
[4] Text and trans. Bailey 1947.

things by combining with one another in various proportions" (*ad* 723). Lucretius shows, through this description of Sicily, that the elements remain distinct: the land is surrounded, the water separates the two lands, fire belches into the air. All is bounded and distinct, even if, as Denis Feeney has pointed out, that distinction is, in the case of the Sicilian straits, only the width of his smallest *elementa* "a" (lines 720-721: "angustoque fretu rapidum mare dividit undis / Aeoliae terrarum oras a finibus eius").[5]

Vergil's passages in Book 3 about Sicily (especially those surrounding the description of Aetna which "atram prorumpit ad aethera nubem . . . sidera lambit" [572, 574] and even the rocks are "liquefacta" [576]) counter this passage from Lucretius, suggesting that, just as Lucretius uses Sicily to rework Empedocles, so Vergil will use Sicily to rework Lucretius. Vergil's Sicily is defined not by its boundedness but rather by its permeability, and the shadowy outlines of Lucretius here makes this all the clearer.

For Dido—and the reader—hear not once but twice of Aeneas' decision, following Helenus' advice, to avoid the divide, the strait where the lands were once joined, and go instead all the way around the island: "praestat Trinacrii metas lustrare Pachyni / cessantem, longos et circumflectere cursus, / quam semel informem vasto vidisse sub antro / Scyllam et caeruleis canibus resonantia saxa" (*Aen.* 3.429-432; and again at 684 *et seq.*); on the advice of Helenus Aeneas avoids Scylla and Charybdis and travels the long way around Sicily. This act clearly separates him from Jason who was caught in the straits "as long as the space of a day is lengthened out in springtime, so long a time did [the gods] toil, heaving the ship between the loud-echoing rocks" until "the heroes caught the wind and sped onward; and swiftly they passed the mead of Thrinacia, where the kine of Helios fed" (*Argonautica* 4.921-981; esp. 960-965) and Odysseus who first "sailed up the narrow strait lamenting" (*Odyssey* 12.234) and then, more memorably, alone, where he hangs on the fig tree and waits as long as a long day at court for his mast and keel to return (12.425 ff.). But this divide is then smudged as Aeneas, in avoiding the straits, distinguishes himself from the earlier heroes and goes around Sicily, both marking and erasing the divide. Where other heroes and authors find and emphasize division, Vergil and Aeneas assert a more complex relationship as a new unity emerges from the divided land.

What I would propose is that the blurred divide introduced by Helenus and the allusion to Lucretius is replicated on the level of structure within the poem as a whole, especially in terms of its two halves. If one were to look at Servius on 7.1, one would expect the second half of the epic to begin with, if not an epic invocation, at least some explicit acknowledgment of a new beginning:

---

[5] Cited in Farrell 2001, 45 n. 17.

Ut et in principio diximus, in duas partes hoc opus divisum est: nam primi
sex ad imaginem Odyssiae dicti sunt, quos personarum et adlocutionum
varietate constat esse graviores, hi autem sex qui sequuntur ad imaginem
Iliados dicti sunt, qui in negotiis validiores sunt: nam et ipse hoc dicit "mai-
us opus moveo."

(As we also said at the beginning, this work is divided into two parts: for
the first six books, which are agreed to be denser in the variety of characters and speeches, are said to resemble the *Odyssey*, while the six books that
follow, which are stronger in action, are said to resemble the *Iliad*: for even
Vergil himself says, "I undertake a greater task" [7.45].)[6]

But, as we all know, Book 7 begins not with a bang but a whimper:

Tu quoque litoribus nostris, Aeneia nutrix,
aeternam moriens famam, Caieta, dedisti;
et nunc servat honos sedem tuus, ossaque nomen
Hesperia in magna, si qua est ea gloria, signat. (*Aen.*7.1-4)

(You also in dying, Aeneas' nurse, Caieta, gave eternal fame to our shores;
even now your honor watches over the spot, and [your] name marks your
grave in great Hesperia, if there is any glory in such a thing.)

The opening two words, "tu quoque," both announce a new beginning (so
Frischer 1983, 238-240)[7] and offer a supplementing echo of the narrator's address to Icarus in Book 6:

. . . tu quoque magnam
partem opere in tanto, sineret dolor, Icare, haberes.
bis conatus erat casus effingere in auro,
bis patriae cecidere manus. (*Aen.* 6.30-33)

(You also would have had a great part in so great a work, if pain had allowed, Icarus. Twice he tried to depict the fall in gold, twice the father's
hands fell short.)

It can, in fact, be argued that the purpose of Book 7 (if not the entire second half
of the poem) is to give voice to the fallen Icarus and all he stands for; the echo of
the tag "tu quoque" at the beginning of Book 7 expands the role of the absent Icarus beyond the frieze into Italy proper even as it undermines the divide expected

---

[6] Text from Servius 1881, *ad Aen.*7.1; translation mine.
[7] They also announce an end: see Horsfall 2000, 46 on funerary epitaph.

between the first and second halves of the poem, in a way that is reinforced by the closer repetition of the name of Caieta at the end of 6 and the beginning of 7.

My point is simple: where we expect sharp divides in the text, especially as it moves further and further along, we get none. Instead we get feints at that division, like Aeneas sailing almost all the way through the straits of Scylla (this is even clearer in Ovid), and then embraces that bridge the divide (*tu quoque* works that way). Book 7 both does and does not begin even as Book 6 both does and does not end.

Sicily would seem to offer up a literary model to Vergil as it did for Lucretius. The question remains: why use Sicily to make this point? The answer, I think, is political. Sicily serves two significant functions in Augustan propaganda. It is the site of one of Augustus' most important victories (*Res Gestae* 25: "Mare pacavi a praedonibus")[8] and, through Cicero, it is known perhaps best for its role as the first province: "Prima omnium, id quod ornamentum imperi est, provincia est appellata; prima docuit maiores nostros quam praeclarum esset exteris gentibus imperare" (*Verrines* 2.2.1) ("[Sicily] was the first of all to receive the title of province, the first such jewel in our imperial crown; she was the first who made our forefathers perceive how splendid a thing foreign empire is"). The acquisition of Sicily as a province, "the jewel in the crown," is, according to Cicero what made empire seem like such a great idea. The line that Aeneas draws around the island, embracing it, drawing it back toward the mainland without fully connecting it, offers a model for empire and for province. Sicily is in the fold. It is one of us, like us, but different, still separate, still divided, but one of ours.

If this is so it is in direct opposition to what might be termed "the poetics of Carthage" (the "France" of this text) which posits an identification and union that only masks ultimate difference. What the story of Sicily suggests, rather, is the reverse—a union that is dependent on division. In the *Aeneid* as a whole, Sicily, in its peculiar relationship to the mainland, in its literary portrayal, in its history as a site of civil war and as reputed first province, stands as an emblem of empire. It also offers a hermeneutic model to the reader that helps explain the blurring of significant divisions within the text even as it helps chart the development of the text overall from discord to compromise, from division to common ground, all by way of the island that is and is not separate from the mainland. Like Wales in Hawkes's reading of *Henry V,* Sicily offers a striking instance of

---

[8] The importance of the victory over Sextus Pompeius in Sicily has long been overshadowed by Octavian's final victory over Antony at Actium. Yet the evidence suggests that both victories figured largely in Octavian's strategies. The temple of Apollo on the Palatine, for example, was vowed at the battle with Sextus Pompeius, completed after the victory at Actium. See Powell and Welch 2002 for further on the importance of Sicily for Octavian.

a location that by virtue of its unique, dependent relationship to Italy provides the "underpinnings of the new national identity." The reunification suggested by Aeneas' journey around the island, which prefigures the inclusion of Juno in the compromise at the end of the poem, includes within it the possibility of an imperial relationship that acknowledges difference. It also, though, offers the spectre of a ground that grows too common, of a line that becomes too smudged, of an annihilation of difference in the interests of power.

Sicily in *Purgatorio*

Let us now turn from Vergil to Dante, at the point where Dante turns to find Vergil gone:

> Ma Virgilio n'avea lasciati scemi
> di sé, Virgilio dolcissimo patre,
> Virgilio a cui per mia salute die'mi;
> né quantunque perdeo l'antica matre,
> valse a le guance nette di rugiada
> che, lagrimando, non tornasser atre. (*Purg.* 30.49-54)

(But Virgil had left us bereft of himself, Virgil sweetest father, Virgil to whom I gave myself for salvation; nor did all that our ancient mother lost keep my dew-washed cheeks from turning dark again with tears.)[9]

Rachel Jacoff (1991, 131-44), among others, has noted the evocation of Orpheus here from *Georgics* 4 (via Statius), an evocation made through the triple echo of Vergil's name. I want to draw your attention, though, to another Vergilian allusion, this one in line 52: "perdeo l'antica matre," the loss of the ancient mother, which the commentaries gloss as referring to Eve. Yet Singleton notes how Latinate and archaizing the phrase "antica matre" is (*matre* instead of *madre*) and as we have noted, the phrase does occur, in its original Latin form, in the prophecy about the journey to Rome, where Anius prophesies to Anchises (an allusion, according to Robert Hollander's latest census [1993, 318], noted by a student of his in the 70s)[10]:

> Dardanidae duri, quae vos a stirpe parentum
> Prima tulit tellus, eadem vos ubere laeto

---

[9] Text from the Petrocchi text ed. Singleton 1970-1975. Translations are those of Singleton.

[10] See also Putnam 1995, 314 n. 40.

> Accipiet reduces. Antiquam exquirite matrem.
> Hic domus Aeneae cunctis dominabitur oris
> Et nati natorum et qui nascentur ab illis. (*Aen.* 3. 94-98)

(Tough Dardans, the same earth that first bore you from parental stock, led back that same earth will accept you with happy breast. Seek out the ancient mother. Here the house of Aeneas, and sons of sons, and those born from them will rule over all shores.)

"Antiquam exquirite matrem": seek out the ancient mother, first thought by Anchises to be Crete, then learned by Aeneas in a dream to be Italy: "non haec tibi litora suasit / Delius aut Cretae iussit considere Apollo. / Est locus, Hesperiam Grai cognomine dicunt, / terra antique . . . nunc fama . . . Italiam dixisse . . ." (*Aen.* 3.161-166) (Delian Apollo does not urge these shores on you, or order you to settle in Crete. There is a place the Greeks call Hesperia, an ancient land now known as Italy . . .).

If the archaizing of *matre* and the phrase *antica matre* in *Purgatorio* 30 refer us to Italy, instead of, or in addition to, Eve as ancient mother, then the question becomes: in what way is Dante like that ancient mother, Italy? Or, what did Italy lose that is parallel to Dante's loss of Vergil? The text offers two clues: the first within the same passage in 30, the other earlier in the canticle. For not only is *matre* archaizing, but so, arguably, is *patre* (cf. *Par.* 24.92 where the *antico padre* refers to Adam). The ancient mother lost the sweetest father. But the father lost to Italy in the *Aeneid* is, of course, Anchises, Aeneas' father who dies on Sicily before the Trojans make it to Rome. At the end of *Aeneid* 3, Aeneas weeps for his lost Anchises (the verb is *amitto*; a use echoed later by the Troades in 5.614 who "amissum Anchisen flebant") even as Dante does for his lost "father," Vergil.

Moreover, Dante offers a further gloss to this passage in *Purgatorio* 18.133-138:

> Di retro a tutti dicean: "Prima fue
>   morta la gente a cui il mar s'aperse,
>   che vedesse Iordan le rede sue.
> E quella che l'affanno non sofferse
>   fino a la fine col figlio d'Anchise
>   sé stessa a vita sanza gloria offerse."

(Behind all the rest they were saying, "The people for whom the sea opened were dead before Jordan saw its heirs; and those who did not endure the toil to the end with Anchises' son gave themselves to a life without glory.")

Here Dante urges a comparison among the souls in Purgatory, the journey of the Israelites in the desert, and those left behind on Sicily in the *Aeneid*, Anchises and the older Trojans. Even as the Israelites who sacrificed themselves led the way to the promised land, so the Trojans who remain behind and Anchises made it possible for the younger Trojans to reach Rome. In addition, both, I would argue, provide a model for Vergil's staying behind in *Purgatorio* 30: Vergil, like Anchises, and like the Israelites, enable progress through their own refusal to go on.[11]

But why? Does Sicily just provide the classical counterpart to the scriptural desert: Egypt/desert/Israel; Troy/Sicily/Rome? That might be the case, and might be enough in any case, if Sicily weren't also critical to Dante's thinking in other ways. It is my argument, rather, that to invoke Sicily as Vergil leaves is to urge a poetico-political lens on *Purgatorio* as a whole.

For Sicily does not come to us in *Purgatorio* just through Vergil but also through Lucan, as is clear in the following passage from *Purgatorio* 14:

> ... Non so; ma degno
> ben è che 'l nome di tal valle pèra;
> ché dal principio suo, ov'è sì pregno
> l'alpestro monte ond'è tronco Peloro,
> che 'n pochi luoghi passa oltra quel segno,
> infin là 've si rende per ristoro
> di quel che 'l ciel de la marina asciuga,
> ond'hanno i fiumi ciò che va con loro ... (*Purg.* 14.29-36)

(I do not know, but it is fitting indeed that the name of such a valley should perish, for from its source (where the rugged mountain-chain from which Pelorus is cut off so teems with water that in few places it is surpassed) down to where it yields itself to replace that which the sky draws up from the sea, whence rivers have that which flows in them ...)

This passage draws heavily on the *De bello civili* of Lucan, in which the rivers of Italy are described in such glorious detail:

> ... tunc Vmbris Marsisque ferax domitusque Sabello
> uomere, piniferis amplexus rupibus omnis
> indigenas Latii populos, non deserit ante
> Hesperiam, quam cum Scyllaeis clauditur undis,
> extenditque suas in templa Lacinia rupes,
> longior Italia, donec confinia pontus
> solueret incumbens terrasque repelleret aequor,

---

[11] It is, of course, the sloth of the Troades that is being lamented in *Purgatorio* 18, yet the mention of Anchises, glorified elsewhere in the *Comedy* (*Paradiso* 15. 25, where he provides the classical antecedent for Cacciaguida), suggests that the action of staying on Sicily is multivalent: negative from some perspectives, positive from others.

at, postquam gemino tellus elisa profundo est,
extremi colles Siculo cessere Peloro. (*De bello civili* 2.430-438)

(Then, fertile for the Umbrians and Marsians and tamed by Sabine
Ploughshare, it embraces with its pine-clad crags
All Latium's native peoples, not abandoning
Hesperia until cut short by Scylla's waves
And stretching its crags to Lacinium's temple,
Longer once than Italy, until the sea's attack
Destroyed the junction and the water drove back the land;
But after earth was smothered by the twin depths,
Its furthest hills became the property of Sicilian Pelorus.)

Here the word choice emphasizes the fact that Sicily is cut off from Italy ("tron-co") even as the enjambement of lines 31-32 and 34-35 sutures the lands back to-gether. In this, Dante echoes Vergil even as he repeats a gesture he made earlier with respect to another passage from Lucan. In the *De vulgari eloquentia* Dante uses the Lucanian description of the unified source of Italy's rivers to describe the diaspora of the Italian vernacular:

Dicimus ergo primo Latium bipartitum esse in dextrum et sinistrum. Si quis autem querat de linea dividente, breviter respondemus esse iugum Apennini, quod, ceu fictile culmen hinc inde ad diversa stillicidia grundat, aquas ad alterna hinc inde litora per imbricia longa distillat, ut Lucanus in secundo describit. (*De vulgari eloquentia*, 1.10.6)

(I say first that Italy is divided into right and left sides; and if anyone asks what is the dividing line, I answer in short that it is the yoke of the Apen-nines, which like the ridge of a tiled roof channels the rainwater into gut-ters on either side, pouring them down alternate shores through long fur-rows, as Lucan describes it in the second book of his *Pharsalia*. [Shapiro 1990, 57-58])

Yet—strikingly, given both Lucan and Vergil's insistence on the divide at Pelorus—here there is no such division. Dante continues: "Et dextri regio-nes sunt Apulia, sed non tota, Roma, Ducatus, . . . sinistri autem pars Apulie, Marchia Anconitana, . . . Forum Iulii vero et Istria non nisi leve Ytalie esse pos-sunt; nec insule Tirreni maris, videlicet Sicilia et Sardinia, non nisi dextre Ytalie sunt, vel ad dextram Ytaliam sociande" (1.10.7) ("The regions of the right are Apulia [but not all of it], Rome, the Duchy of Spoleto . . . ; of the left, part of Apulia, the March of Ancona, . . . Friuli and Istria must belong to the left side, and the islands of the Tyrrhenian Sea; Sicily and Sardinia to the right side, or classed with it" [Shapiro 1990, 58]). Sicily is grouped with, not cut off from, the mainland.

And in a bit of poetic sleight of hand, Dante also makes clear what the true source of the linguistic diaspora is. Certainly not, as for the Arno, Tuscany, nor, as for Lucan, the Apennines: these, instead, are the flawed sources of corruption. By contrast, in the *De vulgari eloquentia*, Dante speaks of the best of the Italian vernaculars, the one pure language, the language of "sì":

> Qui autem sì dicunt a predictis finibus orientalem tenent, videlicet usque ad promuntorium illud Ytalie, qua sinus Adriatici maris incipit, et Siciliam . . . Exaceratis quodam modo vulgaribus ytalis, inter ea que remanserunt in cribro comparationem facientes, honorabilius atque honorificentius breviter seligamus. Et primo de siciliano examinemus ingenium, . . . Si autem ipsum accipere volumus secundum quod ab ore primorum Siculorum emanat, ut in preallegatis cantionibus perpendi potest, nichil differt ab illo quod laudabilissimum est, sicut inferius ostendemus. (1.8.8; 1.12.1-2, 3)

> (Those who say *si* live to the east of Genoa, as far as the promontory of Italy, where the gulf of the Adriatic begins, down to Sicily . . . Now that we have to some extent sifted through the Italian vernaculars, let us compare those that remain in the sieve and briefly select the one which is the most honorable and confers the most honor. First let us test the genius of Sicilian . . . [I]f we mean the language as it is spoken by the ordinary native . . . then this dialect does not deserve preference . . . But if we mean by Sicilian the language that comes from the mouths of the most distinguished Sicilians—as may be observed in the poems cited above—it differs in no way from the most praiseworthy vernacular. [Shapiro 1990, 55, 59-60])

This sentiment is clarified in the *Vita nuova* (25.4-5): "E non è molto numero d'anni passati, che appariro prima questi poete volgari . . . [i quali] quasi fuoro li primi che dissero in lingua di sì."

In *Purgatorio* 31 Dante faces Beatrice across the river Lethe:

> "O tu che se' di là dal fiume sacro,
>   Rispondi a me; che le memorie triste . . . Che pense?
>   in te non sono ancor da l'acqua offense."
> Confusione e paura insieme miste
>   mi pinsero un tal "si" fuor de la bocca,
>   al quale intender fuor mestier le viste (*Purg.* 31.1, 10-15)

> ("O you who are on that side of the sacred river . . . What are you thinking? Answer me, for the sad memories in you are not yet destroyed by the water." Confusion and fear, together mingled, drove forth from my mouth a *Yes* such that the eyes were needed to hear it.)

"Un tal 'si'": in this one word the sources converge—of love, of language, of vision. Dante speaks the language of "Sicily," of unity, of before, as he faces Beatrice across the river that will soon erase all memory of division. If the *antica matre* is Italy and Eve, it is also Beatrice, who rebukes Dante as a mother does a child. He crosses the river from Sicily to Italy, the river that miraculously erases memory and separation rather than causing it. The Sicily where Dante bid his Anchises, Vergil, farewell is also the land associated with the optimal vernacular of the poets. Shapiro (1990, 96-97) sums this up: "Out of the unified cultural climate that had been allowed to evolve in Sicily, Dante swiftly draws the image of a quasi-national poetic movement in which not only Sicilians but all Italians who compose participate in virtue of the foundational quality of its linguistic medium . . . Dante recognizes the potentially unifying character of the poetry, cultivated not by Sicilians alone but by members of a wide aristocratic culture." For Dante, the river that leads to Beatrice and the erasure of memory is also the mark of another unity, of the political unity of Frederick the Second and Manfred, who brought together not only "politics and culture, intelligence and magnanimity" but also ruled over the kingdom of Sicily, marked, not divided by the break at Pelorus.[12] ("And that is why," Dante says in the *De vulgari eloquentia*, "those who were noble of heart and gifted by God sought to be at one with the majesty of such great princes, so that in their time whatever the most excellent minds of Italy produced first shone forth at the court of these sovereigns; and because Sicily was the royal seat, it came about that whatever our predecessors wrote in the vernacular was called Sicilian" [Shapiro 1990, 60]).[13]

In *Paradiso* 8 and 9 Sicily surfaces as a location central to Dante's understanding of empire. In a passage laden with Vergilian themes of father and son, of loss, and of the importance of the past to a construction of the future, Charles Martel laments that "fair Trinacria, which between Pachynus and Pelorus, on the gulf most vexed by Eurus, . . . would yet have looked to its kings born through me" had his grandfather, Charles of Anjou, not lost the island of

---

[12] The *Enciclopedia Dantesca* (s.v. *Sicilia*) confirms this: "la Sicilia federiciana non solo è centro di un'unità linguistico-poetica, per cui tutto ciò che di poetico veniva allora creato in Italia era detto 'siciliano,' ma centro altresì di unità politica, in virtù dei due principi, Federico e Manfredi, che avevano saputo far convergere, in armoniosa, sintesi, politica e cultura, intelligenza e magnanimità." See also Mallette 1998, 84-85.

[13] "propter quod corde nobiles atque gratiarum dotati inherere tantorum principum maiestati conati sunt; ita quod eorum tempore quicquid excellentes Latinorum enitebantur, primitus in tantorum coronatorum aula prodibat; et quia regale solium erat Sicilia, factum est ut quicquid nostri predecessores vulgariter protulerunt, sicilianum vocaretur" (1.12.4).

Sicily in 1282. In Charles's recounting of that event, the separatists at Palermo yell "Mora, mora" ('Die, die'), an anagram of "Roma," the site of the true, future empire "onde Christo è romano." Historical Sicily is thus linked in Dante's work with the scrambling of true lines, be they genealogical or linguistic. The break between Sicily and the mainland, "the gulf most vexed by Eurus," comes to represent a loss that must be repaired through a new understanding of empire.

Further back in Sicily's history, however, that very gulf had been bridged by Frederick the Second who, in *Convivio* 4.3.6, is called "ultimo imperadore de li Romani." With his son Manfred, Frederick not only brought together "politics and culture, intelligence and magnanimity" but also ruled over the kingdom of Sicily, which, before 1282, had encompassed both the island and the southern Italian peninsula and was marked, not divided, by the break at Pelorus. As in Vergil, though, the separation offered by the straits continues to serve a metaphoric purpose: Dante placed Frederick the Second in Hell, arguably for failing to separate the spheres of church and state (Ferrante 1984, 123-24). Through his poetry Dante aims to create the means for establishing an empire like that ruled by Frederick the Second, which, nonetheless, will assert a new clarity and order.

Earthly Paradise where past and future converge, the past having enabled the future to emerge as Anchises did for Aeneas and Vergil for Dante, is where the Sicily of poetry, of unity, will also be found. As Dante says to Matelda in *Purg.* 28.49-51, "Tu mi fai rimembrar dove e qual era / Proserpina nel tempo che perdette / la madre lei, ed ella primavera." (You make me recall where and what Proserpina was at the time her mother lost her, and she the spring).[14] The "where" of this mother's loss, as in the Vergilian prophecy repeated in 30, is again Sicily. The recovery of spring, of Eden, the attainment of the Earthly Paradise with the river that runs through it, is the recovery of the unity of Italy, a unity symbolized for Dante by the language and concept of the kingdom of Sicily.

If, as Joan Ferrante has argued (1984, 198), Dante's Purgatory "is situated on the surface of this earth . . . potentially accessible to the living—Ulysses sailed within sight of it," then, arguably, Purgatory is Sicily, or, at least, the idea of Sicily where poetry and justice unite, where "poets are the only fit guides to contemporary society" (1984, 239). "The words of poets speak to men across time and even across the boundaries of language. Dante moves toward one language in Purgatory, as he is moving towards a unified people under the empire, and he does it through the poets" (1984, 373). While language may be transcended in Paradise—through music, through symbol—in Purgatory it is what there is. Even as the language of "sì" means Sicilian as the best of the Italian vernaculars, so Sicily, whose language, unlike its rivers, is not divided at Pelorus from

---

[14] See also Brown 1971, 33-48 on this passage.

the Italian peninsula, is the land of unity for both politics and poetry. Its relationship to the mainland provides the model for what will become, in Paradise, "legato con amore."

Dante inherits from Vergil the awareness that Sicily, like Wales for Hawkes, provides the underpinning of the Italian identity, but he lays over that his own understanding of its potential as political and poetic inspiration. Sicily, for Dante, is defined not through the delicate balance of trope but through the symbolic embrace of mother and father, through the rejoining of past in future. Where the straits of Pelorus offer the necessary distance for Vergil's poetics, they offer to Dante's a different trope: that of a hinge, linking island and mainland, in the tripartite scheme, a binding that unites even as it redefines. For Vergil the tension between unity and separation proffers a language of Roman empire. For Dante that empire is marked by a new order: the earthly Paradise is modeled on the memory of Sicily under Frederick the Second and a dream of a future empire that will revive that cultural ideal, sharpened by a clearer separation of church and state. Distinguished by the image of empire they envision, politics and poetics are nonetheless joined for these authors in the geography of the land they share.

Works Cited

Brown, Jr. E. 1971. "Proserpina, Matelda, and the Pilgrim." *Dante Studies* 89: 33-48.

Dante Alighieri. 1970-1975. *The Divine Comedy.* Ed. Charles Singleton. Princeton: Princeton University Press.

————. 1968. *De vulgari eloquentia.* Ed. Fredi Chiappelli. Milan: Mursia.

Diodorus Siculus. 1936. Ed. and trans. C. H. Oldfather. Loeb Classical Library. Cambridge, MA: Harvard University Press.

Farrell, Joseph. 1999. "*Aeneid* 5: Poetry and Parenthood." In *Reading Vergil's Aeneid: An Interpretive Guide,* ed. Christine Perkell, 96-110. Norman, OK: University of Oklahoma Press.

————. 2001. *Latin Language and Latin Culture.* Cambridge: Cambridge University Press.

Ferrante, Joan M. 1984. *The Political Vision of the* Divine Comedy. Princeton: Princeton University Press.

Frischer, Bernard. 1983. "Inceptive Quoque." *Glotta* 61:238-51.

Galinsky, G. Karl. 1969. *Aeneas, Sicily and Rome.* Princeton: Princeton University Press.

Hawkes, Terence. 2002. *Shakespeare in the Present.* London: Routledge.

Hollander, Robert. 1993. "Le opere di Virgilio nella *Commedia* di Dante." In *Dante e la "bella scola" della poesia,* ed. A. Iannucci, 247-343. Ravenna: Longo.

Horsfall, Nicholas. 2000. *Virgil,* Aeneid *7: A Commentary.* Leiden: Brill.

Jacoff, Rachel. 1991. "Intertextualities in Arcadia: *Purgatorio* 30.49-51." In *The Poetry of Allusion: Virgil and Ovid in Dante's Commedia,* ed. eadem and J. Schnapp, 131-44. Stanford: Stanford University Press.

Lucan. 1992. *De bello civili, book 2.* Ed. Elaine Fantham. Cambridge: Cambridge University Press.

————. 1992. *Civil War.* Trans. Susanna Braund. Oxford: Oxford University Press.

Lucretius. 1947. *De rerum natura.* Ed. and trans. Cyril Bailey. Oxford: Oxford University Press.

Mallette, Karla. 1998. "Arabic and Italian Lyric in Medieval Sicily." In *The Future of the Middle Ages and the Renaissance,* ed. R. Dahood, 81-92. Turnhout: Brepols.

Miller, Paul Allen. 1995. "The Minotaur Within." *Classical Philology* 90:225-40.

Mitchell, W. J. T. 1994. *Landscape and Power.* Chicago: University of Chicago Press.

Nugent, S. Georgia. 1992. "Vergil's Voice of the Women in *Aeneid* V." *Arethusa* 25: 255-92.

Powell, Anton, and Kathryn Welch. 2002. *Sextus Pompeius*. London: Duckworth.

Putnam, Michael C. J. 1965. *The Poetry of the* Aeneid: *Four Studies in Imaginative Design*. Cambridge, MA: Harvard University Press; repr. Ithaca: Cornell University Press.

————. 1995. "Virgil's *Inferno.*" *Materiali e discussioni* 20 (1988): 165-202; repr. in idem, *Virgil's* Aeneid: *Interpretation and Influence*, 286-95. Chapel Hill: University of North Carolina Press.

Quint, David. 1993. *Epic and Empire*. Princeton: Princeton University Press.

Servius. 1881. *Servii Grammatici qui feruntur in Vergilii Carmina Commentarii*. Ed. G. Thilo and H. Hagen. Leipzig: Olms.

Shapiro, Marianne. 1990. *De vulgari eloquentia: Dante's Book of Exile*. Lincoln, NE: University of Nebraska Press.

Vergil. 1972. *Opera*. Ed. R. A. B. Mynors. Oxford: Oxford University Press.

WOMAN AS MEDIATOR
IN MEDIEVAL DEPICTIONS OF MUSLIMS:
THE CASE OF FLORIPAS

SUZANNE CONKLIN AKBARI

Since the publication in 1975 of Joan Ferrante's groundbreaking study *Woman as Image*, much work has been done on women's roles in medieval literature: not just on their active participation as writers, patrons, and correspondents, but on their passive representation. They are objects of exchange to be circulated among men, beautiful images to be adored from afar, personifications of ideals or of malignant qualities. In the area of French literary studies, in particular, Sarah Kay and Roberta Krueger have done much to catalogue the various roles played by women in medieval romances and *chansons de geste*, and to interpret them within the frameworks of gender and power encoded in the texts (Kay 1993, 1995a, 1995b; Krueger 1993). This essay explores the figure of "the Saracen princess," sometimes also called "the Saracen queen."[1] This figure has received considerable attention during the last several years, perhaps due to the increasing interest in religious and cultural difference as depicted in literature of the Middle Ages, as well as the recent application of postcolonial theory to medieval culture.[2] While some treatments of "the Saracen princess" convention are rather limited due to their focus on a single, paradigmatic exemplar, others provide a broader, more nuanced account of the variations.[3] In this essay, I too will focus on a single exemplar of the convention, the Saracen princess Floripas featured in the romance of *Fierabras*. I do so, however, not in order to suggest that she (rather than, for example, Bramimonde or Orable) ought to be taken as paradigmatic, but in order to illustrate the range and variety to be found in the depiction of medieval Saracen women, even within the portrayal of a single character.

---

[1] I use the word "Saracen" because that is the term used most frequently in the literary texts themselves. This should not disguise the fact that the characters, as followers of "Mahom" or Muhammad, are meant to represent Muslims, as we would call them today. On the development of the term, see Daniel 1986, 53–54; Beckett 2002, 90–104.

[2] On the usefulness of such approaches, see Cohen 2000.

[3] Lynn Tarte Ramey, for example, fixes on Orable/Guiborc as "probably the most remarkable Saracen princess of them all" (Ramey 2001, 41). Jacqueline de Weever discusses several examples of the Saracen princess convention, but assimilates them all into a singular manifestation of the "white" Saracen woman (de Weever 1998). A useful overview of the convention appears in Metlitzki 1979, 160–77, and a more detailed summary in Bancourt 1982, 571–665; neither, however, discusses the significance of the variations. Both Kay 1995a and Kahf 1999 provide useful overviews of the variety to be found within the literary convention.

The romance of *Fierabras* was extraordinarily popular, as is attested by the large number of surviving Old and Middle French manuscripts as well as the wealth of translations and adaptations. These include texts written in Middle English, Provençal, Italian, Spanish, Latin, and Old Irish; oral versions of the romance survived into the twentieth century in South America and, in the nineteenth century, yet another version was adapted as an opera by Schubert (de Mandach 1987, 165–86). On the one hand, the widespread popularity of the *Fierabras* romance reveals what cultures have in common, extending over a long period of time and including a wide geographical range: they share an interest in the matter of chivalric romance—that is, the competition of knights, the alluring pagan princess, defiant and hideous giants, and so on.[4] At the same time, however, the numerous redactions of *Fierabras* reveal how cultures differ from one another, for several of the versions vary in ways which reveal how the narrative was adapted to fit the needs, concerns, and interests of the culture in which it appeared. Some versions, for example, depict the Saracen knight Fierabras as a giant, others merely as a magnificently built knight; some versions minimize the descriptions of the relics of the Passion sought by the Christian knights, while others expand those sections, transforming courtly romance into devotional literature.[5]

Yet the widespread diffusion of *Fierabras* is just one reason that the figure of Floripas merits special attention. She differs significantly from other figures seen as representative of the Saracen princess convention in being the daughter of a Saracen emir, rather than the wife of one, like Bramimonde or Orable.[6] While all of these Saracen women traverse the gap separating pagan and Christian cultures, delivering their Saracen kinfolk into the hands of the Frankish knights, they differ with regard to the nature of the obligations they disavow, and consequently differ both in the nature of their disobedience and in the nature of what they bring to their new environment. Yet Floripas also differs in two significant ways from the Saracen princesses sometimes considered in connection with her, such as Nubie in the *Prise de Cordres et de Sebille*, Malatrie in the *Siège de Barbastre*, or Josiane in *Boeve de Haumtone*. The baptism of the Saracen in *chansons de geste* and romances is conventionally accompanied by a change of name in recognition of the person's spiritual rebirth and renewal: Bramimonde becomes Juliane, Orable becomes Guibore, and so on. Floripas, however, retains her name even after baptism, a fact to which the text ostentatiously draws attention.[7] The

---

[4] On the general appeal of the *Fierabras* romance during the Middle Ages and the insights it offers into the cultural history of the period, see Gourlay 2002.

[5] An overview of the versions of the romance can be found in Ailes 1989. On the Fillingham *Firumbras* as "devotional romance," see Akbari 2005.

[6] On this distinction, see Kinoshita 1995, 274.

[7] This anomaly is found elsewhere only in *Gaufrey*, where Flordespine's baptism similarly results in no change of name. The passage corresponds very closely to the account of Floripas's baptism (verse *Fierabras*, line 6013; compare *Gaufrey*, lines 9163–9164);

omission is rendered all the more remarkable by the fact that the conversion of her brother, Fierabras, is accompanied by a change in name: after baptism, he is renamed Florans.

The second, even more striking difference between Floripas and other Saracen princesses pertains to her status and behavior during the period between her avowal of the desire to become Christian and her actual baptism at the close of the narrative. During this time, Floripas exhibits apparently paradoxical behavior: she is beautiful and delicate, but also aggressive and violent. Floripas is both the exquisite object of men's admiration and the dominant mastermind supervising the Christian victory over the pagan forces led by her father. She speaks out forcefully; she laughs openly, often in response to violent behaviors of which she approves; she even kills with her own hands. In some versions of *Fierabras*, Floripas's behavior is explicitly characterized as unfeminine, and she herself is described as a dangerous combination of masculine and feminine qualities. In others, Floripas's behavior is not characterized as unfeminine, because her Saracen identity is dominant in the determination of what constitutes normative behavior. In each case, however, the extended period during which Floripas is neither wholly Saracen nor wholly Christian repays examination, for it constitutes a liminal phase during which not only Floripas's identity, but also the feminine ideal itself, is in flux.

As Hans-Erich Keller has shown, a comparison of the different versions of the medieval *Fierabras* reveals discontinuities indicative of the changing tastes of reading communities all around Europe, from the twelfth century to the fifteenth (Keller 1993). Keller's work focuses mainly on Floripas's physical beauty. Other aspects of her character, however, also vary significantly; for example, some versions accentuate her violence, while others play it down. In addition, other discontinuities cast an indirect light on the variable role of Floripas. These include the characterization of her brother, Fierabras, and the changing illustration of pagan idolatry in the text. The conversions of Fierabras and Floripas are, in a sense, mirror images of each other. While both siblings convert to Christianity, they do so independently: one is persuaded to believe devoutly as the result of a military confrontation visibly influenced by the hand of God, while the other is led to Christianity more pragmatically, as the only means to achieve marriage with the Christian knight she has come to adore. The emotional softness of Fierabras displayed in the closing scenes of the narrative contrasts sharply with the harsh dismissiveness expressed by his sister as they witness the death of their father the emir. Changes in the depiction of pagan idolatry in *Fierabras* illuminate the figure of Floripas in a different way. Their increasing luxuriousness illustrates a growing

---

perhaps the redactor of *Gaufrey* (which survives in a single manuscript, Montpellier, Faculté de médecine, MS. H.242) based his depiction of Flordespine on that of Floripas in the ubiquitous *Fierabras*.

interest in the sensuous abundance of the Orient, an interest which extends to the body of the Saracen princess herself. Some fifteenth-century versions of *Fierabras* thus amplify both the opulence of the pagan images and the erotic potential of the scene of Floripas's baptism recounted in the last lines of the narrative. Both the jewel-studded image and the shining white body of Floripas are foci of desire, each of them a bridge between two worlds: the image links the material and the spiritual, while the pagan woman links the Christian and the pagan. Both, however, also entail danger, for the pagan image leads to idolatry, while the pagan woman even after conversion may pollute the Christian world she enters.[8]

In the remaining pages of this essay, I will illustrate the variable depiction of Floripas using three French versions of the text. One of these, the verse *Fierabras*, represents a very early version of the work, though the earliest manuscript of the complete text dates from the fourteenth century; the other two, selected for the insights they offer into the evolution of the narrative in accord with late medieval reading tastes, include the anonymous prose *Fierabras*, which survives in two early fifteenth-century manuscripts, and the prose version completed in 1478 by Jean Bagnyon.[9] This last version enjoyed immediate popularity, being published in an English version by Caxton just seven years later and a Spanish version in 1521.[10] A comparison of the versions reveals great variety with regard to both the depiction of Floripas's body (that is, her status as the passive object of desire) and her depiction as an active subject, who directs the actions of the Christian knights and displays violent aggression. After outlining these variations, I will illustrate the alterations in the manifestation of masculine desire for Floripas, giving attention to the ways in which the impurity of the Saracen woman's body is gradually erased in the various texts. The depiction of Floripas's body closely parallels the depiction of the relics stolen by the pagans and eagerly sought by Charlemagne. Like the body of Floripas, the relics are guarded by prohibitions regarding who may touch them, and when they may be touched.

---

[8] See Kahf 1999, 53–54, on the residue of Saracen identity remaining even after the woman's conversion, and the danger it poses.

[9] Quotations from the verse *Fierabras* edited by Kroeber and Servois are noted in the text as "verse F." followed by line number; those from the anonymous prose version edited by Miquet are noted as "prose F." followed by line number, with paragraph number in parentheses; those from the version edited by Keller are noted as "Bagnyon" followed by page number, along with part and chapter number in parentheses.

[10] William Caxton, *The Hystory and Lyf of the Noble and Chrysten Prynce Charles the Grete* (Westminster, 1485), ed. Sidney J. H. Herrtage, EETS e.s. 36 and 37 (Oxford: Oxford University Press, 1880–1881; repr. in one vol. 1967). Nicolas de Piemonte, *Hystoria del Emperador Carlo Magno y de los doze pares de Francia: e de la cruda batalla que ovo Oliveros con Fierabras Rey de Alexandria hijo del grande almirante Balan* (Seville, 1521). Other early editions are cited in de Mandach 1987, 178.

In terms of the narrative, the late fifteenth-century version by Bagnyon corresponds closely to the Old French verse text; it differs remarkably, however, in the extent to which Bagnyon lingers on the image of Floripas's body, both in her initial description and in the concluding description of her nude body at the baptismal font. The verse *Fierabras* itself includes an elaborate description of Floripas, her "car . . . tenre et blance comme flours en esté, / La face vermellete comme rose de pré, / La bouce petitete, et li dent sont seré, / Ki plus estoient blanc k'ivoire replané" ["flesh as tender and white as summer flowers, her face pink as the rose in spring, her tiny mouth, with teeth straight and as white as polished ivory" (verse F. 2008–2011)]. Although this long blazon includes a detailed account of Floripas's luxurious and opulent garments, its last lines seem to see right through her clothes: "Moult estoit la pucele sage et de grant biauté; / Petites mameletes, cor bien fait et molé, / Dures comme pumetes, blankes com flours de pré" ["The young girl was very wise and of great beauty, with small little breasts, a body well made and moulded, hard as little apples, white as flowers in springtime" (2037–2039)]. Bagnyon amplifies this account even more. His detailed description of her face, body, and clothing concludes by telling how the sight of Floripas would affect any man who saw her: "Et estoit Florippes si belle atout ses abillemens que, se une personne eust jeusné trois ou quatre jours sans mengier et il veoit celle belle fille, il estoit remplis et saoullez" ["Floripas was so beautiful that if a person had fasted three or four days and saw this beautiful girl, he would be filled up and sated" (Bagnyon 74 {2.2.2})]. Floripas's beauty satisfies physical needs, even hunger, and appeals not just to the sense of sight, but to the sense of smell: "Et avoit si grande oudeur que c'estoit merveille. Pour quoy de la beaulté d'icelle dame pucelle chescun se merveilloit" ["She had such a great sweet smell that it was a marvel; everyone marveled at the beauty of this noble girl" (Bagnyon 74 {2.2.2})]. For Bagnyon, the effect of Floripas's beauty on those who witness it is as significant as that beauty itself.

This is apparent in the scene of Floripas's baptism which comes at the climax of the *Fierabras* narrative, where Bagnyon seizes the opportunity to give a second elaborate anatomy of Floripas, corresponding closely to the initial one. Even in the verse *Fierabras*, the response of the men to Floripas's beauty is emphasized. She disrobes "voiant tout le barné" ["while all the barons watch" (5999)], and at the sight of her "petites mameletes" ["small breasts" (6000)], shapely body, and golden hair, nearly all of the barons have their desire stirred, and even Charlemagne himself is moved to smile with pleasure.[11] In Bagnyon's

---

[11] A very similar scene appears in the unique manuscript of *Gaufrey*, lines 9149–9165. The staging of masculine erotic desire in these scenes calls into question Sarah Kay's assertion that "the epic poems show little taste for the portrayal of sexual desire as a valid emotional state for men . . . Their representation of male desire . . . is almost invariably tinged with sharp reproof" (Kay 1995a, 235).

version, however, the description both of Floripas's body and of the response of the men is more elaborate. He adds a detailed anatomy of Floripas which corresponds to that given in her initial description, down to the "deux mamelles petites et rondettes, / eslevees sur le corps comme deux petites montaignetes" ["two small and round breasts, lifted up on the body like two small mountainettes"]: "Et si bien fut faite a l'aventaige de ses membres, procedans en toute beaulté et pareillement en toute plaisance amoreuse qu'elle frappa le cuer de pluseurs en desir d'avoir son amour, tant estoit plaisant et belle, et par especial Charles l'empereur, combien qu'il fut cassé et ancien" ["she was so well made with regard to every part of her body, conveying such beauty and also such amorous pleasure, that she struck the hearts of many with the desire to possess her love, because she was so pleasing and beautiful—especially Charles the emperor, even though he was broken down and old" (Bagnyon 171 {2.3.15})]. For Bagnyon, the spectacular nature of Floripas is foremost. Even though he preserves the integrity of the romance's narrative, in which Floripas plots, threatens, and even kills, her agency and aggressiveness are overshadowed by the spectacle of her body, which exerts a powerful effect on those who see it.

The anonymous prose *Fierabras* handles the sight of Floripas very differently. In this version, Floripas is made more conventionally feminine: she does not physically attack the jailer or her governess (both of whom she kills in the other versions), nor does she verbally abuse either the Christian knights or her father, the emir. Yet this feminization of Floripas, interestingly, does not include an increased emphasis on the spectacle of her body. On the contrary, in the anonymous prose *Fierabras*, Floripas is introduced simply as "la plus belle dame qui fust en monde en ce temps, et tante richement ordonnee et vestue" ["the most beautiful woman that was in the world at that time, very richly attired" (prose F. 743–744 {69})]. The concluding scene of her baptism merely states that she "estoit la plus belle creature a regarder que oncques homme e[u]st veue. A ce jour elle fut moult dessiree de plusseurs" ["she was the most beautiful creature that any man had ever seen; that day, she was desired by many" (3133–3134 {287}). The redactor even adds a detail, unique among the different versions: Floripas's body is not seen by "all the barons," as in the verse *Fierabras* (5999). Instead, Charles "fit ouster les jeunes" ["throws out the young men"], keeping with him only the two oldest barons; "non obstant que lé troit fussent bien vieulx, sy rioient ilz et avoient grant plaisir de la voyr ainxi toute nue, tant estoit belle" ["even though the three were quite old, they smiled and had great pleasure to see her naked, she was so beautiful" (prose F. 3136–3139 {287})]. Here, the overwhelming effect of the sight of Floripas's body is acknowledged; but while Bagnyon takes this opportunity to indulge in an extended description of the contours of Floripas's body, the writer of the anonymous prose text as it were censors the scene, keeping out of the chamber those men who would be most vulnerable to the effect of the spectacle.

The magnitude of that effect can be gauged by the reactions of the men who, though old and gray-haired, cannot keep from smiling with pleasure. The depiction of Floripas as an active subject also varies significantly in the various versions. The anonymous prose *Fierabras* presents a neutralized Floripas: in the other versions of the text, Floripas initially saves the Christian knights by striking their jailer with a club so hard that "les ex li fist de la teste voler; / Devant lui à ses piés le fist mort craventer" ["his eyes flew out of his head, and he fell dead at her feet" (verse F. 2090–2091). In the anonymous prose version, however, she merely asks her seneschal to "l'en pugnissez presentement et tellement que ce soit exemple es autres" ["punish [the jailer] right away so that he will be an example to others" (prose F. 732–733 {68})]. In a subsequent episode, both in the verse text and in Bagnyon's prose, when Floripas's governess threatens to reveal that the princess is hiding the Christian knights from her father, Floripas lures the governess to the window and pushes her out; the author of the anonymous prose version simply omits the episode entirely. Again, when the Christian knight Guy is initially reluctant to reciprocate Floripas's love, Floripas "jure Mahomet: 'Se vois ne me prenés, / Je vous ferai tous pendre et au vent encruer'" ["swears by Muhammad, 'If you don't take me, I will have you all hanged and left to blow in the wind'" (verse F. 2812–2813)].[12] In the anonymous prose version, on the other hand, Guy responds to Floripas's avowal of love by saying, "Madame, et je suis tout voustre, tenez vous en sceure" ["Madame, I am entirely yours, you can know that for certain" (prose F. 1026 {91})]. While in the verse text and Bagnyon's prose, Guy has to be forced by his companions to accept Floripas, in the anonymous prose text the knights all desire Floripas, and all envy Guy. Roland states, "Or voi je bien, . . . , Guy, qu'il n'est pas pauvre qui est bel; pour voustre beaulté et voustre jeunesse este le mielx amé et vous devez bien louer Dieu, car vous avez belle dame" ["Now I see very well, Guy, that he who is good-looking is not poor: because of your beauty and your youth, you are the best beloved, and you should praise God, because you have got a beautiful woman"]. Duke Naymes adds, "C'est la plus belle que je veisse oncques mes. Qui pourroit coucher une seulle nuyt avecques elle, il ne luy fauldroit james aultre paradis" ["She is the most beautiful one I have ever seen. Whoever could sleep with her for a single night would never need any other paradise" (prose F. 1028–1034 {92})]. Throughout the anonymous prose *Fierabras*, Floripas is presented as a model of feminine deportment: restrained, demure, and courteous.

Yet while the anonymous prose *Fierabras* stands apart from the other two versions in many respects, it shares with Bagnyon's prose text a tendency to

---

[12] Kay points out how Floripas, like some other Saracen princesses, thus effectively circumvents the conventional process of gift-giving among men, in which the woman is the gift (Kay 1995a, 44, 46).

generalize about women's behavior based on the behavior of Floripas. This can be seen in two episodes in which one of the emir's councilors advises him not to trust his daughter, based on the fact that the nature of woman is essentially changeable. In the verse *Fierabras*, the councilor simply asks, "Sire . . . or vois voi assoté; / Veus tu donc cuer de fame essaier n'esprouver?" ["Sire, now I see you're crazy. Do you want to test the heart of a woman?" (verse F. 2733–2734)]. In both later prose versions, however, this moment serves as the springboard for misogynistic generalizations. In the anonymous prose text, the councilor states, "Sire, vous n'estes pas sage de croire vostre fille. Vous savez que cueur de fame est toust changé et par ma foy, si vous les ly baillés, vous vous en repentirez. Et croiez que homme qui se fie en famme est hors du sens ou enragez, je le sçay bien pour la moye, qui maintez foiz m'a moqué" ["Sire, you are unwise to believe your daughter. You know that the heart of a woman is easily changed and, by my faith, if you trust her with [the prisoners], you will repent of it. And you should believe that a man who puts his trust in a woman is out of his mind or mad — I know this very well because of my own [wife], who has made a fool of me many times" (prose F. 969–973 {87})]. Similarly, in Bagnyon's text, the councilor states, "Sire admiral, ce n'est chose convenable que sur ce fait vous doyés fier en femme a cause de leur mutabilité. Et vous en avez beaucoup ouÿ dire d'exemples et congneu la verité comme pluseurs ont estés deceuz par femmes" ["Sire, it is not appropriate that you should rely on a woman in this matter, because of their mutability. You have heard many examples illustrating this, and know the truth about how many men have been deceived by women" (Bagnyon 93 {2.2.8})].

In each of the prose texts, outside experience — whether the personal experience of the councilor or the examples written down in 'books of wicked women' — is used to support the claim that Floripas, like all women, is at best changeable and at worst a liar. The mutability of women is the central theme of several misogynistic *dits* produced in the fourteenth century: as "La Contenance des fames" puts it, "Moult a feme le cuer muable . . . Feme a un cuer par heritage / Qui ne puet estre en un estage" ["A woman's heart is mutable . . . A woman's heart is just not able / To chart a course that's firm or stable" (Fiero *et al.* 1989, lines 20, 27–28)]. The appearance of misogynistic truisms (that go back to Vergil, *Aeneid* 4.569–70) in the two later prose versions of *Fierabras* marks a dramatic shift from the earlier verse text, in which Floripas's deceit and erratic behavior were evidently motivated by her pagan identity; the two later prose versions, even though they differ from one another in many respects, share the tendency to interpret Floripas's behavior as stereotypically feminine.[13] The anonymous prose *Fierabras*

---

[13] As Kay observes, actions that a modern reader reflexively interprets as masculine may have quite a different value in a medieval text: "The *chansons de geste* are less committed to a categorical view of gender than their critics. On the one hand they can take sexual difference as fundamental; on the other, they may subordinate it to the category of the person" (Kay 1995a, 35).

even includes additional reminders designed to remind the reader of women's 'true' nature. For example, after the emir has become aware of his daughter's disloyalty, his councilor states, "Sire, nous vous disoions bien que vous fasoiez que foul de les bailler a voustre fille en garde; onc sage homme ne se fia en fame, car elle est trop muable" ["Sire, we told you before that you did not do well to give [the knights] to your daughter to guard; a wise man never trusts in a woman, because she is too mutable!" (prose F. 1196–1199 {110})].

The allusions to misogynistic tradition found in both prose versions of *Fierabras* are significant not just because they illustrate the extent to which the story of Floripas came to be assimilated to prescriptive norms of women's behavior, but also because they highlight the paradox at the center of her depiction. What precisely is Floripas? Is she pagan or Christian? Is she a passive object of desire, or an aggressive agent? Is she feminine, or is she masculine? In his prose adaptation, Bagnyon highlights this split at the center of Floripas's character, formulating it in terms of Floripas's gender identity. He interjects the following comment immediately after Floripas avows her love for Guy: "Touteffois, bien considéré cestuy chappitre, grande euvre y fut comprise, quant premierement Florippes la courtoyse, qui estoit payenne, eut le desir de parler és Françoys, et cecy touche bien la voulenté des femmes pour sçavoir nouveaulx. Mais tant qu'il tousche l'euvre qu'elle fit contre le maistre et garde de la prison et comment ilz furent mis dehors, ce fut euvre d'omme bien approuv[é]e" ["All in all, considering the whole of this chapter, there is a great work contained within it: for at the beginning, Floripas the courteous, who was pagan, had the desire to speak with the Frenchmen, and this touches very well on the desire of women to always know new things. But that part which touches on the work that she did against the jailer at the prison, and how [the knights] were brought out of there, that was the very capable work of a man" (Bagnyon 79 {2.2.3})]. The author of the prose text simply erases this paradox, omitting the "capable work of a man" within Floripas, while continuing to interpret her behavior as stereotypically feminine. Bagnyon, conversely, emphasizes the contradiction, heightening it by providing elaborate, erotic portraits of Floripas that awaken the desire of the Christian men who see her.

Carnal desire for Floripas is central to all three versions of *Fierabras* discussed here. They differ, however, with regard to how that desire is constituted, and the freedom with which it is expressed. In all three versions, a pivotal scene takes place in which an evil enchanter is sent out at night by the emir to steal from Floripas the *ceinture* or magical belt which keeps hunger away from those who touch it. By having it stolen, the emir hopes to force the Christian knights out of the tower they have been occupying. Once in Floripas's chamber, however, the enchanter is overcome by the sight of her naked body: "Et puis vint au lit de Florippes et sercha secretement tant qu'il trouva la centure, et la ceint autour de luy. Cecy estre fait, il regarde la fille toute nue, qui estoit moult blanche et belle, et fut incliné a dormir avec elle, tellement qu'il la va accoller toute nue par les flancs" ["He came to the bed of Floripas and searched until he found the belt, and wrapped it around himself. Having done that, he looked at the girl, all naked, who was so white and pretty, and became inclined to sleep with her, so that he began to embrace her thighs, all naked" (Bagnyon 102 {2.2.10})]. She wakes up and screams; this awakens Guy, who rushes in and kills the thief. In this episode, the beauty of Floripas's body awakens the desire of the man who sees it, just as in the baptism scene described above; yet it also awakens the desire of the man who intervenes, that is, Guy. It is necessary to recall that until this point in the narrative, in both the verse *Fierabras* and Bagnyon's text, Guy has accepted Floripas's love reluctantly and only because Roland has commanded it. This scene, then, marks the first time that Guy responds to Floripas and acts on her behalf. Bagnyon's version of this scene differs subtly from the verse *Fierabras* with regard to both the basis of the thief's desire for Floripas's body and the basis of Guy's newly awakened desire. In the earlier version, the thief "Floripas resgarda, qui tant fu coulourée" ["looks at Floripas, who was so beautifully colored" (verse F. 3078)], while in Bagnyon's version, her nude body is "moult blanche et belle" ["white and beautiful" (102 {2.2.10})]. Her body contrasts dramatically with that of the thief, who is (in the words of the verse *Fierabras*) "plus noir d'une pevrée" ["more black than a peppercorn" (3085)]; in Bagnyon's words, "black as a Moor" ["ainssy noir comme meure" (102 {2.2.10})].[14] His blackness makes her look more white; that is, both more beautiful and less alien. In both versions, but more emphatically in Bagnyon's text, the desire of the black pagan man for the white pagan woman awakens the desire of the white Christian man.

This scene is pivotal because it marks a shift in Floripas's status, making her more accessible to the Christian knights, less clearly marked off as alien. Her initially forbidden status is evident in her early encounters with the knights. When she first discovers Guy, for whom she has long cherished a passion, "en la bouce ne l'osa adeser, / Pour ce k'ele est paiene, il est crestiennés" ["she did not dare to kiss him on the mouth, because she was a pagan and he was a Christian" (2822–2823)]. Here, their mutual difference causes the prohibition on physical contact. In the later text, her status alone is the cause: "ne l'ose baisier en la bouche sy non és joues et out menton pour la cause qu'elle estoit payenne" [she did not dare to kiss him on the mouth, nor on the cheeks or chin, because she was a pagan" (Bagnyon 96 {2.2.8})]. Even though the pleasures of Floripas's body are forbidden,

---

[14] "Meure" literally means "blackberry"; by the fourteenth century, however, wordplay on "meure" and "more" was very common. See, for example, usages of the expression, "noirs come mores mëures" ("black as blackberry-dyed Moors") cited in the *Tobler-Lommatzsch Altfranzösisches Wörterbuch*, 11 vols. (Wiesbaden: Franz Steiner, 1925–1989), 6: 267, s.v. "more, meure." The pun appears to be based on the same logic displayed in Brunetto Latini's explanation of the origin of the name Ethiopia: "Etyope ... ou sont les gens noires come meure, et por ce sont il apelé mors" (Latini 1948, 120 [bk. 1, chap. 124]).

she does possess something precious that the knights can kiss freely. Both texts immediately go on to describe how (in the words of Bagnyon) "Florippes joyeusement et par grant amour s'en vint un ung escrin et l'a ouvert devant les barons et fait estendre ung beau drap de soye, puis desvelloppe les reliques . . . Et puis dist a Roland: 'Veez cy le tresor que vous avés tant desiré.' Quant les François furent ainssy devant les reliques, de joye ilz vont tous plourer moult tendrement, et l'un après l'autre les vont baiser a genoulx moult humblement" ["Floripas joyfully and because of great love brought out a chest and opened it before the barons, and displayed a beautiful silk drapery, and then unwrapped the relics . . . and said to Roland, 'Look at the treasure which you have so much desired.' When the French came before the relics, they cried tenderly with joy, and then one after the other came and kissed them, on their knees" (Bagnyon 96 {2.2.8})]. The kisses which cannot be received by Floripas's body, because she is still marked off as pagan and therefore forbidden, can instead be received by the relics that are in her possession, wrapped in the same luxurious silks that the princess herself wears.[15] The desire for Floripas's body is thus deflected onto the relics.

In the anonymous prose *Fierabras*, this scene is simply omitted; it is not necessary, because Floripas's body is not forbidden. On the contrary, Floripas freely kisses Roland himself on the lips, and goes on to say to Guy, "Si vous plaist, vous me baiserez. Ja vous n'y aurez pechié, car je croyroy en Dieu; pour l'amour de vous je seray crestienne . . . Pour Dieu, mon amy, baisez moi, car oncques fame ne fut joyeuse que je suys de voustre venue" ["You can kiss me if you wish. You will never have any sin from it, because I shall believe in God; because of my love for you I will be a Christian . . . For God's sake, my love, kiss me, for no woman was ever more joyous than I am at your arrival" (prose F. 1013–1015, 1024–1025 {91})]. Conversely, in the verse *Fierabras* and in Bagnyon's text, Floripas's body only gradually becomes licit. With the attack of the enchanter, Floripas becomes more appealing to the Christian knight Guy, so that he comes to kiss her "moult amoureusement" ["most amorously" (Bagnyon 120 {2.2.16})]. With her subsequent second display of the relics of the Passion, which takes place on the battlements of the castle, Floripas moves still farther away from her earlier state of impurity. When the Christian knights become demoralized by the prospect of defeat in battle, Floripas restores their spirits by promising to bring out the "reliques c'avés tant desiré" ["relics which you've desired so much'" (verse F. 5222)]. She touches the relics both when she removes them from their casket and when she returns them, in Bagnyon's words, "reveramment" ["reverently" (156 {2.3.10})]. Only with her baptism at the climax of the narrative, however, does Floripas become wholly accessible. By becoming spiritually 'clean,' dipped in the

---

[15] Floripas is wrapped in "paile galacien" (verse F. 2016), as are the relics (5243).

purifying waters of the baptismal font, the pagan princess at last ceases to be a potential source of pollution to the Christian knights.

Significantly, even as she becomes available to the Christian men upon exiting her former liminal state (neither wholly Christian nor wholly pagan), Floripas comes to be affected by conventional prohibitions on women's behavior. In both the prose *Fierabras* and Bagnyon's text, Floripas does not touch the relics she presents to Charlemagne after her baptism, even though she had earlier handled them freely. Instead, the archbishop is summoned to unwrap and display the relics (Bagnyon 172 {2.3.16}; prose F. 3196–3203 {293}). This marks a significant change from the verse text, in which Floripas continues to be able to touch the relics even after her full assimilation into the Christian community (verse F. 6048–6057). This change may indicate the extent to which gender roles dictate the norms of feminine behavior in the late medieval texts, in contradistinction to the earlier verse *Fierabras*; alternatively, it may reflect prohibitions on laypeople touching sacred objects. Similar reinforcement of religious orthodoxy can be found in the digressions on the right use of images in worship found elsewhere in Bagnyon's text (153 {2.3.9}; 168–169 {2.3.15}).

To summarize, then, the three French versions of *Fierabras* described here make very different use of Floripas in her role as mediator between the worlds of Christian and pagan. The earliest version, the verse *Fierabras*, presents a Floripas who must be understood within the terms of the ideology of crusade. Like Orable/Guiborc in the Guillaume d'Orange cycle, she is moved by love to betray not only her countrymen but her family.[16] Her desire for the Christian man magnifies his image, revealing how potent and desirable he himself is, and the righteousness of his cause. Her beautiful exterior belies the savage impulses that lie beneath, impulses that lead her to threaten, lie, and kill. Gradually, however, Floripas's savage impulses are tamed: the two murders take place very early in her encounters with the Christian knights, and after her initial threat to "hang them all" if Guy does not reciprocate her love, Floripas confines her insults to her Saracen father and his henchmen. Correspondingly, Floripas's body, initially untouchable due to her pagan identity, becomes an appropriate object of desire, even (in the final scene) to the emperor Charles himself. Like the relics of the Passion, like Jerusalem itself, Floripas is a beautiful prize which (in the ideology of crusade) is rightfully reclaimed from the dirty hands of the Saracens.[17]

The anonymous prose *Fierabras* is quite another matter. Here, Floripas's paradoxical nature is erased, and she behaves according to the finest standards of women's behavior. The death of the jailer is not even explicitly ordered by Floripas,

---

[16] On Guiborc's behavior, see Ferrante 1974, 43–44. On the interrelated development of the characters of Floripas and Guiborc, see Bennett 1984.

[17] On the rhetoric of pollution in crusade documents, see Cole 1993.

much less committed, and the murder of the governess is omitted entirely. She never threatens the Christian knights, because such rebuke is unnecessary: her kisses are accepted by Guy from the outset, eliciting the envy of the other Christian knights who adore her as well. A particularly striking contrast can be seen in Bagnyon's rendition of the scene in which the emir's councilor reminds him how foolish it is to trust women. Floripas exclaims: "Filz de putain! Traitre desloial! Parjure! Se je ne penssoye plus oultre estre blasmee de moy prandre a toy, je te donneroye tel coup sur le vaisaige que le sang aval en viendroit habondamment" ["Son of a whore! Disloyal traitor! Liar! If I didn't think I would be blamed for doing it, I would give you such a blow from my fist on the nose that the blood would flow right down to your mouth" (Bagnyon 93 {2.2.8})]. The anonymous prose text, however, simply relates that, "quant Floripez ouÿt Bruillant ainsi parler, elle en eut grant despit en son cueur, combien qu'elle n'en fist nul semblant et jura Dieu qu'il ly en souviendroit" ["when Floripas heard him speak this way, she was filled with contempt, even though she didn't let it appear, and begged God to make him pay for it later" (prose F. 978–980 {88})]. Similarly, when a second councilor of the emir comes to Floripas's chamber to investigate the presence of the knights, and is attacked by one of them, Floripas responds with enthusiasm. When the Saracen lands in the fireplace, Floripas says, "Sire . . . or le laisiés caufer; / Moult aime le foier, il n'a soing de lever" ["Sire, now let him cook! He loves the fire, he doesn't care to lift himself up" (verse F. 2941–2942)]. In the anonymous prose text, she simply thanks the knight, saying "vous m'avez fait un tres grant plaisir" ["you've given me a very great pleasure" (1128 {102}), and comes over to kiss and embrace him.

The Floripas of the anonymous prose *Fierabras* is an exemplary woman, given to devout expressions, displaying modesty and restraint. In the scene where she is attacked by the thief, for example, the writer of the anonymous prose text specifies that she was "couchee toute vestue" ["all covered up" (1254 {115})] as she lay on the bed. Perhaps the most dramatic illustration of how neutralized Floripas is, in the anonymous prose version, appears in the closing baptismal scene, when her father has just refused to be christened (and just before Floripas herself disrobes). Floripas's brother is moved, and appeals to their father to convert; not so Floripas. In the verse text, she turns to the emperor and says "Karles, que demourés? Ce est .I. vis diables; pou coi ne l'ociés? / Moi ne caut se il meurt, mais que Gui me donnés; / Je ne plourai moult peu, se j'ai mes volentés" ["Charles! Why are you waiting? This is a living devil; why don't you kill him? I don't care if he dies, as long as you give me Guy. I won't cry much for him, if I have my way about it" (5955–5958)]. In Bagnyon's prose, Floripas is only slightly more polite: "Sire empereur, pour quoy mettés vous tant a fayre mourir celluy deable tant desloyal? Il ne m'en chault s'il meurt, seullement que Guy de Bourgoigne soit mon espoux" ["Sire emperor, why do you wait so long to have this disloyal devil put to death? It doesn't disturb me if he dies, as long as Guy of Burgundy be my spouse"

(169 {2.3.15})]. In the anonymous prose text, however, Floripas falls to her knees to intercede alongside her brother: "Monseigneur mon pere, pour Dieu, aiez pitié de vous et ne vous faictez pas mourir par voustre follie; pour Dieu, faictez le plaisir au roy Charlemaigne" ["My lord and father, for God's sake, have pity on yourself and don't make yourself die because of your folly; for God's sake, do the pleasure of King Charlemagne" (3091–3093 {283})].[18] Here, Floripas is a dutiful daughter and a dutiful subject, appealing humbly to her father to submit himself to the will of their common ruler, which is (in turn) the will of God. While little is known about the circumstances under which the anonymous prose *Fierabras* was commissioned, it is tempting to speculate that it may have been intended for women readers, as a romance narrative with didactic intent embedded both in the misogynistic allusions to women's 'true' nature, and the exemplary submissiveness of Floripas.[19]

The prose text of Bagnyon closely follows its verse model with regard to the progress of the narrative. Unlike the verse *Fierabras*, however, Bagnyon's text no longer partakes fully in the ideology of crusade which governs the role of Floripas in the earlier work. Instead, the rhetoric of the misogynistic texts popular in the fourteenth and fifteenth centuries is brought to bear, explicating the capricious and unrestrained behavior of Floripas in terms of woman's essential nature, rather than in terms of Saracen identity. The spectacle of the woman's body, in Bagnyon's text, is accentuated dramatically, highlighting both the appeal of the desired object and its effect on those who look at it: it fills them up. Recall how, in his opening description of Floripas, Bagnyon inserts a curious phrase into the blazon: "if a person had fasted three or four days, without eating, and he saw this beautiful girl, he would be filled up and sated." This notion of fullness produced through the sight of the woman's body reappears in the scene where the thief pauses in the act of stealing the magical belt, arrested by the sight of Floripas. Like the belt itself, which takes away the hunger of those who touch it, the sight of Floripas fills up the man who looks at her, paradoxically both satisfying and awakening the hunger for more. This satisfaction and fullness is experienced once again in the closing scene of baptism, quoted above: "she was so well made with regard to every part of her body, conveying such beauty and also such amorous pleasure, that she struck the hearts of many with the desire to possess her

---

[18] The Provençal version of *Fierabras* also includes this variation (ed. Bekker 1826). Floripas also intervenes in the Anglo-Norman *Fierabras* (lines 1704–1707), but Ailes argues persuasively that this is due to the scribe's misreading of the abbreviation "F" in his exemplar (Ailes 1989, 46–47); the Anglo-Norman text of London, B.L., MS. Egerton 3028 appears in Brandin 1938.

[19] For an overview of women readers of vernacular romances, see Krueger 1993, 17–30. On women as readers and patrons, see also Ferrante 1997; McCash 1996.

love" (Bagnyon 171 {2.3.15}). At this moment, Floripas is the passive and delightful object of desire.

Sarah Kay suggests that women, in the *chansons de geste*, function as a kind of "colle sexuelle," a glue that brings men together into various kinds of relationships (Kay 1993, 223). In the romance of *Fierabras*, Floripas does indeed bring men together, not just across the boundary separating pagan and Christian but within the Christian community itself, as they bask in the sight of her beautiful body. Her essential nature, however, is defined very differently in the various versions. In the verse *Fierabras*, her verbal aggression and physical violence are attributed not to her feminine nature, but to her eastern origins.[20] In the late medieval prose versions, however, her feminine nature, mutable and unstable, is repeatedly identified as her dominant quality. When Bagnyon states that her "capable work" is that of a "man" he implies that Floripas is a kind of virago, an unnatural woman who exists at the very border of gender norms. The open display of her nude body at the baptismal font and her subsequent surrender of the relics to Charlemagne mark her full entry into the sphere of normative patriarchal culture—reached, paradoxically, through the repudiation of her 'natural' filial obligations to her Saracen father. The multiple redactions of *Fierabras* are striking testimony to the flexibility of the narrative in which Floripas plays such a crucial role: one can readily imagine how her position within the ideology of crusade, found in the early *chansons de geste*, could be adapted for use within the ideology of conquest in the versions of the romance perpetuated in Central and South America. The case of Floripas illustrates the extent to which the "image of woman" is not singular—not even within the tradition of a single romance.

---

[20] On the relationship of climate and physiology (including behavioral predispositions), see Akbari 2000, 23–29; Akbari 2004, 157–166.

Works Cited

Ailes, Marianne J. 1989. "A Comparative Study of the Medieval French and Middle English Verse Texts of the *Fierabras* Legend." Ph. D. Diss., University of Reading.

Akbari, Suzanne Conklin. 2000. "From Due East to True North: Orientalism and Orientation." In *The Postcolonial Middle Ages*, ed. Jeffrey Jerome Cohen, 19–34. New York: St. Martins Press.

———. 2004. "The Diversity of Mankind in *The Book of John Mandeville*." In *Eastward Bound: Travel and Travellers, 1050–1550*, ed. Rosamund Allen, 156–176. Manchester: Manchester University Press.

———. 2005. "The Hunger for National Identity in *Richard Coer de Lion*." In *Reading Medieval Culture: Essays in Honor of Robert W. Hanning*, ed. Robert M. Stein and Sandra Pierson Prior, 198–227. Notre Dame: University of Notre Dame Press.

Bagnyon, Jehan. 1992. *Histoire de Charlemagne (parfois dite Roman de Fierabras)*, ed. Hans-Erich Keller. Textes littéraires français 413. Geneva: Droz.

Bancourt, Paul. 1982. *Les Musulmans dans les chansons de geste du cycle du roi*. 2 vols. Aix-en-Provence: Université de Provence.

Beckett, Katherine Scarfe. 2002. *Arabs, Saracens and Ishmaelites in Anglo-Saxon England*. Cambridge: Cambridge University Press.

Bekker, Immanuel. 1826. "Der Roman vom Fierabras provenzalisch." *Preussische Akademie der Wissenschaften zu Berlin, Abhandlungen aus dem Jahre, Philologische-Historische Klasse*, 10: 129ff.

Bennett, Philip E. 1984. "The Storming of the Other World, the Enamoured Muslim Princess and the Evolution of the Legend of Guillaume d'Orange." In *Guillaume d'Orange and the Chanson de geste: Essays Presented to Duncan McMillan*, ed. Wolfgang van Emden and Philip E. Bennett, 1–14. Reading: Societé Rencesvals.

Brandin, Louis. 1938. "La 'Destruction de Rome' et 'Fierabras': MS Egerton 3028 du Musée Brittanique, Londres." *Romania* 64: 18–100.

Cohen, Jeffrey Jerome. 2000. "Introduction: Midcolonial." In *The Postcolonial Middle Ages*, ed. idem, 1–17.

Cole, Penny J. 1993. " 'O God, the Heathen Have Come into Your Inheritance' (Ps. 78.1): The Theme of Religious Pollution in Crusade Documents, 1095–1188." In *Crusaders and Muslims in Twelfth-Century Syria*, ed. Maya Schatzmiller, 84–111. Leiden: Brill.

Daniel, Norman. 1986. *The Arabs and Mediaeval Europe*. London: Longman.

de Mandach, André. 1987. *La Geste de Fierabras: le jeu du réel et de l'invraisemblable*. Geneva: Droz.

de Weever, Jacqueline. 1998. *Sheba's Daughters: Whitening and Demonizing the Saracen Woman in Medieval French Epic*. New York and London: Garland.

Ferrante, Joan M. 1974. "Introduction." In *Guillaume d'Orange: Four Twelfth-Century Epics*, 1–61. Records of Civilization 92. New York: Columbia University Press.

———. 1975. *Woman as Image in Medieval Literature from the Twelfth Century to Dante*. New York: Columbia University Press.

———. 1997. *To the Glory of Her Sex: Women's Roles in the Composition of Medieval Texts*. Bloomington: University of Indiana Press.

Fierabras, ed. A. Kroeber and G. Servois. *Les Anciens Poètes de la France*, gen. ed. M. F. Guessard. Paris: F. Vieweg, 1860.

Fierabras: Roman en prose de la fin du XIVe siècle, ed. Jean Miquet. Ottawa: University of Ottawa Press, 1983.

Fiero, Gloria K., Wendy Pfeffer, and Mathé Allain, eds. and trans. 1989. *Three Medieval Views of Women*. New Haven: Yale University Press.

Gaufrey, ed. F. Guessard and P. Chabaille. *Les Anciens Poètes de la France*, gen. ed. M.F. Guessard. Paris, 1859.

Gourlay, Kristina E. 2002. "'Faire Maide' or 'Venomous Serpente': The Cultural Significance of the Saracen Princess Floripas in France and England, 1200–1500." Ph. D. Diss., University of Toronto.

Kahf, Mohja. 1999. *Western Representations of the Muslim Woman: From Termagant to Odalisque*. Austin: University of Texas Press.

Kay, Sarah. 1993. "La représentation de la fémininité dans les chansons de geste." In *Charlemagne in the North*, ed. Philip E. Bennett, Anne Elizabeth Cobby, and Graham A. Runnalls, 223–240. Edinburgh: Societé Rencesvals.

———. 1995a. *The Chansons de geste in the Age of Romance*. Oxford: Clarendon Press.

———. 1995b. "Contesting Romance Influence: The Poetics of the Gift." *Comparative Literature* 32: 320–41.

Keller, Hans-Erich. "La belle Sarrasine dans *Fierabras* et ses dérivés." In *Charlemagne in the North*, ed. Bennett et al., 299–307.

Kinoshita, Sharon. 1995. "The Politics of Courtly Love: *La Prise d'Orange* and the Conversion of the Saracen Queen." *Romanic Review* 86: 265–87.

Krueger, Roberta. 1993. *Woman Readers and the Ideology of Gender in Old French Verse Romance*. Cambridge: Cambridge University Press.

Latini, Brunetto. 1948. *Li Livres dou Tresor*, ed. Francis J. Carmody. Berkeley: University of California Press.

McCash, June Hall, ed. 1996. *The Cultural Patronage of Medieval Women*. Athens: University of Georgia Press.

Metlitzki, Dorothee. 1979. *The Matter of Araby in Medieval England*. New Haven: Yale University Press.

Ramey, Lynn Tarte. 2001. *Christian, Saracen and Genre in Medieval French Literature*. New York and London: Routledge.

Lifting the Veil? Notes toward a Gendered History of Early Italian Literature

Teodolinda Barolini

In this essay I am going to sketch a paradigm for evaluating the treatment of women in early Italian literature. In other words, I am going to look at that well worn trajectory—Italian literature from its lyric origins to Dante, Petrarch, and Boccaccio—from a less worn perspective: the perspective of gender.

It may be worth explaining how a critic with a long track record of working on these authors from a non-gendered perspective arrived at this particular intellectual crossroads. The issue of gender is obviously central in early Italian literature and is clearly posed by the texts themselves: Italian literary texts of this period feature male lover-poets and the female figures that they love. The difficulty, for me, was figuring out how to approach this issue in a way that seemed integrated with the complex reality of the texts themselves. I could see the issue: because much of the early Italian tradition deals with desire that is filtered through a cultural system we know as "courtly love," in which the male lover aspires to the love of a lady worshiped as an ennobling ideal, attention to issues of gender seems an obvious enough critical move. I could see the need: there is an absence of sustained analysis of gender in medieval Italian literature which in turn must be set within a broader intellectual context in which the word "gender" in the sense of "gender studies" is not even easily translated into Italian. What I could not see was a satisfying avenue—which at this stage in our critical enterprise must mean an avenue that goes beyond "women in x, y, or z"—by which to approach the issue of gender in these authors.[1]

I reached the paradigm that I will put forth here slowly, over the last ten years, and by working backwards, from Boccaccio, the Italian author who most explicitly places the category "woman" (rather than just a particular woman) at the core of his opus. In a fashion that is contradictory, nuanced, and anything but ideologically doctrinaire, Boccaccio shines a light on the disenfranchisement of women, using them as emblematic for all those who are oppressed, disenfranchised, cloistered away from society, and stripped of agency (Barolini 1993). Female agency came into focus again years later when, through a historicist reconstruction of *Inferno* 5, I uncovered a submerged "feminist" agenda embedded in

---

[1] Joan Ferrante's pioneering volume, *Woman as Image in Medieval Literature*, was published thirty ago. I happened to be in W. T. H. Jackson's office at Columbia University, a graduate student at his office hours, when his advance copy of *Woman as Image* arrived in the mail. I remember well his picking it up and commenting that this was a book that was going to have a major impact: an impact this volume illuminates.

Dante's Francesca da Rimini (Barolini 2000).[2] From Francesca I worked backwards again to look at the issue of gender in Dante's lyrics, drawing in this way nearer to the courtly origins of the Italian tradition (Barolini 2003).

My goal now is to connect the dots: to write a gendered history of early Italian literature. To tell this story we have to follow the trajectory of the non-gendered history; we have to start before Dante, in the lyric pre-history to the *Commedia*, and we have to include both of the key forgers of the aftermath to the *Commedia*—the period that sets the stage for the rest of Italian literary history—namely Petrarch as well as Boccaccio. In this paper I will start with Dante, move back in time to discuss one of Dante's lyric precursors, Guittone d'Arezzo, say little about Boccaccio, and barely mention Petrarch. But I will advance a framework for thinking about gender relations in these authors and their works, a framework that I hope to fill out in a book where I will be able to elaborate on what here I can only suggest.

I argue that the key to approaching the construction of gender in the authors of the early Italian tradition is the ambivalence they display in their treatments of love and desire. This ambivalence is manifested in the competing ideological systems to which they subscribe: on the one hand, they subscribe to the ideology of courtly love, and, on the other, to an often violently anti-courtly ideology that permeates their moralistic poetry. These two ideologies underwrite very different attitudes toward women and toward gender.

The dialectic between courtly and anti-courtly ideologies is a historical constant in the early Italian tradition: it is present not only in Dante (1265–1321), but in poets before Dante, like Guittone d'Arezzo (d. 1294), and it is a major feature of Boccaccio's (1313–1375) work as well. For this reason, the ideological shifts manifested by these authors lend themselves to constructing a historical overview of the issue of gender in this tradition, allowing us to frame a gendered history of early Italian literature in terms of the dialectic between a courtly ideology and a competing set of values.

Courtliness, the set of values associated with what Dante and his peers call *cortesia*, is by definition a gendered issue, since its logic is constructed around a male/female binary. In the courtly lyric, the male lover-poet voices his aspiration to poooeoo the unattainable perfection that the lady represents. On the other side of this binary stands the courtly lady, who represents, embodies, serves as goal and point of reference, but does not, in the courtly lyric, do, act, or speak. Dante started life as a courtly poet; he ended life as the author of the *Commedia*, a text in which women act, speak, and possess moral agency. The question that arose

---

[2] A historicist reading of this sort is a logical development once one has "detheologized" one's reading of the *Commedia* (see Barolini 1992): in the case of *Inferno* 5, detheologizing allows one to postulate interpretive categories more complex than "Dante places Francesca in hell, so his view of her is negative."

for me, the question that offered me the means to get beyond the "women in the *Commedia*" approach to gender issues in Dante and to think in terms of a larger historical paradigm, diachronically, was thus the following: how do we account for Dante's development from a courtly poet into the poet of the *Commedia*, that is, into a poet who assigns moral agency to all human beings, including women? In other words, how do we account for Dante's development into the poet who gave Francesca da Rimini, forgotten by contemporary chroniclers and dynastically unimportant, a voice and a name, indeed the only contemporary historical name recorded in *Inferno* 5? How did Dante become the poet who wrote Francesca's story, who inscribed Francesca's existence into our collective memory, our history?

Poetry based in a courtly logic is always fundamentally narcissistic and centered on the male lover/poet; the female object of desire serves as a screen on which he projects questions and concerns about himself. Whether we are speaking of the early courtly poetry of the Sicilian Giacomo da Lentini (ca. 1230) or the later theologized courtliness of Dante and his fellow *stilnovisti* (poets of the "new style"), the fundamental logic of the courtly poem remains narcissistic. The didactic works of writers like Guittone d'Arezzo, Dante in his late moral canzoni, and Boccaccio, on the other hand, are marked by a utilitarian stamp: women are supposed to *use* this literature, to be instructed by it, to learn from it. In other words, this poetry, precisely by virtue of its moralistic and even paternalistic program, actually needs to communicate with women, to treat them as subjects who can learn, rather than as objects to be desired.

In Dante's work we can see the tension between the courtly approach to women, in which the female figure serves to arbitrate male behavior and exists functionally only as a predicate to the male lover-poet, and a moralizing approach in which women are arbiters of themselves and exist in the poem as potential users of poetry in their own right. Beatrice is a hybrid figure—and I take her hybridity as emblematic of the complex portrait of women's lives and desires that emerges from the *Commedia*. If all the *Commedia*'s diverse female figures and varied perspectives were synthesized, we would see, I believe, a text that is neither fundamentally misogynistic nor free of misogynistic elements.[3]

Beatrice's hybridity has its roots in that paradigmatically hybrid text, the *Vita nuova*,[4] where we can reconstruct the history of this trajectory, the stepping-stones

---

[3] I do not disagree with Kirkham, who notes "a vein of misogyny that shoots beneath the surface of the entire poem" (Kirkham 1989, 34). I am less persuaded by Jacoff's view that the female is the figure of transgressive desire in the *Commedia*, that there is no "image of female desire that is not in and of itself transgressive" (Jacoff 1988, 142). Shapiro, 1975, offers a very negative assessment of women in the *Commedia*.

[4] I use the traditional *Vita nuova*, in Italian, because I have not been convinced by the arguments put forward by Guglielmo Gorni in his edition for changing to *Vita Nova*, in Latin; see *Vita Nova*, ed. Guglielmo Gorni (Torino: Einaudi, 1996).

on the way to the *Commedia*. One such stepping-stone is the unelaborated but nonetheless suggestive last verse of the sonnet *Amore e 'l cor gentil sono una cosa* (*VN* 20). According to this verse, the process of love being awakened in a noble heart that occurs in men occurs analogously in women: "E simil face in donna omo valente" ("And a worthy man does the same to a woman").[5] Also significant are the ladies of *Vita nuova* 18, who question Dante in a way that shakes him from his complacent self-indulgence and alerts him to his true quest: not to write about himself but to praise Beatrice. The complex role assigned these ladies is emblematic of the *Vita nuova* itself, a text in which Dante embeds his early lyrics into a prose frame that ideologically repositions and reconceptualizes them. These ladies, who belong to the prose narration, not to the lyrics, are given the work of cutting through the rhetorical stance of the courtly lover and pointing out the narcissism in his work. They do this work by speaking, and they speak in a way that certainly is novel with respect to Dante's lyrics. However, in that they speak exclusively about *him* and *his* moral state, they are functionally still courtly ladies.

Let us come back to Beatrice's hybridity. On the one hand she conserves many of the erotic markers of the lady in the courtly lyric and, like the lady in the courtly lyric, her poetic existence is predicated on the needs of the lover-poet: Beatrice's existence in the *Commedia* is always predicated around Dante. On the other hand, she possesses an absolutely unprecedented and masculine authority: she develops from the silent icon of stilnovist courtly verse to the talkative figure I once labeled *Beatrix loquax* (Barolini 1992, 303, n. 36). The hybridity (or, as Kirkham puts it, "androgyny") of the *Commedia*'s Beatrice is such that, in the space of two verses, she can, in a signature courtly topos, first ray her lover with a smile "such that it would make a man happy in the flames," and then—in the very next verse—begin a speech with the words "according to my infallible judgment" ("secondo mio infallibile avviso" [*Par.* 7.19]). The use of the adjective "infallible" to qualify female speech is stunning, given the long and documented tradition of female speech as the special focus and target of misogyny; moreover, this is the *Commedia*'s only use of *infallibile* for human speech of any sort, male or female.[6]

Beatrice's speechifying has put off the historically mostly male commentators of the *Commedia*, we note one critic's claim that the "Beatrice [of the *Vita nuova*] appears far more persuasive, enigmatic, explosive, than the recreated and cantankerous figure" of the *Purgatorio* (Harrison 1988, 19). To this we must reply that

---

[5] The text is cited in the edition of Domenico De Robertis, *Vita nuova* (Milano: Ricciardi, 1980). Ferrante singles out this verse for comment: "It is not insignificant that a worthy man can arouse the same response in a woman—the instinct to love what is pleasing and to desire what one loves is common to all human beings" (1975, 130).

[6] The adjective appears otherwise only to qualify God's "infallibil giustizia" (*Inf.* 29.56).

the "explosive" Beatrice of the *Vita nuova* is silent, while the "cantankerous" Beatrice of the *Commedia* speaks. In this context of scant critical appreciation for what is new about the Beatrice of the *Commedia*, an exception is Joan Ferrante, whose 1992 essay "Dante's Beatrice: Priest of an Androgynous God" illuminates Dante's unorthodox handling of Beatrice in the *Commedia*, explaining that Dante puts her "in a role which is specifically forbidden to women by major theologians, as priest, as confessor and teacher of theology . . . in flagrant defiance of Paul's injunction, frequently echoed in the thirteenth century, against women teaching" (4).

While the *Beatrix loquax* of the *Commedia* is the most obvious example of Dante's mature reconfiguration of the gender paradigm he inherited from the courtly lyric, it is by no means a unique instance. In my recent attempt to rehistoricize and repoliticize our reading of *Inferno* 5, I looked at the historical record surrounding Francesca da Rimini and found that *Inferno* 5 breaks the silence of the chroniclers, none of whom saw fit to mention Francesca's murder (Barolini 2000). The first and most authoritative chronicler of Rimini was Marco Battagli, whose history *Marcha* contains a section called "On the Origins of the Malatesta" (1352). Battagli alludes to the event in which Francesca died without naming her, indeed without acknowledging her existence, except as an implicit cause of Paolo's death, which occurred "causa luxuriae": "Paolo was killed by his brother Giovanni the Lame on account of lust." One son of Malatesta da Verucchio, the founding patriarch of the Malatesta dynasty, killed the other; this fact is of interest because it affects the history of the dynasty. Francesca matters not a whit as herself. And, in fact, the only historical document that records her name is the will of her father-in-law, in which he refers to "the dowry of the late lady Francesca." Otherwise, silence.

Dante, who preserved Francesca, recording her name, giving her a voice, and saving her from consignment to historical oblivion, broke this silence. And, as though to make this point crystal clear, Francesca's is the only contemporary name registered in *Inferno* 5: Paolo's name is absent, as is Gianciotto's. In canto 5, she is the protagonist, she is the agent, and she is the one who speaks, while Paolo stands by weeping. Through the intervention of *Inferno* 5, Francesca became a cultural touchstone and reference point, achieving a dignity and a prominence—a celebrity—that in real life she did not possess. The woman who in real life was merely a dynastic pawn, whose brutal death did not even cause a serious rupture between the Malatesta of Rimini and the Polentani of Ravenna, emerges in Dante's version as the canto's unchallenged protagonist. The woman who in real history had no voice and no name emerges in the canto's history as the only voice and only name. Again, the question that arises is: how did a courtly poet, that is a poet raised in the conventions of female silence, reach this point? The traces of this evolution, I have argued in another essay, are to be found in his lyrics (Barolini 2003).

Analysis of the arc of Dante's lyrics from the perspective of gender reveals an evolution in his thinking. As Dante moves away from the courtly paradigm of his early verse toward his moral and philosophical canzoni, which are frequently anti-courtly, his attitude toward gender evolves. I propose that Dante's mature anti-courtly lyrics harbor more progressive positions vis-à-vis gender than his earlier courtly lyrics. For instance, a canzone that I once viewed as merely obnoxiously paternalistic, *Doglia mi reca*, I now view as harboring a progressive attitude toward gender roles along with its paternalism, because it holds women to moral standards. The move away from a courtly ideology makes possible the construction of woman as a moral agent in her own right: as the poet shifts away from an exclusive focus on the male lover, the female can come into focus as a subject, rather than serving solely as backdrop for male subjectivity and commentator on male behavior. Anti-courtliness is the signature move of *Doglia mi reca*, and it makes possible a new approach to the construction of gender.

Doglia mi reca, a late canzone written shortly before the transition to the *Commedia* and fully committed to moral themes, opens with female desire, already anomalous as a focus of attention, and makes its anti-courtly agenda even more explicit by focusing on base female desire — "il vil vostro disire" (6):

> Doglia mi reca ne lo core ardire
> a voler ch'è di veritate amico:
> però, donne, s'io dico
> parole quasi contra tutta gente,
> non vi maravigliate,
> ma conoscete il vil vostro disire (*Doglia mi reca*, 1–6)

> (Grief brings boldness to my heart on behalf of a will that is friend to truth. If then, ladies, I speak words against almost everyone, do not wonder at this, but recognize the baseness of your desires . . .)

As truth's friend, Dante tells us, he will utter "words against almost everyone." Dante is here classifying his canzone's program as profoundly unconventional. He is signaling that *Doglia mi reca* starts within the courtly framework and then turns against it, rather than operating within a different framework from the outset. For, were *Doglia mi reca* operating within the set of conventions we associate with misogynistic writing, for instance, an attack on female desire would be utterly conventional. Thus, in Boccaccio's *Corbaccio*, where female desire is routinely construed as vile and base, Boccaccio is not worried that he will be perceived as antagonistic or unconventional, as Dante is in *Doglia mi reca*. Dante is not adopting misogynistic conventions in *Doglia mi reca*—which is not to say that he may not say some things that strike us as misogynistic—but rather exploding courtly conventions from within.

Doglia mi reca allows female desire to exist as a context, no longer holding women harmless as passive recipients of male love, but forging them as desirers and moral agents in their own right, and starting down a path that will lead eventually to the *Commedia*'s Francesca da Rimini and Piccarda Donati. But at this point Dante is not yet incorporating courtly issues into a broader moral framework, as he does in *Inferno* 5, but rather importing all these moral issues into a constraining courtly framework, which is why his thinking sometimes appears contradictory and muddled. Thus, *Doglia mi reca* begins by bringing female agency to the fore, as we have seen, but then confuses the issue as the first stanza continues. Making female beauty the correlative of male virtue, and love the force that unifies the two — "se vertute a noi / fu data, e beltà a voi, / e a costui di due poter un fare" ("if virtue to us was given, and beauty to you, and to Love the power to make of two things one" [12–14]) — Dante holds that it is a woman's duty to deny her love to men who cannot match in virtue what she offers in beauty. He instructs women not to love, and to cover up their beauty, since virtue, which was beauty's target, is no more:

voi non dovreste amare,
ma coprir quanto di biltà v'è dato,
poi che non c'è virtù, ch'era suo segno (*Doglia mi reca*, 15–17)

(You should love no more, but rather hide the beauty given you, since virtue, that was its goal, is found no more.[7])

By engaging a gendered duality that assigns beauty to women and virtue to men, and so associates women with exteriority and superficial values, men with interiority and ethical values, the canzone's implicit program of non-dualistic gender construction seems to falter. Charting territory that is new to him, Dante does falter, but his attraction to the idea of female agency and responsibility is strong and manifests itself again before the stanza concludes. The first stanza of *Doglia mi reca* ends by declaring that it would be particularly laudable for a woman to bid farewell to her beauty of her own accord:

Dico che bel disdegno
sarebbe in donna, di ragion laudato,
partir beltà da sè per suo commiato. (*Doglia mi reca*, 19–21)

---

[7] The context in no way supports Pézard's thesis that this passage exhorts women to self-blinding, a thesis given undue credibility by Foster and Boyde in their commentary (1967, 299-300). As we shall see, the key word here is "coprir" and the key trope is veiling/unveiling. Translations are mine.

(I say it would be an act of fine scorn in a woman, and rightly praised, to
sever beauty from herself—bidding it farewell of her own accord.)

Dante here puzzles the English editors Foster and Boyde who wonder what
is "the special point of adding 'of her own accord'?" (1967, 300). But precisely these words, "per suo commiato," hold the key to Dante's thought process.
These words bring Dante back to her will, her agency. Moreover, his apparent
need to go in this direction gets him all tangled up. Let us consider: if women
should cover themselves of their own will (in a kind of self-imposed chador),
then women are to make a moral choice to hide their beauty from immoral men.
So, though this passage began with the equation virtue:men=beauty:women ("se
vertute a noi / fu data, e beltà a voi" [12–13]), it soon gets severely tangled, as
Dante exhorts women to deploy the virtue that they theoretically lack against the
men who theoretically possess it.

Although *Doglia mi reca* never fully overcomes this initial confusion, it develops always in the direction of assigning more and more choice to women,
and as a result takes an anomalous interest in communicating with them and
instructing them. Whereas the courtly canzone frequently opens with a conventional address to ladies who then disappear from the poem (Cavalcanti's *Donna
me prega*, Dante's *Donne ch'avete intelletto d'amore*), the female addressees whom
Dante enlists in the struggle against male vice in stanza one of *Doglia mi reca* do
not disappear from view but are summoned again prior to the canzone's midpoint
and again at the conclusion. Dante comes back to his female audience half way
through the third stanza. The passage in question starts out in a metapoetic key,
announcing a change in style toward greater clarity in order to best serve his female audience, and then reaffirms the poet's role as moral guide, whose compensation will be his audience's compliance:

> Ma perchè lo meo dire util vi sia,
> discenderò del tutto
> in parte ed in costrutto
> più lieve, sì che men grave s'intenda:
> che rado sotto benda
> parola oscura giugne ad intelletto;
> per che parlar con voi si vole aperto:
> ma questo vo' per merto,
> per voi, non per me certo,
> ch'abbiate a vil ciascuno e a dispetto . . . (*Doglia mi reca*, 53–62)

(But that my speech may be of use to you, I'll come down from the general to the particular, and to a lighter form of expression, so that it may be
less hard to understand; for seldom under a veil do obscure words reach the

intellect, hence with you one must speak openly. But this I want in recompense (for your own good, certainly not for mine) that you hold every man as vile and as object of scorn . . .)

There is an interesting insecurity in the commentary tradition regarding "sotto benda" in verse 57: does Dante refer to the literal article of clothing (*benda* is the "strip of cloth or silk with which married women wrapped their cheeks, temples, and forehead for ornamentation and to hold their hair") and therefore, by synecdoche, to those who wear it, namely women, or does he refer to an allegorical veil, a veil of language?[8] The allegorical reading has taken precedence in the twentieth-century commentary tradition over the literal. While the Barbi-Pernicone commentary takes a no-nonsense literal approach, glossing "sotto benda" as "in cervello di donna" ("in the brain of a lady" [1969, 613]),[9] Contini gives primacy to the allegorical: "La *benda* è la stessa imagine che *il velame de li versi strani* (*Inf.* IX 63) e il *velo* di *Purg.* VIII 20. Attraente tuttavia la dichiarazione, di più studiosi, che *benda* sia l'ornamento femminile, e s'abbia dunque allusione a una necessità di chiarezza maggiore con donne" ("The *benda* is the same image as 'the veil of the strange verses' of *Inf.* IX 63 and the 'veil' of *Purg.* VIII 20. Attractive, nonetheless, is the declaration on the part of some scholars that *benda* refers to the female headdress, and that therefore we have an allusion to the need to speak with greater clarity to women" [1965, 186]). Foster and Boyde follow Contini, starting with the allegorical and adding that "the other interpretation"— i.e. the literal interpretation—"is also attractive: this takes *benda* as the wimple worn by women" (1967, 304).

I believe that it is important to restore as primary the literal meaning of "sotto benda" in this passage in *Doglia mi reca* and, along with the literal meaning, to recuperate the gendered nature of Dante's intervention. Indeed, the result of focusing on the allegorical reading of "sotto benda" is to elide out of the text the gendered aspect of what Dante says. Contemporary evidence, in the form of lexical usage and responses to Dante's verses by other poets, suggest that the literal meaning should be taken as primary.

If we look at the entries for *benda* and *velo* in the *Grande dizionario italiano* we see that *benda* is much less given to metaphorical extrapolation than *velo*. Dante's own usage corresponds to this perception: the noun *velo* and the verb *velare* are used frequently across the gamut of Dante's works (*Rime, Fiore, Vita nuova,*

---

[8] The definition is from Muzzarelli 1999, whose Glossary defines *benda* thus: "striscia di tela o di seta con cui le donne sposate si avvolgevano guance, tempie e fronte per ornamento e per trattenere i capelli" (353).

[9] Barbi's material was published posthumously by Pernicone; hence, despite the 1969 date, it is of earlier vintage.

Convivio, Commedia) and across a semantic range from literal to metaphorical. Moreover, even the literal *velo* has a more poetic quality than *benda*, so that in the ethereal and abstracted context of the *Vita nuova* we find two uses of *velo* as covering, but never the more socially attuned *benda*. Dante uses *benda* infrequently: first in our passage in *Doglia mi reca*, and then three times in the *Commedia*, where it is always a signifier of a woman's marital status, either in the secular sphere (never married or widowed and remarried) or in the monastic. Thus, the remarriage of Beatrice d'Este is signified through the change in the color of her *bende* ("che trasmutò le bianche bende" "she exchanged her white veils" [*Purg.* 8.74]), the nubile young lady of Bonagiunta's prophecy "non porta ancor benda" ("does not yet wear a veil" [*Purg.* 24.43]), and "sacre bende" ("sacred veils" [*Par.* 3.114]) signify that Costanza is the bride of Christ. *Benda* is a word deployed by Dante univocally to refer to socially mandated and regulated female covering.

The verses in *Doglia mi reca* indicating women through the synecdoche "sotto benda" elicited responses from two important contemporaries, the doctor and astrologer Cecco d'Ascoli (1269–1327) and Petrarch (1304–1374). Both interpret "sotto benda" literally as referring to women. In the conclusion to the political canzone *O aspectata in ciel*, Petrarch writes that love resides not only "sotto bende" (*Canzoniere* 28.113), "under veils," in order to make the point that a canzone inspired by a non-erotic form of love can nonetheless take its place with pride among its fellows. In his commentary to Petrarch's canzone, Santagata cites *Doglia mi reca* as the source for "sotto bende" and notes that Petrarch evidently interprets the debated verses from Dante's canzone in the same manner as Cecco d'Ascoli in *Acerba*.[10] Cecco d'Ascoli cites the verses from *Doglia mi reca* in his encyclopedic *Acerba*, in the context of a misogynist *capitolo* dedicated to his negative views of women. Here Dante is used as an *auctoritas* on female intellectual limitations: "Rare fiate, como disse Dante, / S'intende sottil cosa sotto benna" ("Rarely, as Dante said, are subtle thoughts understood [by those] beneath a veil" [*Acerba* 4.9.4397–4398]).

Cecco's response to Dante is extremely interesting, for he both appropriates and changes *Doglia mi reca*. Thus, while it is true, as the Barbi-Pernicone commentary points out, that Cecco understands Dante correctly, in that he takes "sotto benda" to refer to women, it is also true that Cecco works considerable changes on Dante's passage, which he appropriates to his own misogynist ends. Because Dante *wants* to communicate with women, he voices his concern that rarely will an obscure word ("parola oscura") reach the intellect of one under the veil, that difficult language will make communication with women difficult to achieve, and uses this concern as a platform from which to announce a shift toward a more

---

[10] See Petrarca 1996, 154.

accessible style.[11] Cecco, on the other hand, changes "parola oscura" to "sottil cosa" — a "subtle thought" — and uses the passage from *Doglia mi reca* as a platform from which to launch a savage invective against women, who are beings without intellect and "fruit of all evil": "La femmina ha men fede che una fiera, / Radice, ramo e frutto d'ogni male, / Superba, avara, sciocca, matta e austera, / Veleno che avvelena il cuor del corpo, / Iniqua strada alla porta infernale" ("Woman has less faith than a wild beast, root and branch and fruit of all evil, proud, miserly, foolish, mad, severe, poison that poisons the heart of the body, path of iniquity to the gate of hell" [*Acerba* 4.9.4403–4407]). Moreover, Cecco takes the citation from *Doglia mi reca* as an opportunity to pen one of his sardonic indictments of Dante (most of which are focused on the *Commedia*). Here he paints Dante as a foolish naïf whose belief that women possess intellect is the equivalent of looking for the Virgin Mary in the streets of Ravenna: "Maria va cercando per Ravenna / chi crede che in donna sia intellecto" ("He who believes that there is intellect in women is looking for Mary in Ravenna" [*Acerba* 4.9.4401–4402]).

Cecco's misogynist diatribe and passing dig at Dante offer us a valuable perspective from which to gauge the force and direction of Dante's gendered intervention in *Doglia mi reca*. We remember that Dante interrupts his canzone to address the ladies. Because he desires his speech to be of use to them, he writes, he will descend from the general to the particular, and to a lighter form of expression, so that it will be less difficult to understand. Seldom, Dante explains, does obscure language reach the intellect of a woman; hence with a woman it behooves him to speak openly. No doubt the patronizing tone of this passage is annoying. At the same time we do well to keep in mind that these verses testify to Dante's genuine concern that the women to whom he writes understand him, that they be authentic comprehenders and recipients of his message — maybe even authentic interlocutors, given that this poem's *congedo* explicitly sends it to a woman. Most of all, as Cecco's response helps us see, Dante's intervention is founded in a belief in women's intellect — an intellect whose existence is taken for granted and that he seeks to reach. In order to reach it, in order to communicate with women, he says he will change his discourse, lowering it to the level of their comprehension. Cecco, who dismisses as foolish the belief that women possess any intellect at all, gives us the vantage from which to see that Dante's paternalism is an affirmation: women possess intellect, he is saying, and it is up to me as poet to figure out how to reach it.

---

[11] The ideological import of this passage is if anything heightened by its being misleading: the style of the canzone is *not* noticeably lightened — in the sense of simplified — after the poet's declaration. It is, however, more dramatic, especially in the stanza that immediately follows.

There can never be problems of communication in dealing with an idealized—or demonized—projection of our own desires; problems of communication arise only when we deal with an authentic other, like the women of this canzone. The women of *Doglia mi reca* are not the idealized stilnovist muses of Dante's youth, who possess "intelletto d'amore" in the *Vita nuova*'s canzone *Donne ch'avete intelletto d'amore* ("Ladies who have intellect of love"). Rather they have plain "intelletto"—"che rado sotto benda / parola oscura giugne ad *intelletto*"—enough to receive the poet's instruction, if not in its obscure form, "parola oscura," then as "parlar . . . aperto." Dante here combines a self-consciousness about rhetorical and poetic technique rooted in vernacular poetics ("lieve," "grave," "oscura," "aperto" echo Provençal categories such as *trobar leu, trovar clus*), with a pedagogic pragmatism that may well be a hallmark of texts addressed to women: the emphasis on the utility of discourse—"perchè lo meo dire *util* vi sia"—reminds one, as we shall see, of the *Decameron*, another text addressed to women and determined on communicating with them.

No attentive reading of this canzone, so genuinely and vigorously in dialogue with women, can bypass the literal meaning of these verses, which place women at the very heart of this poem addressed to them. Because the women of *Doglia mi reca* are genuine interlocutors, not vehicles for writing about the self, Dante must alter his rhetoric to be of use to them, for "rarely beneath the veil do obscure words reach the intellect; hence with you one must speak openly" (57–59). Dante then builds on the literal veiling of women to suggest the metaphorical veiling of their intellects that he is working to breach. The verse in stanza 1 enjoining women to cover their beauty—"ma coprir quanto di biltà v'è dato" (16)—with its key word *coprir*, may be seen in retrospect to initiate the key trope of veiling/unveiling. Thus "ma coprir quanto di biltà v'è dato" in stanza 1 will be echoed by "rado sotto benda" and "aperto" in stanza 3, indeed will be picked up and reversed—literally, as *coprir* gives way to *aperto*—by the poet's need to penetrate "beneath the veil" with his words, his "open speech" ("parlar . . . aperto"). The literal *benda* becomes ever more elaborately metaphorical: in a deliberate recall and inversion of the exhortation that women veil their physical beauty, the poet will throw the veil of obscurity off the text and speak openly, using the verb *disvelare* (based on the more metaphorically charged *velo* rather than *benda*, this verb is a hapax in Dante's *rime* that occurs only once in the *Commedia*) to unveil the truth for his female audience. "I have unveiled for you, ladies"—"Disvelato v'ho, donne" (127)—says the poet in his conclusion, to show that he has turned their literal *bende* into a trope of *revelatio*. Here the male poet does the work of unveiling for his veiled female audience; in the *Commedia* Beatrice will unveil first herself, in the poem's only instance of *disvelare*,[12] and then—through her speech, her *parlar aperto*—she will unveil the mysteries of the universe for her audience, both female and male.

In the *congedo* to *Doglia mi reca* Dante instructs his canzone to await the commands of its female recipient, who is not an idealized *senhal* but a specific "lady from our country: beautiful, wise and courteous" ("donna / ch'è del nostro paese: / bella, saggia e cortese" [148–150]). It will be her task to dispose of the canzone: "prima con lei t'arresta, / prima a lei manifesta / quel che tu se' e quel per ch'io ti mando; / poi seguirai secondo suo comando" ("stay first with her, to her manifest what you are and why I send you; then continue as she commands" [155–158]). Commentators show some surprise at the *congedo*'s praise of a woman: "a perhaps rather surprising conclusion to the stern exhortations preceding it," say Foster and Boyde (1967, 296). But it is all of a piece with *Doglia mi reca*'s treatment of women as moral agents who are held accountable for their desires and actions. As moral agents, they are individual subjects and, like the lady to whom the canzone is sent, they even receive names: in this case she is "Bianca, Giovanna, Contessa" (153), later she will be Francesca, the only person named in her canto. At stake are discretion, choice, responsibility, agency. To the degree that a woman is "saggia," she will make appropriate decisions, in this case the decisions regarding the canzone. If she is not *saggia*, she may make inappropriate decisions, and—despite the poet's best efforts—she may perish. This strong sentiment from *Doglia mi reca*'s seventh and conclusive stanza anticipates the *Commedia*, in which a woman's moral choices, like a man's, may in fact cause her to perish.

Although at first it may seem counterintuitive to read the harsh paternalism of *Doglia mi reca* in a progressive light, Dante accomplishes quite a lot in this canzone. The ladies of *Doglia mi reca* are definitely off the courtly pedestal. They have more to worry about than the behavior of their male lovers: they have their own selves, including their immortal souls, to take care of. They have acquired the status of moral agents and although they do not yet speak—an activity for which we have to await the *Commedia*—they are expected to be able students, fully receiving and intellectually digesting the poet's message. Moreover, if we put *Doglia mi reca* into the context of options available to the courtly poet, we see that Dante here bypasses altogether the courtly paradigm, according to which a lady is conceived in negative terms not on moral grounds but on the basis of her perceived cruelty to her male lover (in Dante's personal lyric constellation, this would be the stony lady of the *rime petrose*). In *Doglia mi reca* a woman possesses her own actions and her own desires and it is up to her whether she develops into "Bianca Giovanna Contessa" or someone else—someone like, say, Francesca.

---

[12] *Disvelare* occurs in a moment charged with the memory of lyric eros, when the theological virtues beg Beatrice to unveil and reveal her mouth for the pilgrim: "Per grazia fa noi grazia che *disvele* / a lui la bocca tua" (*Purg.* 31.136-137). The *Commedia*'s one use of *svelare*, in *Purg.* 3.33, carries no physical connotations.

While the substance of Dante's message to women in an anti-courtly and moralizing poem like *Doglia mi reca* may be paternalistic, the fact that he addresses them directly, "lifting the veil" to speak to them clearly and intelligibly, is highly significant: it means he construes them not as objects of desire but as subjects who desire and who must take responsibility for their desires. Dante's precursor in this matter of women and the utility of poetic discourse—as in so many of his moves as a morally committed poet—is Guittone d'Arezzo, a Tuscan poet who died circa 1294. Guittone d'Arezzo wrote a didactic poem on female chastity, *Altra fiata aggio già, donne, parlato*, that opens by addressing the ladies and establishing the poet as their defender: "Altra fiata aggio già, donne, parlato, / a defensione vostra ed a piacere" ("On another occasion, ladies, I have already spoken in your defense and for your pleasure" [1–2]).[13] *Altra fiata* influenced *Doglia mi reca*: while *Doglia mi reca* is indebted to Guittone's poetic manifesto, *Ora parrà*, for its anatomy of desire, a philosophy of desire that is non-gendered and that indeed will be of great import for the *Commedia*, it is indebted to *Altra fiata* for its gendered discourse to and about women.[14]

The importance of *Altra fiata* as an intertext for the gendered issues of *Doglia mi reca* leads one to wonder if Guittone is a precursor also with respect to the signature move of *Doglia mi reca*, the anti-courtliness that allows Dante to attack women for their "vile desire," rather than focusing exclusively on male desire. In other words, does Guittone's didactic and paternalistic stance toward his female audience in *Altra fiata* open the door to their free agency, as Dante's does in *Doglia mi reca*? To what degree does Guittone pave the way for Dante's handling of gender in *Doglia mi reca*? My suggestion is that *Altra fiata* does indeed offer an early model of the *Doglia mi reca* paradigm whereby paternalistic morality defeats courtliness and ironically enhances the status of women by conceiving them as moral agents.

Women are moral agents in Guittone's canzone, albeit weak-minded ones, who need to be prodded and pushed in the direction of virtue. Guittone's anti-courtliness is quite different from Dante's, and would repay study as a model that Dante both attended to and rejected. Guittone is more attuned to popular religiosity and less to philosophical models than Dante (for instance in his adoption in strophe 2 of an explicit Eve/Mary template for female behavior). And he differs from Dante in using an autobiographical stance that gives his presentation a more personal urgency: the premise for his sermon is that he himself was

---

[13] Guittone is here referring to his canzone in defense of women, *Ahi lasso, che li boni e li malvagi*. Translations are mine.

[14] See Barolini 1997 for *Doglia mi reca*'s philosophy of desire. As my work on *Doglia mi reca* has proceeded I have become progressively aware of its boldness and subtlety. In the 1997 essay I was dealing with Dante's handling of desire in the canzone, *tout court*; the gendered aspects of *Doglia mi reca*'s analysis became apparent only in a later stage of my work on the canzone.

once a seducer who deceived and corrupted women.[15] Now that he has changed his ways, he will defend women from such as he was; he writes, as we have seen, "a defensione vostra" ("in your defense" [2]). As a former entrapper he owes a debt to women: "ma debitor son voi, chè fabricate / ho rete mante e lacci a voi lacciando" ("I am your debtor, for I have made many nets and snares for the purpose of trapping you" [10–11]). He plans to discharge his debt by helping them to stay "free" — "libere": "se libere star, più che lacciarvi, amate" ("if you prefer to be free, rather than ensnared" [16]). Guittone's choice of adjective here seems to allude to the human faculty that is the prerequisite for moral behavior, namely *libero arbitrio* or free will, as well as to conjure all the associations of sin with bondage and virtue with freedom.

Guittone exhorts women to pursue all virtue but most especially chastity. He commends above all a woman who is chaste both in body and spirit: "Oh, che molto io commendo / donna che tene casto corpo e core!" ("Oh, how much I commend a lady who keeps chaste her body and her heart!" [75–76]). To live in the flesh without fleshly desire ("Vivere in carne for voler carnale" [77]), he says, is better than angelic, since angels have chastity but without the temptations of the flesh ("Angeli castitate hanno for carne" [79]). At the same time that he praises total chastity, however, Guittone is open to chastity within marriage for a woman who cannot or will not choose absolute chastity, a woman who has or desires a husband: "Chi non pote o non vol castità tale, / che ha marito overo aver desia" (83–84). A woman who lives chastely with a husband is considered virtuous; even more significant, a woman can virtuously desire a husband she does not yet have. Noteworthy here are the verbs of volition "vol" and "desia" that allow females free will to participate in these crucial life decisions: it is important that Guittone allows that a woman may choose marital chastity over absolute chastity, and that he acknowledges a woman's right to desire a husband.

With respect to unchastity, Guittone is explicit about the double standard that applies to the sexes: carnal vice is bad in men, but much worse in women. Guittone sets a precedent for Dante in *Doglia mi reca*'s argument regarding female unchastity leading to death. His view is that it is better for a woman to die than to take a lover:

Ohi, quanto fòrate, donna, men male,
se l'amadore tuo morte te desse,
che ben tal te volesse!
Chè pregio vale ed aunor più che vita.
Oi donna sopellita

---

[15] Interestingly, Dante seems to pick up on this Guittonian persona in another of his moral canzoni that deal with courtliness and women, though he does not adopt it for himself: Guittone casts himself in a role like that of the false knights and corrupters of women whom Dante castigates in the canzone *Poscia ch'Amor*.

in brobio tanto ed in miseria, aviso
che peggio d'onne morte è vita tale. (*Altra fiata*, 108–114)

(Oh, how much would it be less evil for you, lady, if your lover were to give
you death, than that he should love you thus! For worth and honor are more
valuable than life. Oh, lady buried in such shame and misery, I consider
such a life worse than any death.)

While *Doglia mi reca* presents a complex scholastic analysis of different kinds
of desire and concludes with the idea that a woman who fails to discriminate between lovers deserves to perish ("Oh cotal donna pera / che sua biltà dischiera
/ da natural bontà per tal cagione, / e crede amor fuor d'orto di ragione!" "Oh
let such a woman perish, who for such reasons sunders her beauty from natural
goodness and believes that love exists outside the garden of reason!" [144–147]),
Guittone simply exhorts women to remain chaste at all costs, for even death is
better than unchastity.

Altra fiata also anticipates *Doglia mi reca* in connecting a discourse on female
chastity to the necessity for women to cover their beauty: *Doglia mi reca*'s "You
should not love, but rather hide the beauty given you" ("voi non dovreste amare, /
ma coprir quanto di biltà v'è dato" [15–16]) echoes Guittone's "Ladies, if you like
chastity, let honor cover your beautiful face" ("Donne, se castità v'è 'n piacimento,
/ covra onestà vostra bella fazone" [157–158]). The key word in both passages is
coprire: rather than the elaborate metaphorical play around the trope of veiling/
unveiling that we saw in *Doglia mi reca*, Guittone is matter of factly concerned
with the importance of covering and protecting that which one treasures. The importance of cover is one of the topoi common to moralizing discourses on female
conduct that we find in *Altra fiata*, along with the stress on appropriate speech
and the caution against ornamentation. Female conduct is about respecting limits, staying within the accepted norms or constraints: as female speech is only appropriate within limits ("garrendo" [140] or garrulous speech is not acceptable), so
ornamentation is perilous, since outward signs are an indication that a good is for
sale. A horse that is not for sale will not carry a sign; a man who shows his treasure
is not sufficiently protective of it. Similarly, if a woman is not for sale, she should
not expose herself; if she values her chastity she should cover herself:

Ben dona intendimento
che vender vol chi sua roba for pone.
Caval che non si vende alcun nol segna,
nè già mostra che tegna
lo suo tesoro caro om ch' ladroni
lo mostri ed affazioni.
Donne, se castità v'è 'n piacimento,
covra onestà vostra bella fazone. (*Altra fiata*, 151–158)

(He who puts his goods outside shows his intention to sell. A horse that is not for sale does not carry a sign, nor does he who shows his treasure to thieves demonstrate that he values it. Ladies, if you like chastity, let honor cover your beautiful face.)

It is significant that the above instructions on not exposing a woman's beauty are not directed to a male protector in charge of covering the woman, but, as in *Doglia mi reca*, are offered directly to the woman, who is thus placed in charge of covering herself.

Dante may have had the last strophe of *Altra fiata* in mind as he composed *Doglia mi reca*'s central metapoetic strophe. *Altra fiata* ends with a strophe in which Guittone defends the difficulty of his poetry from detractors who say his writing is too hard and difficult to savor: "E dice alcun ch'è duro / e aspro mio trovato a savorare" (163–164). They may be right, Guittone says, but the difficulty of his verse is the opposite of decorative, frivolous, and unmotivated; rather, it is the direct result of how much material he needs to include, and how pressing is his need to communicate:

E dice alcun ch'è duro
e aspro mio trovato a savorare;
e pote esser vero. Und'è cagione?
che m'abonda ragione,
perch'eo gran canzon faccio e serro motti,
e nulla fiata tutti
locar loco li posso; und'eo rancuro,
ch'un picciol motto pote un gran ben fare. (*Altra fiata*, 163–170)

(And some say that my poetry is hard and difficult to savor; and it could be true. What is the reason? That I abound in discourse, so that I make a great canzone and bind together words, and never can I find a place to place them all. Hence I regret, for a little word can do a great good.)

Guittone ends *Altra fiata*, a poem that addresses women and what we could call "women's issues" throughout, with a strong statement of personal regret: he regrets, he says, that he cannot fit in everything he would like to say in defense of women. His last word touches on the moral agenda of his canzone: he ends by saying that even a small word can do a great good—"ch'un picciol motto pote un gran ben fare." Guittone thus concludes *Altra fiata* by emphasizing first the difficulties of communication but ultimately the moral value and utility of his discourse.

The conclusion of *Altra fiata* is directly connected to the central passage in *Doglia mi reca* in which Dante says that he will now write more clearly in order to be of greater use to his female audience: "perchè lo meo dire util vi sia." Utility is a key feature of this tradition, clearly articulated in Boccaccio's *Decameron*, another text addressed, not just once or twice but consistently and indefatigably, to women. Boccaccio defends his targeting of female readers precisely on the basis of their greater need. Women are cloistered and enclosed, constrained by the wishes of their families and immured in their rooms: "ristrette da' voleri, da' piaceri, da' comandamenti de' padri, delle madri, de' fratelli e de' mariti, il piú del tempo nel piccolo circuito delle loro camere racchiuse dimorano" ("constrained by the wishes, the pleasure, and the commandments of their fathers, their mothers, their brothers, and their husbands, most of the time they remain enclosed in the small compass of their rooms" [*Proemio*, 10]). Therefore, argues Boccaccio, women have most need of what he has to offer; indeed his discourse will be of greatest utility to them:

> E quantunque il mio sostentamento, o conforto che vogliam dire, possa essere e sia a' bisognosi assai poco, nondimeno parmi quello doversi più tosto porgere dove il bisogno apparisce maggiore, sì perchè più utilità vi farà e sì ancora perchè più vi fia caro avuto. (*Proemio*, 8)

> (And though my nourishment, or comfort if we want to call it such, may seem to the needy to be rather slight, nonetheless it seems to me that it should be offered more readily where the need seems greatest, both because it will be of greater utility in that quarter and because it will be more appreciated.)

As he embarks on his book, he states that the ladies who read it will be able to derive from it both delight and useful counsel—"utile consiglio" (*Proemio*, 14). And he ends the *Decameron* on the same note, turning again to his female audience and asking us to remember him, if what we have read has proven of any service: "E voi, piacevoli donne, con la sua grazia in pace vi rimanete, di me ricordandovi, se a alcuna forse alcuna cosa giova l'averle lette" ("And you, sweet ladies, with His grace remain in peace and remember me, if some benefit has come to some of you from reading these" [*Conclusione dell'Autore*, 29]).

I have argued elsewhere that, for all its programmatic ambiguity, the *Decameron* does indeed offer benefits to its female readers (Barolini 1993) Boccaccio uses verbs to signify male freedom in the Proem of the *Decameron*, where we find the alignment of deeds and verbs with men. The pains of love are alleviated for men, says Boccaccio, because, while women are forced into immobility that increases melancholy, men have access to a host of distracting activities, expressed as nine successive infinitives: "per ciò che a loro, volendo essi, non manca l'andare a torno, udire e veder molte cose, uccellare, cacciare, pescare, cavalcare, giucare o mercatare" ("so that men, if they want, are able to walk abroad, see and hear many things, go fowling, hunting, fishing, riding and gambling, or attend to their business affairs" [*Proemio*, 12]). These same activities are used throughout the *Decameron* to generate metaphors for sex, with the result that the text is hard-wired, through the metaphors that equate sex with various masculine activities, to contaminate the world of women and the world of men, allowing women access to the male world of mobility, deeds, and accomplishment. The *Decameron's* sexual metaphors are literal bridges (metaphor from *metapherein*, to carry over) between two gendered activities that are accorded different status and worth along gender lines: the metaphors serve to transfer or carry over some of the worth accorded men's work to women's work, thus transferring to women some of the symbolic worth accorded to men and appropriating for women the larger frame of reference—the broader playing field—usually reserved for men.

My point here is that the *Decameron* can be inscribed within a specific tradition, which, if not in itself feminist, is arguably the tradition in which feminism could later take root. This is the tradition in which female interlocutors are not just tropes, not just part of the poet's self-construction, as they are for courtly poets. Standing between courtliness on the one hand and misogyny on the other, this is the tradition that is moralizing, didactic (to the point of frequently being paternalistic and obnoxious), utilitarian, pragmatic—and that truly addresses issues of women in society. This is the tradition whose hallmark is a stress on the utility of discourse, a feature of the *Decameron* that has not typically been connected to its proto-feminism but that I would firmly connect to a certain kind of writing to and about women.

I am suggesting that we can identify the moralizing, utilitarian, pragmatic strand of Italian letters—starting with Guittone d'Arezzo and going forward to Boccaccio—as the more open and progressive toward women. It is extremely interesting, from this perspective, that Petrarch did not write such poems. Put very succinctly, I would take my analysis here as yet one more demonstration—this time in the area of gender roles—of what it means that Petrarch triumphed over Dante as the model for subsequent generations of Italian poets. Petrarch forged his identity against Dante's by going back to the courtly paradigm that Dante abandoned, thus institutionalizing a model of gender relations that endured for centuries and that, through the extraordinary internet that was European literary Petrarchism, became a cultural trope. To go back to the case of Francesca, we could say that the reading of *Inferno* 5 that ultimately emerged—depoliticized and stripped of much of Dante's agenda—is precisely a Petrarchan reading. Dante took on the task of being the historian of record with respect to Francesca's story, and whether or not his treatment of her can be classified as feminist, it is certainly culturally anomalous in the respect and dignity accorded the personhood of the dynastic wife, a dignity that derives from the text's commitment to her historicity, her identity, her self. The commitment to female historicity and selfhood is not a feature that we associate with Petrarch, however, and it is Petrarch who set the agenda for the subsequent Italian literary tradition.

Works Cited

Barolini, Teodolinda. 1992. *The Undivine* Comedy: *Detheologizing Dante.* Princeton: Princeton University Press.

———. 1993. "*Le parole son donne e i fatti son maschi*: Toward a Sexual Poetics of the *Decameron* (*Dec.* 2.10)." *Studi sul Boccaccio* 21:175–97.

———. 1997. "Guittone's *Ora parrà*, Dante's *Doglia mi reca*, and the *Commedia*'s Anatomy of Desire." In *Seminario Dantesco Internazionale: International Dante Seminar* 1, ed. Zygmunt B. Baranski, 3–23. Firenze: Le Lettere.

———. 2000. "Dante and Francesca da Rimini: Realpolitik, Romance, Gender." *Speculum* 75:1–28.

———. 2003. "Beyond (Courtly) Dualism: Thinking about Gender in Dante's Lyrics." In *Dante for the New Millennium*, ed. Teodolinda Barolini and H. Wayne Storey, 65–89. New York: Fordham University Press.

Battaglia, Salvatore. [1961]–2002. *Grande dizionario della lingua italiana.* Vols. 2 and 21. Torino: Unione tipografico-editrice torinese.

Cecco d'Ascoli (Francesco Stabili). 1927. *L'Acerba.* Ed. Achille Crespi. Ascoli Piceno: Cesari.

Boccaccio, Giovanni. 1980. *Decameron.* Ed. Vittore Branca. Torino: Einaudi.

Dante Alighieri. 1965. 2nd edition, original 1946. *Rime.* Ed. Gianfranco Contini. Milano: Einaudi.

———. 1967. *Dante's Lyric Poetry.* Ed. Kenelm Foster and Patrick Boyde. 2 vols. Oxford: Oxford University Press.

———. 1969. *Rime della maturità e dell'esilio.* Ed. Michele Barbi and Vincenzo Pernicone. Firenze: Le Monnier.

———. 1980. *Vita nuova.* Ed. Domenico De Robertis. Milano: Ricciardi.

———. 1996. *Vita Nova.* Ed. Guglielmo Gorni. Torino: Einaudi.

Ferrante, Joan M. 1975. *Woman as Image in Medieval Literature: From the Twelfth Century to Dante.* New York: Columbia University Press.

———. 1992. "Dante's Beatrice: Priest of an Androgynous God." *Center for Medieval and Early Renaissance Studies: Occasional Papers, 2.* Binghamton, NY: State University of New York Press.

Guittone d'Arezzo. 1940. *Le Rime di Guittone d'Arezzo.* Ed. Franco Egidi. Bari: Laterza.

Harrison, Robert Pogue. 1988. *The Body of Beatrice.* Baltimore: Johns Hopkins University Press.

Jacoff, Rachel. 1988. "Transgression and Transcendence: Figures of Female Desire in Dante's *Commedia*." *Romanic Review* 79:129–42.

Kirkham, Victoria. 1989. "A Canon of Women in Dante's *Commedia*." *Annali d'Italianistica* 7:16–41.

Muzzarelli, Maria Giuseppina. 1999. *Guardaroba medievale: Vesti e società dal XIII al XVI secolo.* Bologna: Il Mulino.

Petrarca, Francesco. 1996. *Canzoniere.* Ed. Marco Santagata. Milano: Mondadori.

Shapiro, Marianne. 1975. *Woman Earthly and Divine in the* Comedy *of Dante.* Lexington: University of Kentucky Press.

Afterword: In Praise of a Nonpareil Colleague

Robert W. Hanning

For more than forty years it has been my privilege, and my joy, to have known Joan Ferrante, first as a fellow graduate student, then as a colleague, and long since as a cherished friend. Our shared experiences in Columbia University's Department of English and Comparative Literature—a title recently truncated to Department of English for reasons of institutional politics that perforce ignored Joan's departmental presence as a distinguished comparatist—have made me aware, again and again, of her unique gifts not just as a medievalist but as a teacher, a liberal intellectual, and a human being.

As I look back over our long association, which has so enriched my academic and personal life, I can easily isolate several of Joan's virtues that make her the special person she is. The first and foremost is her extreme, indeed breathtaking, honesty. Don't ask Joan a question about a piece of your writing, about a graduate student or colleague, about a university policy or a required undergraduate course, if you aren't ready for a completely candid answer. But it's crucial to add that such candor, which comes as naturally to Joan as obfuscation or polite mendacity does to most of us mere mortals, is a character trait and not a strategy; it lacks even a scintilla of nastiness or self-righteousness. At some point in her life—perhaps following the example of her admirable parents, now departed?—she simply decided that honesty is indeed the best policy. And which of us can honestly deny the wisdom of her choice? (I suspect it's a main reason for her enjoying the eight hours of sound sleep she insists her system needs.)

Closely related to Joan's honesty is her equally extraordinary courage. I have never seen her back away from speaking truth to power or defending unpopular causes in which she believes. Again, a disclaimer: she does this without rancor or recklessness; there is no permanent chip on her shoulder, nor is she exorcising inner demons. If something is *wrong*—if injustice is being done; if exclusionary practices characterize institutional policy; if the human rights of anyone, but especially women and children, are being ignored or trampled; if racism, religious bigotry, or political privilege are seeking yet another triumph—and even if the rest of us respond with fear or indifference, Joan will speak out against it and, even more important and more admirable, will set to work, alone or with like-minded others, to resist or reverse it.

Her efforts on behalf of justice link Joan's courage to a third memorable virtue: her generosity with her time, efforts and resources in aid of a good cause. As a prime example, her contributions to the Human Rights Center at Columbia are as many as they are substantial: she is a member of its board, and each year she and her husband, Carey McIntosh, host an orientation weekend at the McIntosh family farm for front-line human rights advocates from around the world who have been awarded a semester's residency at Columbia. Perhaps the clearest sign of her commitment in this area is her decision, about a decade ago, to create an undergraduate seminar on women, religion, and human rights which she teaches every year, thus dedicating one quarter of her pedagogical energies to this enterprise of great potential political and humanitarian efficacy. Concurrently, Joan's long service in the University Senate, particularly with the Commission on the Status of Women and the Faculty Affairs Committee, has repeatedly involved taking courageous (and in some quarters unwelcome) stands against the inequitable or unjust treatment of both women and men within our academic community.

In paying homage to Joan Ferrante's virtues, I have risked painting the picture of a dour do-gooder whom one can admire from afar, but might well avoid close contact with. The facts are, however, quite different. Here is a person who loves laughter—especially directed at herself—trips to the zoo with her grandchildren, new adventures of all kinds, and (when she can arrange them) rides on real trains and playing with model ones. As she has often admitted, in her soul of souls, she is a ten-year old boy, and getting younger all the time. (I remember with particular pleasure going with her and a mutual friend to a railroad memorabilia shop in, I think, St. Louis, and watching her eyes get wide with delight as they took in the artifacts and mementos of America's Golden Age of rail transport.)

Joan is a devoted fan of the New York Mets (though she usually turns off her radio if the Mets are ahead going into the ninth inning, lest she jinx them) and has become an enthusiastic mountain climber under Carey's tuition. But above all, she is devoted to music, as an accomplished pianist and violist, a lover of opera (especially Verdi's, which have been favorites in her family for generations), and an enthusiastic participant in chamber music with a wide variety of friends. (I have seen her considerably more nervous about getting the viola part right in tomorrow night's living-room performance of a Brahms sextet than about delivering a major address to a meeting of one of the many scholarly organizations—the Medieval Academy of America, national Phi Beta Kappa, the Dante Society of America—over which she has presided during her illustrious career.)

Mention of those organizations reminds me all the occasions their meetings provided for Joan to laugh at herself (and me). We often traveled together to conferences, occasionally turning a routine itinerary into an adventure by our general cluelessness. We have had to race down endless miles of airport corridors to makes flights we were *sure* left an hour later than they did; and we have sat insouciantly in airport waiting areas watching passengers board a flight we were *sure* was not ours, until we noticed, about two minutes before the doors shut, that indeed it was ours. But if travel mishaps of a simple kind provoked Joan's sense of humor, more challenging ones provided opportunities for her matchless problem-solving abilities, combining unflappableness with that vein of courage that I have already applauded.

On one occasion, we flew out of New York's La Guardia Airport en route to a conference in Tennessee, only to have to return to Kennedy Airport when the pilot discovered one of our engines had gone dead ("never saw that happen before," he confided when we ran into him after deplaning). The airline in question was quite content to strand us at Kennedy all day, and we might still be there had Joan not insisted to several levels of airline bureaucracy that they had better get us on a plane soon, or else . . . ! ("Doing my Italian thing," she calls these moments.) As it is, when we got to our destination just in time for the opening session of the conference, I discovered that my checked bag had not accompanied us, and would not arrive until the next morning. Joan, who has mastered the art of traveling with only a backpack and never checking any baggage, suggested I take a census of my carry-on bag, and when it was clear that what I most needed was a necktie for a session at which I was speaking later that afternoon, she immediately bought me one ("an early birthday present," she said, waving aside my attempt to pay), and hustled us off to the conference hotel. Hand-wringing (except at the outcome of a recent national election) isn't in Joan's repertory of responses to life's difficulties.

It's appropriate that I end this tribute to Joan Ferrante by conveying some impression of her gifts as a teacher and adviser. (Teodolinda Barolini does justice to Joan's career as a scholar in the Introduction to this volume.) The most important characteristic of her pedagogy is its total lack of flamboyance. I have both taught with Joan and sat in on one of her specialty courses (Provençal), and can testify with complete conviction to her eschewal of the tricks and techniques that some academics use in and out of the classroom to establish their authority over, or impose their opinions on, their students. There's no game playing in a Ferrante classroom; no inflated rhetoric or cultivation of a persona. And this is equally true outside the classroom, with respect to her supervision of graduate students. In both milieux, what you get is impeccable scholarship and a sincere, thoughtful response to whatever text or issue is under discussion, delivered by a consummate professional who is always ready to listen to another point of view (as long as it's based in careful reading), and is never afraid to admit imperfect knowledge when such an admission is necessary. It is this no-nonsense attitude and absolute honesty that have endeared Joan Ferrante to so many generations of her students, and have fostered in the best of those students the commitment to learning and excellence in its pursuit that is evident in the essays published here. Joan's retirement from the academic profession in 2006 will truly be the end of an era. *Beati noi*, who lived in that happy time and place.

ABOUT THE EDITOR

Teodolinda Barolini *(Department of Italian, Columbia University)*
Teodolinda Barolini is Lorenzo Da Ponte Professor of Italian at Columbia. A Fellow of the American Academy of Arts and Sciences and of the Medieval Academy of America, she served as fifteenth President of the Dante Society of America. She is the author of numerous essays on Dante, Petrarch, Boccaccio, and the lyric tradition; most recently her essay "Editing Dante's Lyrics and Italian Cultural History: Dante, Boccaccio, Petrarca ... Barbi, Contini, Foster-Boyde, De Robertis" appeared in *Lettere Italiane* (2004). Her books are *Dante's Poets: Textuality and Truth in the* Comedy (1984; Italian trans. 1993), and *The Undivine* Comedy: *Detheologizing Dante* (1992; Italian trans. 2003); with H. Wayne Storey she edited the volume *Dante for the New Millennium* (2003). She is currently working on a commentary to Dante's lyrics for *Biblioteca Universale Rizzoli* and a gendered history of early Italian literature.

Notes On Contributors

Suzanne Conklin Akbari *(Department of English, University of Toronto)*
Suzanne Conklin Akbari studied at Johns Hopkins and Columbia, and is currently Associate Professor of English and Medieval Studies at the University of Toronto. She recently published *Seeing Through the Veil*: *Optical Theory and Medieval Allegory* (2004), and is now working on a book called *Idols in the East*: *European Representations of Islam and the Orient, 1100-1450*. Her most recent articles are "Alexander in the Orient: Bodies and Boundaries in the *Roman de toute chevalerie*," in *Postcolonial Approaches to the European Middle Ages* (2005), "The Diversity of Mankind in *The Book of John Mandeville*," in *Eastward Bound* (2004), and "Placing the Jews in Late Medieval English Literature," in *Orientalism and the Jews* (2004).

Joan Cadden *(Department of History, University of California at Davis)*
Joan Cadden is an alumna of Joan Ferrante's NEH Summer Seminar, the source of her first article about Hildegard of Bingen (*Traditio*, 1986). Her book *Meanings of Sex Difference in the Middle Ages*: *Medicine, Science, and Culture* (1993) earned the History of Science Society's 1994 Pfizer Prize for best book in the field.

Anne L. Clark *(Department of Religion, University of Vermont)*
Anne L. Clark is Associate Professor of Religion at the University of Vermont. She received her Ph.D. in Religion from Columbia University in 1989. Her research focuses on the religious lives of medieval women and especially women's visionary literature. She has published two books on Elisabeth of Schönau (*Elisabeth of Schönau: The Complete Works*, 2000; *Elisabeth of Schönau: A Twelfth-Century Visionary*, 1992) and has also written on Hildegard of Bingen and Gertrude of Helfta. She is currently at work on a project on medieval nuns and their valuable religious objects.

Susan L. Einbinder *(Hebrew Union College-Cincinnati)*
Susan Einbinder earned her Ph.D. from Columbia, with Joan Ferrante as her main advisor, in 1991, and is Professor of Hebrew Literature at Hebrew Union College-Cincinnati. Her study on medieval Jewish martyrological poetry from northern France, *Beautiful Death: Jewish Poetry and Martyrdom from Medieval France*, appeared in 2002. In 2005, she was on leave at the Institute for Advanced Study, where she began work on a new interdisciplinary project on Jewish literary responses to the fourteenth-century expulsions of French and Provençal Jews.

Robert W. Hanning *(Department of English, Columbia University)*
Robert W. Hanning is Professor of English and Comparative Literature at Columbia University, where he has taught since 1961 and where he and Joan Ferrante were together responsible for the medieval graduate program for many years. His publications include *The Vision of History in Early Britain* (1966), *The Individual in Twelfth-Century Romance* (1977), and a translation, with Joan Ferrante, of *The Lais of Marie de France* (1978). With David Rosand he edited the volume *Castiglione: The Ideal and the Real in Renaissance Culture* (1983), and with Joan Ferrante he edited the essays of W. T. H. Jackson, under the title *The Challenge of the Medieval Text: Studies in Genre and Interpretation* (1985). He has published articles on Old and Middle English literature, medieval romance, Chaucer, Boccaccio, Ariosto, and Castiglione. A Fellow of the Medieval Academy of America and a former Trustee of the New Chaucer Society, Hanning gave the New Chaucer Society's Biennial Chaucer Lecture at the Sorbonne, Paris, in 1998. *Reading Medieval Culture: Essays in Honor of Robert W. Hanning* (2005), edited by Robert M. Stein and Sandra Pierson Prior, has been published in his honor.

Laura Kendrick *(Department of Humanities, Université de Versailles)*
Laura Kendrick is Professor in the Department of Humanities of the University of Versailles. She has published widely on Chaucer and Provençal lyric, and her books include *Animating the Letter: The Figurative Embodiment of Writing in Manuscripts from Late Antiquity to the Renaissance* (1999), *The Game of Love: Troubadour Word Play* (1988), and *Chaucerian Play: Comedy and Control in the Canterbury Tales* (1988).

Margaret Pappano *(Department of English, Queen's University, Ontario)*
A graduate of Columbia University, Pappano was also Assistant Professor of English and Comparative Literature at Columbia University from 1997 to 2003. She was a fellow at the Erasmus Institute at the University of Notre Dame in 2001–2002. She has published articles on medieval drama, Chaucer, troubadour lyric, Marie de France, and Eleanor of Aquitaine. Many of these articles were inspired by her work with Joan Ferrante as a graduate student and colleague. She is completing her book manuscript, *The Priest's Body in Performance: Theatre and Religious Identity in Late Medieval England and France.*

Roy Rosenstein *(Department of Comparative Literature and English, The American University of Paris)*
Professor of Comparative Literature and English, Roy Rosenstein is a Romanist who has taught at American universities (Rochester, Oregon, CUNY), in Greece and Brazil, and at the Sorbonne. He co-edited *The Poetry of Cercamon and Jaufre Rudel* (1983) and *Etienne Durand: Poésies complètes* (1990). He has published on the troubadours, trouvères, Dante, Malory, Rabelais, Montaigne, Cervantes, Shakespeare, and many other subjects.

Sarah Spence *(Department of Classics, University of Georgia)*
Professor of Classics at the University of Georgia, Sarah Spence has published widely on ancient Latin and medieval vernacular texts including: *Texts and the Self in the Twelfth Century* (1996), *Rhetorics of Reason and Desire: Vergil, Augustine and the Troubadours* (1988*), The French 'chansons' of Charles d'Orléans* (1986). Most recently she has edited two volumes of essays on Vergil's reception: *Poets and Critics Read Vergil* (2001), and *Re-Presenting Virgil* (*Materiali e discussioni* 52, with Glenn Most).

H. Wayne Storey *(Department of French and Italian, Indiana University)*
H. Wayne Storey is Professor of Italian and Director of Medieval Studies at Indiana University (Bloomington). His research interests include textual editing, pre-Dantesque poetry, manuscript studies, and Tre- and Quattrocento literary and cultural history through manuscripts and early printed editions. He is the author of *Transcription and Visual Poetics in the Early Italian Lyric* (1993) and of numerous essays on thirteenth- and fourteenth-century manuscript traditions and the editorial features of medieval codices, including his commentary on Petrarch's ideograph of the *Rerum vulgarium fragmenta* ("All'interno della poetica grafico-visiva di Francesco Petrarca," *Rerum Vulgarium Fragmenta. Codice Vaticano Lat. 3195, Commentario all'edizione in fac-simile*, Antenore, 2004, the companion volume of the facsimile of Vat. Lat. 3195, of which he is also the co-editor). He is the editor of the forthcoming diplomatic-interpretative edition of Petrarch's *Fragmenta* (*Francesco Petrarca, Rerum vulgarium fragmenta secondo la lezione dell'autografo e dei codici del tardo Trecento*) and the co-editor, with Teodolinda Barolini, of *Dante for the New Millennium* (2003).